ADRSYA

ADRSYA

Hidden Marvels of the Mahabharata

Curated and Edited by
Aditi Banerjee

ink | OCCAM

ISBN: 978-93-6547-775-7

First published in India 2025
This edition published 2025

BluOne Ink Pvt. Ltd
A-76, 2nd Floor, Sector 136, Noida
Uttar Pradesh 201301
www.bluone.ink
publisher@bluone.ink

Printed and bound in India by Gopsons Papers Pvt. Ltd., Noida

Kali and Occam are imprints of BluOne Ink

ink | OCCAM

CONTENTS

side? Please … please take care of my dear cousin today. He is a gem! And you have to protect him.'

Duhshala thought that the simple prayer would brighten her mood and give her a sense of peace, but, instead, she felt anxious. An unknown worry was nagging her.

She was earnestly looking at the sun, trying to decipher the meaning of her nightmare. *Early-morning dreams always come true*. Her mother had told her once in childhood. She whispered to herself, 'I hope Arjun is safe!'

She heard the tinkling of jewels and the rustle of garments behind her. *The maid? I wonder what brings her in at this early hour,* she thought, and turned in time to see an elderly chambermaid bow deep down in salutation.

'Long live the Princess!' the maid said.

A faint smile crept up on Duhshala's lips. Even after so many years of her marriage, the people of Hastinapur still addressed her as their princess. At first, she would get irritated and insist that she was now a queen and should be addressed as one. Later, her mother made her understand that it was a measure of the people's love and affection for her. They thought of her as their own and did not want to change the perception.

'Yes? Why are you here at this time? Didn't I make it clear that I am not to be disturbed before my morning prayers are over?' she asked the maid, who was still bowed down and waiting to be acknowledged.

'I am extremely sorry, Princess, but there's a messenger waiting at the door. The King has sent a message for you,' the chambermaid replied, her head still bowed.

'Oh! I see. Bring him here. Let us see what Father wants,' she replied, a little puzzled by the latest development. Why would her father bother sending her a message? She glanced at the sun and silently prayed for her cousin Arjun's safety once again.

The old messenger crossed over the threshold and stepped onto the balcony with his head bowed. To Duhshala, he appeared as worn out as his humble cotton clothes. But his stride was strong and conveyed his determination to serve his king.

'What's come over you, Father? Why a messenger at this hour?' she muttered under her breath, as she waited impatiently for the old messenger to get done with the ritual of salutations.

'Long live the Princess!' he said as he bowed in front of her.

'What is it that Father wishes to say, sevak?' she asked impatiently.

'Princess, there has been a development on the battlefield that he wanted to let you know about,' the messenger began hesitantly.

'Sure. Carry on.'

'Prince Arjun took a vow last night.'

'So?' she asked with a frown. 'How does that concern me?'

'The mighty prince has vowed to kill your husband, Sindhu Raj Jayadrath, by sundown today, failing which he would self-immolate.'

'What did you say?' she asked unbelievingly.

When the messenger repeated the message word by word, it was still beyond her comprehension. She was prepared for loss, for that is what a war brings about. But this vow was not what she had signed up for.

'Did you just tell me that my beloved cousin Arjun has taken a vow to kill my husband?' she asked, stupefied.

'That is what Sanjayji said, Princess. I am merely repeating what he told the King.'

'Oh!' she said mechanically. Her uncle Sanjay, her father's charioteer-cum-companion, had the divine vision given to him by none other than Maharshi Vyas. He had the ability to see every corner of the battlefield. *He would never report something without confirmation. But still...*

'Arjun would never do something like that. Never!' She was sure of it. Especially since he and his brothers had decided against killing Jayadrath after his foolish attempt to kidnap their wife, Draupadi, she thought.

Arjun had let Jayadrath go because of his affection for his cousin Duhshala...

'Why would he suddenly try to kill the person he had pardoned earlier? There must be some misunderstanding!' she thought to herself.

'Princess! Please calm down,' the messenger said.

'Calm down? You are asking me to calm down after telling me that my husband is going to be hunted like prey by none other than *the* Arjun? And why, pray tell me, would Arjun do that?' she asked with an edge in her voice. 'Warriors don't single out and target each other in the dead of the night for no reason, especially when they are not fighting a duel. Wasn't that a rule? Isn't that still a rule? Or am I missing something?'

The messenger looked up at Duhshala with sorrowful eyes, and she felt a sudden chill.

'Tell me, what has Sindhu Raj done now, to irk the righteous Pandava Prince?' she asked, dreading the answer.

When the messenger did not reply and kept nervously staring at the floor, her voice went up a notch. 'Speak up, sevak! I want a clear picture. I need to know what happened. Please! Tell me what's going on.'

'I am not supposed to know anything more than the message, Princess,' he replied, with his head still bowed.

'But you do know. I want you to tell me. It's an order!' she thundered.

'Prince Abhimanyu was slain yesterday. Prince Arjun seeks vengeance for his son,' the messenger blurted out.

'Doesn't Arjun know that warriors get killed on battlefields?' she asked, puzzled. 'It is not something new for a seasoned warrior like him. Then why this vow?'

'The Kaurava army used unfair means. The brave heart was killed by deceit,' the messenger replied sadly.

'Did my husband kill Arjun's son?' she asked.

'No. Sindhu Raj was nowhere in sight when the young prince was slain,' the messenger confirmed.

'I don't understand. If Sindhu Raj was not around when Abhimanyu was killed, then why is Arjun adamant on killing him? How can Sindhu Raj be responsible for something done by others?'

'Because it was Sindhu Raj who did not let anyone reach and help Prince Abhimanyu. Sindhu Raj Jayadrath did not let any of the Pandava warriors get inside the Chakravyuh formation.

'Sindhu Raj fought with them all together? That was very brave of him!' she commented, momentarily distracted. Then, as she started listening to the messenger, she stood rooted in her spot.

Seven mighty warriors ganged up and murdered a young, sixteen-year-old defenceless boy. The young prince had now become immortal in death, with his act of heroism...

'Seven experienced war veterans had to gang up to defeat a young, inexperienced boy?' she exclaimed.

He overpowered everyone single-handedly. They could not beat him. When the great Maharathis could not digest defeat at the hands of a mere sixteen-year-old prodigy, they ganged up against him and pounced on him like a pack of hyenas. They beat him to death mercilessly. As if that was not enough, to showcase their bravery and excellence in warfare, they performed a celebratory dance around the mutilated body of the child they had together slain...

A chill ran down her spine.

'The young warrior was trapped because of King Jayadrath. Prince Arjun says there is blood on his hands,' the messenger concluded.

'Oh! There is plenty of blood, alright. But it's not Abhimanyu's,' she shouted, agitated.

'I am sorry, Princess,' the messenger replied in a subdued voice. 'Permission to leave, Princess?'

Duhshala dismissed him with a wave of her hand, as she turned towards the rising sun.

'Why is Sindhu Raj at fault? Because he performed his task to perfection?' she shouted, glaring at the sun. 'And what about the seven supposedly great warriors who actually murdered that boy? They literally bathed and danced in Abhimanyu's blood! How can Arjun lay the blame so squarely on my husband's shoulders? How can he ignore the fact that the hands that stabbed his son belonged to others? And what about those incompetent fools in his own army who failed to aid his son? Are they not to be blamed? Haa! They went scot-free. Why? Because they are technically on his side, they cannot be charged with murdering his beloved son, is it?' Duhshala felt out of breath; she felt her heart hammering loudly against her chest.

As the initial shock and anger subsided, she realized the gravity of the situation and felt bile rising in her throat. Unsteady, she reached for the nearest railing and leaned on it. She could visualize Arjun taking a deadly aim at her husband. Involuntarily, her eyes squeezed shut, and her hands tightened around the railing.

'Why???' she screamed internally as a set of fresh tears rolled down her cheeks and plummeted to the ground somewhere beyond the railing.

The most accomplished warrior—the peerless Arjun—her favourite cousin Arjun had singled out her husband for something done by seven lesser mortals.

Her heart was beating erratically, like the pallu of her sari in the early morning wind. She took hold of her pallu and brought the long, unruly fabric under control. Then she wrapped it around herself securely, trying to reign in her panic.

An image of Arjun aiming his bow at her husband again flashed in front of Duhshala's eyes. This time, Arjun's torso was wounded and bleeding, just like it had been in her dream earlier. She had not known it then, but now she knew the meaning of her dream.

It was not Arjun's but Abhimanyu's blood. And Abhimanyu's father had sworn vengeance.

Duhshala looked up at the sun, now much higher in the sky, and prayed again. 'Oh Lord! Take care of my husband. Be with him today. Arjun will not spare Sindhu Raj if he gets his hands on him. Please … please take care of him!'

The old chambermaid appeared by her side again and bowed, saying, 'Long live the Princess!'

'Wha … what is it, daasi?' Duhshala asked, taken aback by the chambermaid's sudden appearance.

'Your bath is ready, Princess. Would you like to begin your daily routine?' the maid asked courteously.

Duhshala blankly stared at the maid. She failed to understand what the maid was saying. A moment passed, and Duhshala finally realized what the maid wanted to say. Routine. A princess or queen is supposed to be always decked up in the finest of yarns and tons of jewellery. Help was always required to get in and out of the whole ensemble. And today, she was going to need more than a few pairs of hands for assistance, Duhshala thought. 'Yes, sure. Let's go,' Duhshala replied, as she let go of the railing.

Duhshala turned to go inside her room. As she neared the threshold, the sun's rays landed on her from behind, and her shadow fell across the floor in front of her, the head inside the room while the torso was on her side, still on the balcony, separated by the threshold. She paused momentarily as realization dawned on her. 'The curse!' she gasped. 'Oh dear! What have you gotten yourself into, Arjun? You emotional fool!'

Jayadrath had expressed his desire for immortality to his father, Sage Vriddhakshatra. In response, the sage expressed his inability to grant his son the boon of immortality. Instead, he placed a curse on the person who would kill Jayadrath. Whoever caused Jayadrath's head to drop on the earth would instantly have his own head burst into a thousand pieces.

Whatever the outcome, she would lose her beloved cousin today. It saddened her. Arjun! Her dear cousin and best friend since childhood. The prospect that he might be able to kill her husband before he fell prey to the curse caused her even greater agony.

Arjun was always courteous and treated her with so much love and respect that she soon forgot that they were cousins. She felt more connected to him and his brothers than to her own hundred brothers.

Duryodhana, her elder brother, had been so upset with the Pandava brothers' arrival in Hastinapur! Her maternal uncle, Shakuni Mama, had expressed his hatred even more fervently.

'But they are mere peasants!' Shakuni Mama had said. 'You shouldn't let their presence worry you whilst I am still around. And I am not going to leave your side, ever. I will make sure, my dear nephew, that nothing and no one gets in your way to the throne. Now go and welcome your cousins. Mere peasants, they are! Give them a few alms for sure, but never let them sit on the same level as yours.'

Duhshala took her bath and, with the help of her aides, draped a heavy red and gold silk sari around herself. It matched the colour of the vermilion on her forehead, Duhshala noted. Her dutiful attendants helped her with an ensemble of jewellery, and she finally settled in front of her dressing table, where an aide started arranging her hair into an elaborate hairstyle.

Her hair was being decked up with fresh flowers and beads. Every strand was being meticulously pulled back, rolled, or twisted and pinned up neatly. The scene around her made her wonder whether this would be the same routine tomorrow or the day after. Might she end up with only one aide helping her into a simple white cotton sari, like her Kakima Kunti? The mere thought made her shiver involuntarily.

She was contemplating how to distract herself from thinking more about the coming battle when she saw another chambermaid bow down in salutation.

'Long live the Princess! The King sends his best wishes to the Princess,' the chambermaid said, still bowed down.

Duhshala's reverie was broken. 'Huh? What? What is it that Father said?' she asked earnestly.

'He has asked me to inform you that the battle is about to begin. Both armies have taken their respective positions and are awaiting further orders. The commanders will blow their conches any moment now.'

'Okay. Anything else?' she asked with a sharp edge to her voice.

'He did not say anything else, Princess,' the maid replied courteously. Duhshala wondered if the maid was privy to Duhshala's inner turmoil and her apprehensions. She briefly glanced at the maid, but the chambermaid's face was as impassive as ever. Her expressions might as well have been carved out of wood, thought Duhshala. If the maid felt something, she did not show it. Duhshala decided to ask for her views. She felt that it would be a good distraction.

'Daasi, what do you feel will happen today?' she asked tentatively. 'Who do you think will win by sunset?'

'How am I supposed to know what lies in the future, Princess? It is for God Almighty to decide which side wins,' the maid replied politely.

'I know … but still, what is your hunch?' Duhshala persisted, out of curiosity. Surely, the woman must have her own opinion. She wanted to hold on to hope. Hope that everything would be fine at sunset today.

'How can I predict what will happen in a war, my lady!' the maid replied hesitantly. 'It is but a game of uncertainty.'

'But don't you have some opinion on the matter?' Duhshala asked.

'I am a mere bonded labourer in this palace, my lady. My opinions do not count in the general scheme of things. I have seen and heard enough to understand my position in the life of royalty. It is as minuscule as a grain of sand. The princes and princesses of the kingdom do not need opinions from the likes of me. It is up to the Almighty to do justice.'

'That He will do. We all must face our own judgement day at some point in time, Daasi. Mine is today. I wonder what is in store for me at the end of the day,' Duhshala said, crestfallen.

'All I can do is pray for your well-being, Princess. The rest is all God's will.' The maid folded her hands and bowed down in salutation. 'Shall I get you something to eat, my lady? You haven't even touched your breakfast yet.'

'I do not feel like having breakfast. You may leave, Daasi,' she replied with a sigh.

'As you wish, my lady. Still, I suggest you eat something. You need strength. Permission to leave the food here?' the maid asked.

Duhshala merely nodded.

Long after the maid had left, the fruit bowl lay untouched on the side table. So did the breakfast plate. Duhshala had no appetite for food. All she craved was news. A word here, a word there … whatever her ears could pick up. She contemplated going to her father's chambers and listening to the first-hand account from Uncle Sanjay. He had the divine vision to look into any corner of the battlefield. She was sure he would indulge her anxious queries. But she was not so sure about her father.

From the first day of war itself, her father, King Dhritarashtra, had restricted his movements to his inner chambers. From sunrise to sundown, he sat in his royal chair in the confines of his living quarters and listened to the live reports from the field. Seldom had he allowed anyone to come within earshot. From time to time, he would send for a messenger, who would, in turn, relay his messages, or rather updates, to the other members of the royal family.

Even Uncle Vidura, the prime minister of the state of Hastinapur, was not allowed to stay beyond the minimum time that his call of duty permitted. Since the day her grandfather, the mighty Bhishma, had bowed out of the war, Vidura had been expressly told not to disturb the King and to carry on with the day-to-day administration as he deemed fit.

Duhshala had her doubts. If Uncle Vidura was not allowed within hearing range, would she be entertained? She was but a mere princess who did not even understand the basics of warfare.

Duhshala wished that she was like Empress Draupadi in that regard. Draupadi was the driving force behind this war. The most beautiful, enchanting, and fiery lady ever to walk on this earth, Draupadi was an enigma. Duhshala had experienced her hundred brothers and her own husband go weak in the knees for her. Especially her husband. He had drawn a lot of flak for making unjust advances towards her during the Pandava brothers' vanvas. His life was spared, but he was duly punished for his unjust efforts to abduct her.

But then, Draupadi's life had always been in peril. As the shared wife of five husbands, she was always in the public eye, ready to be scrutinized. She was subjected to such horrific humiliation that the entire Kuru clan was put to shame.

'Never! I don't want to be in her shoes ever … in any of my lifetimes,' she cried in distress. 'No. Not one living woman on earth would want to be in her shoes ever.'

Even if mundane and not noteworthy, her life was much better than Draupadi's, she decided. No matter whether Draupadi had the liberty of living her life on her own terms. Terms be damned. Duhshala did not want to live on the edge.

But that was precisely what she was doing now, as she realized with a sickening feeling. She was suspended in deep uncertainty.

Duhshala quickened her pace as she walked down the long and winding corridors of the palace to reach her father's chambers. She glanced out of one of the huge windows. The sun was now high in the sky. It was nearly afternoon, she realized. She took a hasty turn and abruptly came face-to-face with her uncle, Vidura.

'Oh! My apologies, Uncle. I was not paying attention. Did I hurt you?' she asked, courteously.

'Duhshala, my child! You don't have to apologize, dear. I am fine. You came to a stop just in time.'

'Still, I could have hurt you,' she said apologetically.

'You are one of the last people on earth who could hurt someone, child. Don't be so harsh on yourself,' Vidura said.

'That's very kind of you, Uncle.' Duhshala replied. 'Are you headed towards Father's chambers? Would you mind if I tag along?' she asked.

'I was going that way, yes, but now I have changed my mind. Maharaj may not be interested in discussing what I have in mind. You may carry on, though. You need his audience more than ever today,' he said, meaningfully.

'Why do you say so? You are the prime minister of the state. Surely, what you want to discuss must be very important.'

'Everyone has their own definition of importance, my dear. And it keeps evolving from time to time and from situation to situation. Today is not the time to discuss droughts and famines. It's about time that we paid attention to our daughters and their families.'

'Uncle, did you hear? Arjun has vowed…'

'I heard. He seeks justice.'

'But is it justice? Don't you think he is being impulsive? How is killing my husband going to bring justice? Sindhu Raj wasn't even present when Abhimanyu was killed. Why is my husband being punished for someone else's sins?'

'When does a person sin?' Vidura asked her.

'When he commits a crime knowingly.'

'And what about a person who is an accomplice in someone else's crime? What would you say about a person who creates a situation for others to sin? Is he not one of the criminals?'

'But he was only carrying out the task assigned to him! Isn't everything fair in a war?' she cried.

'Is it? If everything were fair, we wouldn't have laid rules before the start of the war in the first place. Moreover, the rules were made by none other than the Kaurava army chief, your Pitamah Bhishma. The Pandava army agreed to abide by them without any misgivings or arguments. We had rules, and they were broken unnecessarily and unjustly—by our own people. We cannot and must not justify that.'

'Haven't the Pandavas broken any rules so far? How did Pitamah Bhishma collapse? Wasn't that a sin? Why did no one punish Arjun and Shikhandi then? Surely, they were at fault that day,' she argued.

'There is a difference between committing a sin and being at fault. Moreover, Arjun did exactly what was expected of him. Today, too, he is doing the same.'

'And what is that?'

'Fighting for justice.'

'You mean killing people mercilessly.'

'That is something I would credit the Kaurava warriors with. They surpassed every criminal on earth when they killed Abhimanyu yesterday.'

'I don't deny what they committed was a crime. But my Jayadrath was not one of the seven warriors. He was merely...'

'...aiding them?'

Duhshala was speechless for a moment. When she finally found her voice, she asked him, 'How can you say that? Do you wish for Sindhu Raj to die today?'

'Why would I wish for something like that?'

'You said that he has sinned. You were favouring Arjun.'

'I was not favouring anyone, my dear. I was only stating the facts for you. Think for yourself.'

'You are definitely not in favour of my husband's survival today,' she persisted.

'I am definitely not in favour of the war. But we are still in the middle of one, and favouritism is not going to make anyone win this bloody war,' Vidura sighed.

'I am sorry, Uncle. I didn't mean to argue with you.'

'I understand your predicament, child. You yourself have always favoured Arjun all your life.'

'I have idolized him.'

'And today he has taken a stand against you. You are at a difficult crossroads in life and don't know which way to turn.'

'I don't want either of them to die,' Duhshala said, teary-eyed.

'And yet, someone will,' Vidura said.

'Oh God! What will happen today?'

'Only time will tell. Hold on till sunset, my child. We will know by then,' Vidura replied. 'I will take your leave now. I hope you get the answers you seek.'

'Thank you, Uncle.' Duhshala folded her hands and bowed her head with respect.

'God be with you, my child. May he give you strength and peace to hold on to life.' Vidura blessed her, gently placing his palm on her head. The wise old man suddenly appeared very sad to her. Vidura turned and left the same way he had come, as Duhshala kept staring at his retreating form. She was disturbed by what he had just said and became apprehensive about going to her father.

Duhshala approached her mother's chamber in a hurry. She needed answers. Her restless heart yearned for comfort. And where else would she find that other than in her mother's embrace!

'Long live the Princess!' the chambermaid at the door bowed deep in salutation.

'Let the Queen mother know I wish to have a dialogue with her. If she is not too busy, I would like permission to enter.' Duhshala spoke in a flat tone. She marvelled at the steadiness in her voice, for her heart was beating erratically. Her mind was in a deep vortex, and she felt ill at ease the moment she thought about the impending duel between her brother and her husband. Rationality was fast slipping away from her, and she was beginning to feel like an emotional mess.

'Your wish is my command, revered Princess. But I am unable to help you in this regard,' the maid replied apologetically.

'Why?' Duhshala asked, worried. 'Is Mother not keeping well? Have you sent for the raj vaidya?'

'The Queen is in perfectly good health, Princess. There is absolutely no reason to worry in that regard,' the maid replied.

'Then what is the matter? Why can't I go inside and meet her?' Duhshala asked, confused. 'Because,' the maid said, 'she is busy in her saadhanaa and has asked not to be disturbed by anyone.'

'Oh!' Duhshala replied, crestfallen. 'I didn't realize she would be in meditation.' She made to go. Then, with an afterthought, she turned back and asked the maid, 'If it is alright, I would like to go and seek blessings from the Lord Mahadev. I won't disturb Mother's prayers, I promise.'

The maid started wringing her hands, and her eyes wandered everywhere but refused to meet Duhshala's. Duhshala understood that the lady was torn between her sense of duty and her compassion towards her princess. While the maid contemplated how to answer, Duhshala turned to leave with a heavy heart.

'Princess!' the maid called out to her from behind. 'Please don't make any sound that might disturb the Queen. I have already lost my husband and my brother in the war. I cannot afford to lose my job. I have three children who depend on me for their daily bread.'

'Don't worry. I will keep in mind not to make a sound,' Duhshala managed to reply. She was grateful to the maid.

Duhshala entered the place of worship in her mother's chamber. Lord Mahadev was situated, in the form of a Shivaling, at the centre of the room. Her mother, Queen Gandhari, sat in front of the idol, deep in meditation. So poised, so pious that she seemed like a celestial being. Even when not in meditation, she came across as a saintly, detached, and dispassionate person. But she had to be loving and caring towards her children and their well-being, Duhshala reflected. Gandhari's persona and the ambience of the room resonated with the immense love that she had bundled up underneath the calm exterior of a queen.

The huge space was lit with a hundred oil lamps, each one signifying one of Gandhari's sons. There was no draught, and yet, Duhshala noticed, a few flames had already been extinguished. They still had oil reserves up to their brim. She did not bother to check the number. She knew in her heart that it would be equal to the exact number of brothers that she had lost so far. A few had started flickering. More lives were on the line today. She was going to lose a few more brothers by sunset. Will Arjun be one of them? But there was no lamp alight with the telltale signs for her. Her husband's fate was still hanging in uncertainty.

Duhshala gathered herself, and, after she had offered her prayers to the God Almighty, she bowed in reverence to her mother. Then, taking care not to make any sound that might disturb her, Duhshala left the place. Once outside, she noticed the maid was still anxiously wringing her hands. When she saw the princess coming out of the chamber, the maid relaxed visibly, and Duhshala gave her a reassuring smile. She continued ahead, but the maid suddenly called out to her. 'Princess, I know how difficult this must be for you. May God give you strength to survive this day.'

Duhshala did not reply. She could not. She was in a trance. She had hoped to find peace by her mother's side. But, instead, the visit had agitated her further. She could not forget the sight of those extinguished lamps. She did not want to lose any more brothers. She loved them all. Even the Pandava brothers. They were all her own. And she was losing them one after the other. The battlefield demanded blood to honour the outcome. The blood of innocent people, her people, her brothers, her cousins, her husband …

Were they innocent, she wondered? No, she knew they were not, and she was less than proud of all their unfair achievements so far. But that did not mean they had to die. The gods of war were just. Rules or no rules, the odds were always stacked against the sinners. And the Kaurava brothers had a fair share of sins in their account book, Duhshala realized.

When would the massacre stop? When would the madness be over? There was only one way. The war had to stop. But how? If only … somehow, Arjun could fail in his task today… Her husband would live to die another day, and her brothers would have a better chance of winning the war at hand. Yes. Instead of losing a hundred, why not sacrifice one? In return for them all, safe and sound … including Jayadrath!

'Long live the Princess!' A servant bowed deeply.

The greeting broke her trance, and Duhshala realized she was walking aimlessly through the palace. She turned her attention towards the servant. 'Yes?'

'Prime Minister Vidura has asked me to inform you about the latest happenings on the battlefield. I went to your quarters, but you were not available. Would you like to receive the message here, my lady? Or shall I come after some time?'

'Now would be fine, messenger. What is it that Uncle Vidura wishes to convey?'

'He has asked me to brief you about the multiple battle formations of the army today. Acharya Drona has constructed a very difficult Sakata Vyuha to safeguard King Jayadrath. Acharyaji is himself stationed at the front gate, with many brave kings, some mounted on their chariots and others on their steeds or elephants, and countless foot soldiers to accompany and assist them in their endeavour. In the rear, he has made another impenetrable lotus formation. Inside that lotus is a needle formation. Sindhu Raj Jayadrath is ably guarded at the rear of this very needle formation. Vidurji says you need not worry about your husband's safety anymore. Enough precautions have been taken, and the army of battle-hardened soldiers will create a human wall between Sindhu Raj and Prince Arjun.'

'Thank you. Please convey my regards to my uncle. You may leave now.'

The messenger gave another respectful bow and took his leave. Duhshala was relieved after hearing Vidur's message. It was very kind of him to step in and let her in on the latest happenings on the battlefield. Her father had broken the news to her at daybreak, and her uncle was trying his level best to keep her abreast of the current happenings throughout the day. She felt grateful towards both for the efforts they were making.

She took a moment to see where she was in the palace. To her utter amazement, she was in the vicinity of her aunt Kunti's residing quarters. Even without her realizing it, her feet, of their own accord, had taken her there … towards her kakima's chambers. Her kakima was not only her aunt but also her best friend. Time and again, when Gandhari was too busy worrying about her sons and managing their mischiefs, Kunti had stepped in as Duhshala's mother. Today, too, Duhshala needed a mother, and Gandhari was not available. Duhshala was sure she would find solace here, in her kakima's embrace.

Duhshala noticed that the doorkeeper was surprised as she approached. She inwardly reprimanded herself for being in the wrong place at the wrong time. 'Gosh! She must be wondering why I am here today, of all the days. I should probably not be here. What will we say to each other anyway? Her son wants to kill my husband. But there is no one else I can go to. I am sure Kakima will understand.'

The chambermaid hastily closed her open mouth and tried to recover from her initial shock at seeing Duhshala approach. The maid bowed politely and said, 'Long live the Princess!'

'Ahem! Is Kakima Kunti free? I can come any other time if she is not ready to receive me,' she stammered.

'You may step inside if you wish to, Princess. Rajmata Kunti will be happy to receive you. In fact, she would be extremely unhappy to know that you had come this far and yet didn't meet her.'

'Why would I not meet her?' she replied. 'Why don't you announce my arrival to her?'

'It is perfectly okay to go inside without announcing your arrival. Rajmata does not like to keep people waiting.'

'I know. It's just that … she might not want to see me today…' She mumbled to herself as she took a step forward and went past the doorkeeper.

The room was spacious but nothing compared to the décor in her mother's chambers. Understandably so. Her aunt had chosen to stay with Uncle Vidura and his wife at their humble residence on the palace grounds. Kunti was still sour with King Dhritarashtra for the way he had treated, or rather mistreated, her sons and their wife.

Duhshala's eyes scanned the room and zeroed in on a figure dressed in white robes, hunched by the window. Kunti straightened after a moment and backed away. With her back still at Duhshala, she prayed in front of the lamp she had lit.

'Should I bring a protective cover, Kakima?' Duhshala asked. 'It might blow out by the window.'

Kunti turned and smiled at Duhshala. 'It's okay, dear. This lamp does not need protection. It will survive for whatever time it is worth.'

'But isn't it for Arjun's safety?' Duhshala blurted out. 'You have lit this for him today, haven't you?'

'Arjun?' Kunti sounded confused for a moment. Then clarity dawned on her as she remembered a hundred lamps in Maharani Gandhari's temple. 'Oh! Arjun does not need a lamp to protect his life. He has Krishna by his side to do that job.'

'Then why have you lit a lamp in broad daylight?' Duhshala asked, perplexed at Kunti's calm demeanour.

'This one? It is in the memory of the departed soul of my dear little grandson, Abhimanyu. This lamp is to honour his bravery,' Kunti replied. She continued in a wistful tone, 'My Arjun is so lucky he had a son like Abhimanyu. He is a proud father today.'

Arjun was always a proud father, reflected Duhshala.

She stood admiring the goofball that she called a cousin. It was adorable, the way Arjun played with his sons and nephews, the way he engaged them, channelled their energies, and enjoyed with them. He used to become a child with them, not caring about what people would say about his antics!

It was during the Rajasuya ceremony that Duhshala got to stay with the Pandava brothers for a brief period. She remembered how proudly Arjun used to carry his son on his shoulders. Abhimanyu had always been the centre of his universe. The eldest son of the Pandava, Abhimanyu was the apple of everyone's eye for every single person in Indraprastha. Even as a toddler, he had won hearts!

The distant memory made the day-old tragedy even more profound, and before she could contain herself, she blurted out her concern. 'Do you also think he should have lived a little more? That his life was abruptly cut short rather ruthlessly? That his death should be avenged?' Duhshala asked, with an edge in her voice.

Kunti did not reply but simply returned a sad smile. Duhshala had a feeling that her kakima endorsed what Arjun had set out to do today. And why not? She would want her son to succeed, thought Duhshala.

'But … but such things happen in war. People lose their lives fighting for their cause,' she persisted.

'I am glad you remember that,' Kunti replied in a gentle voice. 'I hope you don't forget that ever. After all, you too are a Kshatriya by birth. You cannot, and you must not, forget that you belong to the warrior clan. The last thing you should fear is the death of your loved ones in a battle.'

Kunti's words, and the calmness with which she uttered them, evoked a sense of peril in Duhshala's mind. An image materialized before her eyes—an image of her husband and his arrogant laughter. Then, without any warning or predetermination, an image of him lying headless on the battleground flashed across her eyes. She blinked and the image cleared. A cold fear gripped her heart, and she became worried sick for her husband. The confidence and hope she had felt a moment ago were no longer there for her to fall back on.

Duhshala was barely holding on to the few memories she had as a wife. Jayadrath had never been a particularly loving or ideal husband. But she had loved him with all her heart and had always prayed for his well-being as a dutiful wife. He needed her prayers more than ever today, she realized in those difficult moments.

'Duhshala?' Kunti asked as she picked up her needlework and settled on the couch opposite Duhshala.

'Yes, Kakima?' she replied, distracted.

'Do you want to have your lunch here? I can ask the maid to bring it in, whenever you like.'

'I don't feel like having lunch, Kakima,' Duhshala replied as she gazed out of the window. It was well past noon, and the sun was now moving towards the west.

'Are you not feeling well, my child?' Kunti asked her, worried.

'I am fine. It's just that I am not hungry now.' Duhshala brushed the topic away.

'Okay, dear. Let me know whenever you feel like having something. Do you want me to cook something specific for you?' Kunti asked, putting the needlework aside.

'No, no. Don't trouble yourself for my sake, Kakima. I am absolutely fine.'

'It is no trouble, my dear. I wish there was something else that I could do to make you feel better,' Kunti said, as she got up.

'That is very kind of you, Kakima. If you do not mind, I will take your leave now. I have to be somewhere else,' Duhshala said, lowering her eyes. She stood there, staring at the floor while Kunti approached her.

'Sure, my child. Take care!' said Kunti, taking Duhshala in her embrace.

'You too,' Duhshala whispered back, as she held on to her aunt a little longer.

Duhshala quickened her pace and adjusted her pallu, lest anyone noticed the moisture gathering in her eyes. A messenger was waiting for her when she reached the threshold of her own quarters. It seemed that Arjun was making good progress in the killing field. He had evaded a duel with the Acharya and had intelligently slipped past the commander-in-chief.

With every message that she received, Duhshala became more and more aware that it was his playground, and he played his game on his own terms and conditions. He had a firm grip on his favourite weapon—the revered Gandiva Bow—and wherever he went, warriors dropped like dominoes left, right, and centre. Whenever he faltered, his friend, philosopher, and guide, Vasudev Krishna, was right there by his side to give him moral support and strengthen his wavering resolve. It seemed to her that Arjun, the warrior, was on a rampage today!

At this rate, Duhshala feared he would succeed in his quest. Her question remained the same though. Why was her husband being singled out and made to pay for something others had done? She looked outside her window in frustration. Was it a figment of her imagination, or were the skies outside darkening? Surely it was still afternoon, but the light outside suggested dusk was fast approaching. Was there still hope?

She received a string of messages from her uncle's messengers, who were delivering the updates at the speed with which Arjun was making progress. At one point, she was bewildered to hear that he had unfastened his horses in the middle of the field and that Krishna was tending to their wounds. Who rests their horses in the middle of a raging war? Apparently, Arjun and Krishna did. As if that were not enough, to her utter astonishment, her cousin created a small pool of water to quench his horses' thirst in the middle of the battlefield.

Then there came a time when Arjun did a U-turn and went straight back to where his eldest brother, Dharmaraj Yudhishthir, was stationed. Apparently, safeguarding his elder king brother was more important than saving his own neck. Duhshala could only marvel at his loyalty to his brother.

In no time, Arjun was back to where his target was. Jayadrath was flanked by eight mighty warriors. She knew that her husband would not go down without a fight, and she was not disappointed. He did not cower down as most of the Kaurava rank and file had expected. She heaved a sigh of relief as the messengers told her how he was engaged in battle with the mighty Arjun, albeit from behind the cover that the eight warriors provided him.

And then, it was sunset. For Duhshala, it was like a curtain coming down on an ongoing play. She kept receiving the updates. Elsewhere, Vrikodar Bhim had wreaked havoc on the opposition army. The Kaurava brothers were further reduced in number. Suddenly, all that did not matter—to anyone.

When Duhshala received the message that her husband was alive, she heaved a sigh of relief. With the happy news came a bitter realization—that Arjun would self-immolate. But it would not be in vain, she thought. It would be for the greater good. Without Arjun, the war was bound to be over in a day or two. Peace would prevail yet again. As a wife, she was immensely relieved that her husband had survived the day, but she could not be happy about what was about to transpire on the battlefield.

'There's hardly anything to be done about it! How can I feel bad for Arjun when he himself is to blame for his predicament? He should have thought well before taking such a difficult vow,' she tried to convince herself. 'I hope he doesn't go back on his words. He seldom breaks his promise. No, he never breaks his promise,' she went on.

Barging into Draupadi's chambers while she was in the company of Yudhishthir was a different matter altogether. And he did accept the punishment that time. He will have to comply with the rules this time too.

'And imagine how much bloodshed would be avoided if he were out of the equation. This is right. So right!' Duhshala whispered to herself.

Duhshala raced towards her father's chambers. She wanted to make sure that it had happened. She needed a first-hand account of the events unfolding on the battlefield. If the news was positive, King Dhritarashtra would not hesitate to admit her inside, she concluded. Then, she could ask Uncle Sanjay all that she wished to know and see.

She was elated at the sight of the gigantic double doors of her father's chamber. She hurried to reach them and meet her father and Uncle Sanjay. Her father must be so happy, she thought. This was by far the biggest victory for the Kaurava army. 'Oh, how wonderful is this news!' she squeaked happily. 'Just like the beautiful patterns of sunlight on the floor of this passageway.'

Sunlight!

She stumbled and tripped on her feet. She was stumped. How could there be sunlight? Confused, she looked out of the decorated archways of the corridor, and there it was. The sun shone brightly in the sky in all its majestic beauty. This had to be her worst nightmare, she thought. The shock of seeing the sun still shining brightly after apparently setting made her realize that Jayadrath's fate was now sealed. It had to be Krishna, she decided.

'Why, Krishna? Why? I know it was you. It could only have been you. You tricked my husband. You tricked an entire army. You … you tricked us all…' Duhshala was half yelling, half sobbing as she lay twisted on the floor. A bright beam of sunlight set a spotlight on her, blinding Duhshala to the world around her.

With great difficulty, Duhshala gathered herself. She was in pain, and it had nothing to do with the sprained ankle, or so she thought. She hobbled to the nearest pillar and, with bated breath, waited for the doors to open and her father to dispatch yet another messenger. She did not have to wait for long. The messenger stood in front of her with folded hands and delivered the heartbreaking message. Although it was as expected, it still bore a hole through her heart to listen to its finality.

'And Arjun?' she asked in a detached manner.

'Prince Arjun won,' replied the subdued messenger.

'No. I mean, did he … did he survive? After Sindhu Raj's severed head fell on the ground?' she asked hesitantly.

'No, Princess. His head didn't fall to the ground,' the guard replied in a low voice.

'How is that possible?' she asked. 'It should have fallen on the ground, and Arjun's head too should have exploded into a thousand pieces.'

'No, Princess. That did not happen. If what Sanjayji said is to be believed, Prince Arjun made the head travel a considerable distance to where Sage Vriddhakshatra was in meditation. The head is said to have landed on his lap, and he caused it to fall to the ground. It was King Jayadrath's father who died with him.'

A single tear rolled down her ashen face as the finality of the news struck her. It had indeed happened. An anguished father's wrath had destroyed her life. Her husband was left a head shorter and lifeless for that matter. With the loss of love and life, a deep sorrow settled in her heart. Strangely, though, no fond memories of the time spent with her better half came rushing to her. Only a strange emptiness and an eerie silence kept her company.

She tried to think of a few good memories she had shared with her husband but could not come up with anything noteworthy, apart from her son's birth. The whole time that she had been married to him, he was either plotting against his arch-enemies or busy chasing women.

Duhshala noted dispassionately that the sun had now set, and, with that realization, it finally dawned on her that her husband had not paid for the sins of others. He had actually paid the price for his own wrongdoings. Arjun had merely delayed the execution of his sentence. With a heavy heart, she accepted that her husband should have been long dead. He had been living a borrowed existence ever since the day he misbehaved with Draupadi. Instead of rectifying his mistakes, he had plotted to bring down the very people who had pardoned his life. And what had he achieved other than causing eight Akshauhini of his sena to be slaughtered in one single day? Nothing is noteworthy other than losing his own precious life.

Duhshala realized that the guard was still standing in front of her with his hands folded and his head bowed. 'Dismissed,' she ordered mechanically.

'Long live the Princess!' He bowed deeply before he departed.

'I will,' she thought. 'At least till the day I get to meet my beloved cousin again. I know he will come once the war is over, and he has enough time to devote to lesser mortals like this unfortunate cousin.'

Whatever happened today, deep down, Arjun did care. Surely, he would come. And he would have a lot of explaining to do. Until then, she could do nothing but hold on…

With great effort, she dragged her feet towards her father's chamber. As Duhshala stepped into the most important wing of the palace, the grandeur and splendour of the King's chambers were lost to her. The huge room was deathly silent and cast in dark shadows. She found her father sitting in a bent posture, defeated, on his makeshift throne at the centre of the plush décor. Uncle Sanjay was seated next to him, looking equally subdued. She folded her hands and bowed to her father's aide out of an age-old habit, for he was more than a mere charioteer to her father. Duhshala knew that Sanjay had been King Dhritarashtra's good friend and confidant too. Sanjay acknowledged her greetings silently, and she was grateful for the compassion that she could see in his eyes.

'Maharaj, the Princess is here.' Sanjay politely informed the King of his daughter's arrival.

'Duhshala?' Dhritarashtra jerked up his head. 'Why are you here?'

'Father!' She managed a whisper. 'Sindhu Raj…'

'Yes, yes. I know. What a great loss.' Duhshala kneeled in front of him, expecting him to say a few words of comfort. She had lost her husband, but she would not be mourning alone all by herself because her family was here with her. They would see her through these times, she thought. At that moment, she was grateful to be in her father's presence.

'How I wish Jayadrath's head would have fallen to the ground. We could have at least gotten rid of that stubborn Arjun. With him gone, it would have been child's play for Duryodhana and my remaining sons to gain victory in this war. *Oh! Why didn't the head fall?* Dhritarashtra blabbered as a shell-shocked Duhshala stared at him, aghast. She was disappointed in her father beyond measure.

She took her leave silently. At the door, she turned back to look at her father one last time. He had not even acknowledged her departure. Dhritarashtra continued his monologue about how disappointed he was for the lost opportunity as a sad Sanjay looked at him with pitiful eyes.

With a heavy heart, she realized that Dhritarashtra was more upset that Arjun was still alive than that his only daughter had become a widow. On the other hand, her mother Gandhari was solely concentrating on her sons' safety, and, if Duhshala knew her mother well, it was only a matter of time before she joined her beloved son Duryodhana in Kurukshetra. This was the family she had come to extend solidarity to. She had stood by them in their hour of need, but they could not even relate to her grief. It was time she redefined the meaning of home and family. And she realized that it was not Hastinapur. She did not belong here. She belonged to Sindhu Rajya. That was where her home and her family were. She might have lost her husband, but she still had a family and a kingdom to look after. It was time for her to get back to her home, she thought. Her son needed his mother, and the people of Sindhu Rajya awaited their queen. As for the king and queen of Hastinapur … well, they were perfectly capable of taking care of themselves, she realized sadly.

2

Saraswati Nadi Flows as Always

Shivakumar G.V.

'My son.'

'Yes, my mother. Just looking at you is so delightful. Wait, I have never seen you. Why do I think I know you? Your smile—it looks like you know me.'

'My dear, I have always known you. You have, too. You're just seeing me for the first time.'

'Who are you, my mother? Why am I even calling you my mother?'

'Because I am your mother, great Yadava. I am the mother of all of you.'

'Then, why haven't I ever met you?'

'You have, and you do. You see me every day. You just don't recognize me. You will, hereafter.'

'Mother, if that is so, hear me out. I am angry. My brother says he will not help the Kauravas. He has sent his army to serve them in the war. But why does he not want to help them? I am uncomfortable.'

'I know, my son. That is why I came to meet you. Leave all this aside, come to me. You need to see me. There is something that you have to do. You have to tell a story. Through you, I will speak to the future.'

'I do not understand, oh divine lady. But I will come to see you. Your smile, your white attire, that beautiful instrument in your hand. When you speak, it rings a bell in my mind. Oh, is there water all around me? And when I speak, why are your lips in sync with what I say? Who are you, my mother?'

'My son, I am river Saraswati. Come and meet me at Prabhasa Kshetra. Come very early in the morning tomorrow. And just follow me.'

'As you say, my mother. How can anybody say no to you?'

Balaram woke in the morning. 'Why did Mother Saraswati say that there is something that I have to do? When was the last time that Krishna ever said that?' There was nothing to wait for. Balaram had refused to join either side. What was there to choose? Duryodhana, his favourite disciple. Pandavas, his brothers-in-law. Krishna was not participating, either. But he agreed to steer the chariot of Arjun. Balaram urged Krishna to help Duryodhana too in some way. Krishna had refused. 'What if our army is going to Duryodhana? Krishna is on the side of the Pandavas. I am not going to witness my brother aiding the side fighting against my clan. Mother Saraswati, here I come.'

The word spread like wildfire. Balaram was leaving for a tirthayatra to the river Saraswati. Soon the Vrishni chieftains, Brahmins, and the common people of Dwarka gathered around him. 'Make arrangements,' said Balaram. Balaram's command was always acted on first, and any questions asked later. Dwarka began to get ready for his tirthayatra. The accompanying troupe was soon ready. 'Brahmins,' said Balaram. He took a while to speak the next sentence. The troupe waited until he spoke. When was the last time he was absorbed in his own thoughts? 'Oh, Brahmins, lead me and guide me. We are going to the river Saraswati. We shall march along her banks.' At other times, the Brahmins would have been mighty pleased. To the Saraswati? Any time! But there was an impending war. Their champion was on one side, while their army was on the other. To top it all, the leader himself is walking away.

'Chieftains, gather as much wealth, as many animals, and a big troupe as possible. A lot of preparation is needed before we proceed. We shall perform austerities and donate as much as possible. This is my pilgrimage. It is for dharma and my peace of mind. Prabhasa it is, my chieftains. We shall proceed to Prabhasa. It has been a long time since I went there.' Any time, Prabhasa! Those waves, the messengers of Surya Bhagavan in the evenings. It would be lovely if Krishna, Balaram, Satyaki, and Kritavarma were all at Dwarka at once.

'Dear Brahmins and my chieftains, I hear Mother Saraswati is in distress. I may be of service to my mother. Proceed to Prabhasa.'

Preparations complete, the tirthaytra began on the day of Pushya Nakshatra.

'Prabhasa is hardly any distance. There, the mother is meeting the ocean.' Balaram's mind was churning out thoughts. 'Krishna, why do you always make it so difficult for me? Why can't I say no to you? Even this expanse of water cannot get you out of my mind.'

'My dear Balaram,' said a voice. Such a gentle voice. Balaram was filled with it for a while.

'Mother, it is you.' The air was filled with her voice. He looked around but could not fathom from where she spoke. 'Oh Mother, where are you?'

'I am right in front of you, Balaram. You're in front of me, aren't you?'

'Ah, yes, Mother. I see you as the greatest of the rivers, meeting the ocean. But please do appear in front of me with your smile, like you did yesterday.'

'I shall, Balaram. But I shall do so only for you. Your troupe will not see me. Neither will they hear me, Balaram.'

'Why so?' thought Balaram. But he said, 'As you please, Mother.'

'Stand beside me and look at the ocean, Balaram.' At a distance, in the meeting waters, Balaram saw a movement. The ocean turned quiet. Swans came from nowhere. The wind blew, carrying music with it. Balaram could see her gently rising from the meeting waters. She moved over them slowly. Each step she took brought a sweet wave to the shore. As she came near, Balaram could see her clearly. The same smile, that spotless white attire with golden lining, that motherly gaze. Balaram did not take his eyes away for a second, not even to blink. It seemed like an eternity. Balaram forgot his tiff with Krishna for a while.

Balaram, the great Yadava, came to his senses. Mother was right in front of him. 'I am happy you responded to my call, Haladhara.'

Balaram bent to touch her feet. The troupe thought he was bending to touch the waters of the river. 'Mother, I shall not ask you why you called me. I am just pleased you thought of me. You said you were going to speak through me. Is there anything better than becoming your instrument and being the reason for your music? I am at your service, my mother. I will follow where you take me. I just want to forget Kurukshetra.'

Saraswati wore a serious look. 'You shall, Sankarshan, you shall. You will be the reason for people to remember me in the future.' Balaram was puzzled, but he tried not to show it.

'Balaram, do you know the greatness of Prabhasa? This is in your kingdom.'

'Mother, are you testing me? I have learnt it well under the feet of Guru Sandipani. This is the place where Chandra took his final dip to wash away his karma for having insulted his wives. But, Mother, can I have the grace of hearing the story from you again?'

Saraswati obliged and repeated the story. 'You see, Chandra was excessively in love with Rohini, ignoring his other wives. When the other wives complained to Daksha, his father-in-law, he gave him enough warning. Then came a point when Daksha lost his patience and cursed his son-in-law to suffer from Rajayakshma. Soon, Chandra lost his shine. Finally, he was cleansed of his karma through a dip in these meeting waters of mine.'

Balaram recollected. 'Ah, Mother, I am equally strict with anybody insulting a woman. Daksha said the same to Chandra, didn't he? Women ought not to be insulted.' Away from his raja karya after a long time, Balaram felt his mind and body fully present in all the austerities he was performing at Prabhasa. He thanked the Brahmins as he made the first daan.

Saraswati instructed Balrama to proceed to Chamasodbhava from Prabhasa. Balarama and the troup complied and bathed at the Chamasodbhaava Tirtha.

The journey continued.

'That is Adi Tirtha, Balaram, also known as the Udapana Tirtha.' Balaram looked around. He could not put a word to what he felt. One moment, he felt overwhelmed. In the very next moment, he felt as if he was missing something. The place seemed adorned with siddhas and sannyasis like a bueatiful women enhanced with jewels and flowers. The trees and plants were tender. Balaram gently touched them. It was the same as standing next to Mother Saraswati. The ground was wet. Balaram looked around for the river. Mother was there, but the river was not to be seen anywhere.

'Mother, you are very different in this place!' Saraswati kept quiet. He wondered if she was unhappy. She seemed the same, but her smile had diminished.

She finally spoke, 'Do you see that the ground is wet, Halayudha?'

Balaram nodded. 'I also flow beneath Mother Earth here. Leave that aside, Balaram. Listen to the story of Sage Trita. He was the brother of sages, Eka and Dwi. The brothers were jealous of Trita's prowess and popularity. They left him here in a well and went away with cows Trita received in donation. Trita did not lose heart. He performed a yagna within the well. I came as a Pravaha from within the well and lifted him onto the surface. What a great sage he was, Balaram!'

'I now understand, my mother.'

'You do not understand yet, Balaram.' Saraswati smiled.

It was a smile that made Balaram feel heavy. 'Mother…'

The great mother's smile completely vanished. Balaram did not pursue it. 'Finish your austerities here, Balaram. Let us then go to Vinashana Tirtha.' He followed. The power of her words echoed with Balaram. When was the last time I ever followed others? The troupe simply followed Balaram wherever he went. They did what was asked of them.

The view of Vinashana Tirtha struck like a gada blow to Balarama.

'Mother!' Balaram almost screamed. He was not ready for what he saw. How could the mother not be seen suddenly? Where was she? The river was completely missing.

'I told you, Balaram, you will understand soon. Do you now?' Saraswati consoled Balaram like a mother consoles her child. 'This is Vinashana Tirtha, Balaram. Do not worry; it is not that I have stopped flowing. I am simply invisible here. There were too many attacks on me. The hunters hunted. They wanted my water for all activities I did not approve of. I just disappeared. That is why this is known as Vinashana Tirtha.

I am always there, Balaram, just invisible to those who should not see me.' Balaram wondered if this was what Mother wanted him to know. 'Let the people perform the right austerities, and I shall appear here again. I wait for a good tapasvi, Balaram.'

'Mother, Mother! I was about to raise my plough in anger against those who made you disappear here.'

Saraswati laughed heartily. Balaram was relieved. 'Why do you want to get angry so fast, Balaram?'

Balaram brought his plough down. 'Mother, you deal with Krishna every day. I will then see if you can hold this smile for any longer than I can.'

Saraswati smiled once again and seemed to say, 'My dear Balaram, I meet Krishna every day,' but not aloud. 'Let us go, Balaram, we are getting late,' was all that fell on Balaram's ears. 'Take a bath in what is left of me, Balaram.'

The pilgrims accompanying Balaram, wondered when it was that they had last seen their leader being led about like a child. They, after all, couldn't see river Saraswati.

'Ah, Mother,' said Balaram. 'What a relief this is! Why can't you flow like this everywhere?' Balaram almost jumped in relief like a child who has been missing his mother.

'That is why this is called Subhoomika, Balabhadra.' Saraswati's smile told Balaram that she was filled with anticipation. 'Mother, take me along with you like a child.' The place was full of apsaras, Brahmins, devatas, gandharvas, beautiful trees, and flowers. Saraswati stood on the banks of the river. Balaram and his entourage went everywhere and visited everyone. Balaram felt something was filling within him.

'Rauhineya, when was the last time you fought with Krishna?'

'Ahem … Mother, you should just flow like you are here, everywhere, all the time, Mother.' He was in another world.

A little later, he realized he had heard the Mother speak. 'Did you ask me something, Mother?'

'I did, Balaram. But it does not matter. Come, let us go further now. Let us be fast. The next two are Gandharva Tirtha and Gargasrota Tirtha. They are highly praised by the Brahmins. Vishvavasu did his austere penance at Gandharva Tirtha. At Gargasrota, Vriddha Garga earned his status as a Trikala Gnani, one who knows the past, the present, and the future through severe austerities. From there, we will go to Shankha Tirtha. There are all kinds of yakshas, rakshasas, pishachas, vidyadharas, and siddhas out there. Each follows a different path of austerity. They live invisible to common eye, in a huge tree called Shankha Vriksha. These are my favourite places, Balaram. I quietly flow there, just as I want, unhindered. There are so many around me, but nobody disturbs me. There is so much peace with so much happening.'

'I understand, Mother. Be like this always. Whatever makes you excited, I am eager to see.'

'You shall, my son.'

'This is an amazing place, Mother. I am no longer angry with Krishna.'

'I knew, Yadavendra.'

'But Mother, what made me content was something else,' Balaram said after a while. Saraswati did not respond immediately. 'It is your flow, Devi. It has brought me to a state of stillness. I just want to be there forever.' Saraswati only smiled.

'Where are we going next, Mother?'

'Balaram, we are now going to those very places I wanted to take you to. We are entering the realm of Dwaitavana. From ancient times, this forest has been an abode of tapasvis. Do you remember that the Pandavas spent a part of their forest time there? There is the beautiful Dwaita Sarovar here. The tapasvis belong to different traditions. You can recognize them from their costumes. There is a very special place called Nagadhanva Tirtha there. That is where the devas crowned Vasuki as the king of the Sarpas. The Sarpas there do not cause any harm. Dwaitavana forest is an abode of many tirtha kshetras.'

'When you say so much, one must experience it for oneself, my mother,' Balaram said as Saraswati led. The men following Balaram, in turn, followed in their leader's footsteps.

'Ah, I can feel it, my mother,' Balaram said, as they stepped into the dense Dwaitavana. 'The sages, their austerities, and their power. They leave their imprint, don't they? Can I ever forget the day we entered the Sandipani Ashrama?'

Tears trickled down from Balaram's eyes as he remembered Guru Sandipani and how eager Balaram was to learn from him. Just sixty-four days he spent with his Guru. Sixty-four days he has always cherished and always regretted the duration of the stay. Balaram realized he had stopped walking while he was reminiscing. He walked faster to catch up with river Saraswati.

'Why didn't I go to meet the Pandavas when they were here during their exile?' wondered Balaram. 'In any case, the Pandavas may not have come this far into Dwaitavana. But they probably did, they spent a large portion of their exile doing Tirthayatra.' Coming back to present, Balarama again focused on Mother Saraswati.He never tired of watching her flow. From her banks, from a distance, from on top of a hill, and in her very depths. In every way, Balaram loved to watch Sarasvati flow—the majesty, mellifluousness, and eternity.

Suddenly, Balaram stopped. Saraswati once again smiled at him. He hurriedly climbed a small mound nearby. He could see the long stretch of the great river Saraswati. He kept looking at the stretch until she gently patted him on the back. 'What puzzles you, my dear Balabhadra?'

Her indulgent face told Balaram that she knew what was on his mind. 'Mother, you know everything, yet you ask me.'

'Yes, Balaram. I have suddenly turned east here. It should not be very difficult for you to understand why.'

'Mother, I see that you have entered the Naimisha Forest from here.'

'You have understood it right, Balaram. I had to. Where penance is, I am always there. My flow is decided by the penance of the sages and of the learned. You must know this story. Once, there was a congregation on my bank. Sages from all over the universe came to take a bath in me. It was a great Satra Yagna—twelve years long. At the end of it, the sages of Naimisha came to bathe in me. Balaram, I could not provide them with a place. There were so many of them—the Vaalakhilyas, Ashmakuttas, Dantalolookhas, Prasankhyanas, Vaayubhakshas, Jalaahaaris, and Parnabhakshas. These austere sages just lived on air—some on water, some on leaves. The Naimisha sages sought to bathe on my southern banks. But they did not get a chance at all. My banks were full. In the end, they performed their penance wherever they were and returned. Know this, Balaram, when a true sage calls, I always find myself there. I turned east, created tirthas for the Naimisha sages to bathe in, and then returned back to the west to flow further south. All these tirthas are called Naimisheya Kunjas.'

Balaram wondered if Saraswati was kind or if the penance of the sages was so great. As the story sank in, he wondered how Saraswati had appeared in his dreams at Dwaraka. Did he call her knowingly or unknowingly?

'I will soon be a guptagaminee (flowing beneath the earth), Balaram.'

'That is too harsh on us, Mother.'

'You are not to worry, Balaram. You will return to your heavenly abode before I become invisible. But know that, whenever great sages of immense austerities call, I shall always appear.'

'Will there be such in the future, Mother?'

'Rest assured, Balaram.'

'How were you born, Mother?'

'Perfect timing, my son. Like I said, my son, great sages call, and I come down in ways that they call me. Close your eyes, and you will see everything very clearly.'

Once upon a time, in Brahmalok, Lord Brahma came out of his sadhna and opened his eyes. 'The leela of Shriman Narayan,' he observed. 'Lord, we do not understand you, but we have your grace to experience your leela.' At once, Brahma decided to perform a penance and yagna. He came down from Brahmalok onto Mrtyulok (the world of humans) in search of a right place. Finally, he chose Pushkara, where he began his yagna. Despite his austerities, Mother Saraswati did not descend. The sages came to Brahma and wondered if there was any dosha (error) in the yagna. Brahma smiled. He chanted the most sacred mantras of Saraswati, who was flowing as a saras (lake) in his mind. As soon as she heard Lord Brahma chanting the mantras, she appeared as Suprabha (one with auspicious shine). The sages were relieved that the yagna was without any blemish and expressed their heartfelt thanks.

The sages of the Naimisha Forest were performing a long satra—the congregation of the sages. The forest was filled with the sound of their conversations that reached Saraswati in the exalted worlds. Saraswati descended as Kanchanakshi (one with the golden eyes). King Gaya was performing a yagna at Gaya Tirtha, made famous for Vishnu slaying Asura Gaya there. Gaya was devoted to Saraswati. He sought her to come down in all her flow and bless the universe. Saraswati came down as Vishala (the expanse). Sage Uddhalaka, too, invited her for his yagna. Who does not want the power of her flow and words? From the sides of the Himalayas, towards the northern Kosala, came down Saraswati as Manorama (pleasing to the mind). The dance of her movement, the music of her flow, Saraswati was so beautiful in that form that the devas decided to reside in her and were worshipped by all witnessing the yagna.

King Kuru—the great king of the Bharata dynasty—performed great penance in the Kurujangala region to please the devas. The devas were pleased to grant him several boons, and Saraswati came down as Surenu (golden dust) to bless the region of Kurujangala. Daksha Prajapati, many years ago, performed a yagna at Gangadvara (the entrance of Ganga). Saraswati flew there too, as did Surenu. Kurukshetra is where Saraswati was destined to flow. Vasishtha sought her flow for dharma to be established in Mrtyuloka. Saraswati came down with as much love as Oghavati (with the great flow).

It was Brahma who first brought Saraswati to Mrtyuloka. Finally, he meditated on her in the Himalayas again. Saraswati appeared as Vimalodaka.

Suprabha Kanchinaaksheecha Vishaalaa cha Manoramaa
Saraswati Choughavatee Surenurvimalodaka

Balaram opened his eyes. In his mind, he was still chanting the shloka. 'Mother, I see that you came down as seven divine streams. When did you become one and the mighty Saraswati?' Balaram could clearly hear the Vedaghosha (the chant of the Vedas) of the sages at a distance.

'It is here that all my flows merge into one, Balaram. Hence, this region is called the Sapta Saraswata Tirtha (waters of the seven Saraswatis). This place is holier than the holy Balaram. Do you hear the Vedaghosha at a distance? You can feel the Vedaghosha here, even if nobody is chanting. This is the place for the best of everything. Look at all these beautiful trees. Look at all the sages of different varieties performing their penances.'

Balaram went silent. Mother, too, became quiet. They both sat down. Copying their leader, Balaram's entourage too sat in meditation alongside him. There was absolute silence for a long time. There was only Vedaghosha. There was Saraswati everywhere.

'Open your eyes, Balaram.' Balaram jolted from his reverie. 'You will never get enough of Sapta Saraswata Tirtha, Balaram. But we have a lot of distance to cover.'

Balaram smiled. 'Mother, look. I have shed my anger. I have learned to smile like you.' Saraswati laughed.

'Balaram, I am eager to take you to Vasishtha Pravaha Tirtha. But, before that, we will visit Oushanasa, Brahmayoni, Avakeerna, and Yaayaata Tirthas on my banks. They are not to be missed.

'At Oushanasa, Vishwamitra performed his penance. There is an ashrama of Sage Rushangu. Very close, there is another tirtha called Pruthoodaka. That is where the great Sage Rushangu left his body. This is where Mahodara Muni could get rid of the head of a rakshasa stuck to his knee. Hence, it is also called Kapalamochana Tirtha. At my abode, the penitent can get rid of whatever burden they are saddled with. Like you were relieved of your anger, child.'

Saraswati continued, 'A little ahead of you, there is the Brahmayoni Tirtha. Chaturmukha Brahma created the universe by performing meditation here. You are aware of the Rajarshis—Sindhudwipa, Vishwamitra, and Devapi—the great Kshastriyas. They all attained Brahminya here through their penance. Arishtashena Muni, too, attained Brahminya at the same place. It is at my abode that great men perform austerities to transform themselves from one form to another. Arishtashena Muni was so pleased with me that he gave me three boons. Those who perform austerities on my banks shall attain the punya of performing Ashwamedha. At my abode, the Sarpas do not harm. Those who perform austerities here shall realize what they seek.'

Saraswati continued, 'Avakeerna Tirtha is closely associated with the Kuru dynasty. Once, Bakadaalbhya, the son of Daalbhya, was performing penance. He sought suitable gifts from the Panchalas. They obliged with great offerings. At Hastinapur, Dhritarashtra was the king. Cows had died at his place. When Bakadaalbhya sought cows, an angry and distraught Dhritarashtra offered the dead cows as gifts. A grieving Bakadaalbhya performed a sacrifice from the meat of the dead cows. That resulted in a deep famine in the Kuru kingdom. Finally, Dhritarashtra sought forgiveness, after which the Kuru kingdom was restored. Sage Brihaspati, too, performed a yagna there to help the devas kill the asuras. Avakeerna Tirtha is the place where one can seek the material one wants.'

Balaram knew of Dhritarashtra's unstable mind. 'No wonder,' he thought. His mind wandered around the Kauravas, the Pandavas, and Duryodhana—his favourite. 'No, not again. Mother. Protect me from these thoughts.'

Varshneya shed his mind off the Kaurava-Pandava thoughts and set his eyes again on her flow.

'I understand, my son.' Saraswati was not smiling now. She was serious. 'My dear Balaram, we shall quickly visit these tirthas. At each of them, please perform all your austerities to attain the desired fruits. Take your time. We shall then go to Vasishtha Pravaha. That is where I have been wanting to take you for a long time.'

'Mother, as we walk along, please begin to shower me with the knowledge of Vasishtha Pravaha.'

'So be it, Balaram. You shall, as you walk, by my grace. You will see the entire episode in your mind.'

On the eastern shore of Saraswati was Vasishtha's ashram and on the west was Vishwamitra's. Their rivalry was famous across the Bharatavarsha and crossed boundaries of human lifetime by extending across their subsequent births. Even, in their tapas, the sages continued their great conflict. Sage Vishwamitra performed austere tapas that surpassed the intensity of Sage Vasishtha. Yet, he was concerned about the Brahma tejas (grace) of Vasishtha. The urge to surpass Vasishtha swept Vishwamitra onto a destructive path. He imagined Saraswati as sweeping Vasishtha away from his ashrama towards him, enabling him to end Vasishtha's life through his powers. Vishwamitra concentrated his powers and thought on Saraswati. That great river Saraswati was compelled to bring herself to the sage. She knew Vishwamitra's mind; she knew the act that was to follow against her wish. But she had to bow in front of his divine power. She summoned herself in grief. Vishwamitra expressed his design to Saraswati whose grief multiplied. She stood with folded hands, tears sparkling in her eyes. Vishwamitra ordered her to not judge between right and wrong and bring Vasishtha to his mercy.

Saraswati cursed her fate for having to be part of an evil act by Vishwamitra. She decided to go to Vasishtha and tell him what transpired between her and Vishwamitra. She knew of Vasishtha's unmatched powers derived from his tapas and was anxious that she might have to pay a price for Vishwamitra's misadventure. On the contrary, Vasishtha expressed his concern for her well-being. He urged her to protect herself first and asked her to sweep him towards Vishwamitra and leave the rest to fate. If not, Vishwamitra would be sure to curse her to a hapless fate. He had decided to face this destructive power by himself. Otherwise, it would burn the world. Saraswati did not give up. She repeatedly thought of a way to act in a way that would be good for all. At last, she decided that she would sweep Vasishtha away when Vishwamitra was performing his japa, homa, and tapas. Bound by the rules of his performances, Vishwamitra would not complete any act in violation. Saraswati would get enough time to save Vasishtha.

At an opportune moment, Saraswati swept away Vasishtha's ashrama on the eastern shore. Even in those moments of distress, Vasishtha praised the divinity of river Saraswati through a stotra. Upon reaching Vishwamitra's ashrama, Saraswati announced many times that Vasishtha was at the mercy of Vishwamitra. The latter did not have enough time to finish his austerities and find an appropriate weapon. Saraswati knew the ferocity of Vishwamitra's vengeance. She did not waste a moment. She quickly drove Vasishtha further away, towards the east, far away from his ashrama. All the while, Sage Vasishtha was praising Saraswati.

Saraswati, you live in the Sarovara of Brahma
Saraswati, you flow from the drift of his mind

Saraswati, the world is full of your divine waters
Saraswati, you reside in the clouds and make waters
Saraswati, we study the Vedas by your grace
Saraswati, you are the seven forms of the Devi
Saraswati, you are Para, Pashyanti, Madhyama, Vaikhari
Saraswati, within you is the whole world

She had performed all that was expected of her by the word given to Viswamitra. Yet, she had saved Vasishtha from an ill fate that seemed difficult to avoid. This place, where Vasishtha was saved, became famous as Vasishtha Pravaha Tirtha, which echoed the forceful flow of the river.

Vishwamitra felt robbed of his opportunity to achieve his vengeance. He did not take this kindly. Even though Saraswati had fulfilled Vishwamitra's wishes, she had to pay a price for her conduct. Vishwamitra cursed Saraswati to turn red with blood and be sought after only by the rakshasas. As a result, her shores were inhabited only by rakshasas eagerly seeking blood to quench their thirst.

After many years, austere sages began to visit Vasishtha Pravaha. These sages were disturbed to see Saraswati flowing with blood and rakshasas inhabiting the banks of such a divine river. One fine day, they invited Saraswati for a conversation and sought to know what caused her that ill fate. Upon learning the curse from Vishwamitra, the sages tasked Saraswati on an austere path, full of vratas and tapas, seeking Mahadev's grace. Finally, Mahadev was pleased and blessed Saraswati. She was once again filled with her divine waters. Thus, the sages released Saraswati from Vishwamitra's curse.

The rakshasas were now robbed of their blood. They did not have enough power to confront the austerity of these sages. Instead, they submitted themselves and presented their situation. 'O sages, we are now full of hunger without being able to drink blood. Once part of the Sanatana tradition, we have gone far away in disgrace. We are cursed to perform acts so extreme that sages such as you will not show any mercy towards us. As a result, we have become Brahma rakshasas. We troubled the Brahmins, made fun of ritvijas, troubled the gurus, and made life difficult for the old and weak. Thus, we are born here as rakshasas. We seek to be released from this fate through your divine powers.'

The sages took pity on the rakshasas. They set them on an austere path and urged them not to perform any of the ill acts that enhanced their Rakshasa attributes. The sages then prayed to river Saraswati and invoked her powers to liberate the rakshasas from their ill fate. Compassionate Saraswati transformed herself into an oily-red colour that could wash away all the ill performances of the rakshasas. The rakshasas bathed themselves in the river, released themselves from their rakshasa bodies, and attained salvation.

'Mother, I know the *Rig Veda* has praised you. Sages and gods revere you. You have the power to transform rakshasas and release them from their destructive beings. You can transform a conflict into a larger good. Your shores are abodes of ashramas. You can face a destructive situation all alone. You don't hesitate to sacrifice yourself for the good of us. Through your austerities, you can revive anything. Yet, Mother, this conflict of Vasishtha and Vishwamitra shook me.'

'Spardha, the competition, escalates itself into a bloody conflict, my son. But Vishwamitra had a larger purpose. He sought equality with Vasishtha as a rishi. Duryodhana, on the other hand…' Balaram dropped his eyes. Saraswati did not press further.

'Balaram, we will reap what we sow. Karma is not something any of us can defy. You create a rakshasa, be ready to face it. Penance is to be performed to gain the power of transformation. Anything created that goes wrong will need to be transformed into something good. Otherwise, a larger destruction is always on the anvil.'

Balaram said, 'You must flow, my mother, as always. Only then can we release rakshasas from their natural tendencies.' Who will liberate future generations from any tamas? To think of us as their ancestors? Who will take us into their future? What am I saying? Did I indeed say what I said? Balaram wondered.

'Yes, you did, my son,' she said, reading his mind. 'That is why I appeared in your dreams. That is why I brought you here.' Balaram seemed to understand something, but it was not clear to him yet. 'Yadukulottamma, by the end of this journey, you will see it more clearly. Let us now proceed further.'

'You must visit another tirtha called Saraswata Tirtha. But, before that, let me tell you, Vishwamitra's ashrama was on the West Bank—there.' She raised a finger to show the direction. 'Here on the east bank was Vasishtha's ashrama. The place where you see me flow very fast is Vasishtha Pravaha Tirtha, where I moved swiftly and carried him away to save him from Vishwamitra's wrath.'

Saraswati continued, 'This place is more than the Vasishtha–Vishwamitra conflict. Sthaanu prayed to me and established me here. None other than Skanda, the commander of Devas, was crowned here. He killed Tarakasura right at this place. Indra, after killing Namuchi, cleansed himself of his illness here. Aruna Devi joined me here, and hence it is called Aruna Tirtha. Soma himself performed Rajasuya Yagna here in Vasishtha Pravaha Tirtha. Please perform your austerities here along with your men.'

Balaram was still digesting the enormity of what he had been told. 'Mother, I have killed many rakshasas. We have faced down Jarasandha. There is hardly a thing that Krishna and I have not gone through. Yet, I feel very heavy listening to this story.'

'My dear son, have you studied the *Rig Veda* under Maharshi Vyas? Do you know of the Kuru ancestor, Samvarana? The Panchala King Sudasa—do you know him?'

'Mother, Sandipani Maharshi narrated everything to us. You are the one who has seen it all, Mother. As long as you are visible and people see you, they will see themselves very clearly. I now know why you appeared in my dream.'

They walked together for a very long time. There was absolute silence. 'What we attain is after a lot of conflict, striving, and resolution. It is not worth losing what we have. Yet, when it is beyond us, I leave it to Krishna to decide whether it is possible or not.'

'Balabhadra, a Parva-kaala is a Parva-kaala (a bend in the curve of time).'

'Balaram…' Saraswati broke the silence.

He turned with a sigh. 'I am alright, Mother. Let us continue.'

After another brief silence, Saraswati continued, 'My son, we need to proceed to Saraswata Tirtha. But, on the way, there are a few more important tirthas. Let me tell you about them.'

'Taijasa Tirtha is where Varunadeva was crowned as the deity of waters. At Agni Tirtha, Agnideva hid himself in between the Shami trees due to the curse of Maharshi Bhrigu. Finally, he attained a different form and released himself from that curse. That is how we have a new Agni. At Kubera Tirtha, Kubera earned the title of a Dikpala and the ownership of all the wealth of the universe. At Badara Pachana, Sage Shrutavatai, daughter of Sage Bharadvaja, performed an austere tapas to marry Indra. Arundhati performed tapas here when the Saptarishis left for the Himalayas during the twelve-year drought. There is no place like Badara Pachana for austerities, my son. At Indra Tirtha, Devendra himself performed severe penance and performed a hundred yagnas. At Rama Tirtha, Bhargava Rama performed a big yagna to give all his wealth obtained from Kshatriyas to Sage Kashyapa. Varuna performed another Rajasuya yagna. At Adiya Tirtha, Surya attained his status as Aditya to brighten the universe. After killing the rakshasas Madhu and Kaitabha, Vishnu himself took a dip here. The great sages, Asita Devala and Jaigeeshavya, lived here. Asita learned renunciation from Jaigeeshavya and finally attained mukti. What's more, none other than Sage Krishna Dwaipayana performed austerities here and earned siddhi (special powers).'

Hearing the name of Ved Vyas, Balaram closed his eyes for a few minutes and went into deep meditation. Saraswati was still speaking of Soma Mahatirtha, where Chandra performed a glorious Rajasuya, but Balaram was not listening. He was so engrossed in his meditation that he could envision Chandra performing the Rajasuya.

Balaram visited each of those tirthas with Devi Saraswati guiding him, tirthas, where the devas themselves had performed austerities to attain greater fruits. He performed austerities along with his followers and performed donations of many riches he had brought, to Brahmins and others.

He was now ready to visit Saraswata Tirtha.

'Lo and behold, Balaram—this is Saraswata Tirtha.' He said nothing. His eyes said everything. 'There was a devastating drought, Balaram, for twelve years. It was here, during that time, that Saraswata Muni performed severe penance and continued to study the Vedas even in those distressing times.'

'Mother, who was Saraswata Muni? How did he survive the drought? I know I am in for another heavy feeling. But I am eager.'

'Balaram, Sage Bhrigu had a son by the name of Sage Dadhichi. His ashrama was situated on my banks, right here. He was a man of great austerity. Even Devendra was quite cautious with him. Dadhichi had very special powers. He was a man of great physical strength as well as austere powers. Devendra, worried about his powers, sent an apsara—Alambusha—to distract him from his penance. Alambusha was not greatly successful. But, one day, Dadhichi was overcome by seeing Alambusha. His retas fell into my waters. I did not seek to waste the great powers of an austere rishi. I protected his retas in my womb. After nine months, I gave birth to a divine boy. I took him to Dadhichi, who was overjoyed to learn about the boy from me. He gave me special boons. He accepted the boy as his son and named him after me—Saraswata. Soon after, Indra sought Dadhichi's backbone for his Vajrayudha with the gigantic Asura Vritra. Dadhichi gave his consent without blinking his eyes and attained mukti.

'Saraswata had performed special adhyayana under Dadhichi and was a master of all knowledge of Vedas. He continued to live here on my banks. Alas, soon the drought struck. There was no food available anywhere. People began to die. The sages barely managed to survive and abandoned the practice of the Vedas. Soon, they began to forget the sacred texts. Saraswata too sought to move away to a farther place of abundance. But I dissuaded him. I shall flow, my son, and I shall give you fish every day as well. Please continue to be here and with me. Saraswata agreed and, by doing so, survived the twelve years of drought. Throughout, he continued his study of the Vedas without taking a break.

'Soon, the devas smiled. Nature flowered. There was everything in plenty again. The sages came back. However, they had completely forgotten the Vedas and were awestruck when they saw Saraswata's knowledge of them. They sought to learn from him and asked him to help them practice. Saraswata very clearly said, "Accept my shishyathwa, oh sages. Declare me as your guru. I shall get your practice started." This upset many sages. "Saraswata, we are older than you. You are still a boy. How can we accept you as a guru?" Saraswata stood his ground. Finally, they accepted him as guru and attained knowledge of the Vedas. Once again, the Vedas brightened the universe.'

Balaram smiled. 'Mother, oh Mother, who else other than you can revive us after everything is gone. You know how to protect what must be protected. You knew the powers of Dadhichi. You saw the future and protected his retas. You flow during a drought. If only we could see you during drought…' Balaram praised Saraswati greatly.

'Oh, Time, retain your abilities to see Saraswati. She will find the Saraswata in you. Saraswata will bring back the Vedas and destroy all tamas,' pleaded Balaram.

Balaram wondered, 'Who is the Saraswata of our times? Is it Yudhisthira, or is it the entire Pandavas? Or Krishna himself?' Balaram abandoned the thought. Instead, he immersed himself in the thoughts of river Saraswati in deep meditation.

They went further north and slowly approached the origins of the river Saraswati. They passed through the Vriddha Kanya Tirtha. That is where Kunigarga's daughter, Vriddha Kanya, had performed deep austerities. Attaining old age, she left her body and tried to raise herself to the heavens. The devas refused her entry, as she was not complete without the ritual of marriage. Vriddha Kanya invited the sages to marry her and offered half her austere powers. Shringavanta, son of Galava, accepted on the condition that they could stay together for a day. Vriddha Kanya transformed herself into a beautiful young lady, spent the night with Shringavanta, and left for the heavens. Shringavanta, smitten by her beauty, followed her suit.

At Vriddha Kanya Tirtha, Balaram received the news that the last of the Kaurava commanders at Kurukshetra, Shalya has fallen in battle and Kauravas have lost the War. But Balarama did not interrupt his pilgrimage.

At last, they were at Samanta Panchaka Tirtha, the Kurukshetra region. The Kaurava–Pandava battle was close, yet Balaram's mind was devoted to river Saraswati. This was the region once ploughed by King Kuru. The devas had to bestow him with special powers to stop his powerful austerities. They assured him that those who performed fasting or those who died here in battle would attain Brahmalok. Kuru sought Brahmalok from anybody who lived there. But the devas altered his aspirations a little. 'Anyone dying or fasting at Kurukshetra,' they said, 'will attain Brahmalok.' Further along, Saraswati showed Balaram the ashrama of Sage Shandili. She performed severe austerities throughout her life and had lived as a brahmacharini throughout. She attained exalted worlds after she left her body. Saraswati continued flowing.

Finally, they were on the trail to Plaksha Prasavana Tirtha. Saraswati was in tears. They climbed up the Himalayas. Saraswati stood at a distance. Balaram saw where the mother started her flow. There, he saw Krishna smiling.

Balaram visited Karapavana Tirtha, Mitra Varuna Ashrama, and the Yamuna River. He was now left with nothing but silence.

Sage Narada appeared. Balaram knew it was time to return. 'Balaram, the Kulakshaya is complete. Your shishyas are about to begin their final fight. It is time for you to return.' Narada then narrated the course of all eighteen days of the war that had transpired at Kurukshetra. Duryodhana and Bhim were, after all, his dear shishyas. Balaram decided to return. 'I must at least witness this fight.'

He gave instructions to his troupe and made arrangements for the return of the Brahmins. As he rode his horse, Balaram kept looking back until he lost sight of Saraswati's flow.

Saraswati, being near you is such a delight
Saraswati, being with you we acquire divinity
Saraswati, your people go to heavens direct
Saraswati, there too they think of you, always
Saraswati, the divine of all rivers
Saraswati, the auspicious one for all
Saraswati, those who live by you
Saraswati, do not suffer the sins of their ills

Balaram then climbed down the Himalayas and hastened towards Samanta Panchaka Kshetra, the Kurukshetra.

'Who among you has the flow of the river Saraswati? Bhim, is it you, or is it Duryodhana?' He began to take big strides towards Kurukshetra.

It was Shravana Nakshatra. The journey had ended. The flow, of course, was eternal.

Meanwhile, river Saraswati was flowing, as always.

3

Ambalika: The Third Sister

Ramanjaneya Sharaph

The morning after our arrival in Hastinapur, after our abduction from our wedding venue at Kashi, by Bhishma, a messenger arrived from Kashi. He brought our father's blessings and congratulations at our impending wedding to Vichitravirya, the king of Hastinapur and Bhishma's younger half-brother.

Kashi had acquiesced to our abduction. Joyfully.

Amba, my eldest sister, had pledged her heart to the king of Shalva and was given leave to join her paramour. She was happy.

Ambika, my middle sister, was preparing to be the empress of Hastinapur. She was joyful too.

But I was not.

Amba was busy preparing for her departure to Shalva, and I had Ambika for company.

'Aren't you angry?' I asked Ambika.

'Why should I be angry?'

'Because it is Vichitravirya who will be marrying us, not Bhishma.'

'So?'

'What do you mean "so"!' I threw my hands up in the air. 'It was Bhishma who carried us off from the swayamvar, defeating the assembled princes. As per the Kshatriya code of honour, he is required to marry us!'

'A woman is first the daughter-in-law of the house she marries into, and then a wife. Whether we marry Bhishma or Vichitravirya, we will still be daughters-in-law of the House of Kuru.' Ambika was always the practical one.

'But … the code of honour?'

'Do you think the man who incurred the wrath of the kingdoms of Kurujangala to secure brides for his half-brother will break his vow of eternal celibacy and marry you?' She sank the sharp point of a knife into a ripe apple that she had picked up and punctured the skin. A drop of apple juice dribbled down the side, filling the room with sickly sweet apple fragrance. 'And let's be practical, Ambalika,' she chided, 'Vichitravirya is king. It is by marrying him that the son born to me will be the next chakravartin, not by marrying Bhishma, only a caretaker, howsoever capable he may be!'

Ambika's words pricked my ears. 'What do you mean the son born to you!'

'Well, I am your elder, therefore, my son will have precedence to the throne over yours!' She put a piece of the ripe apple into her mouth.

If Amba had not been marrying the king of Shalva, Ambika would not have been so smug.

'Did you know about Amba and Shalva?' I asked Ambika.

'No,' Ambika replied. She was now busy sifting through saris from among a heap of silks, selecting the ones she would wear during the wedding.

'I wonder how they met. And when did they get Father's approval? Oh, how exciting! To be able to choose one's own husband!' I said.

'Hmmm?' Ambika responded, without even taking her eyes off the piles of shimmering fabric. The silks interested her more.

Leaving Ambika to her saris, I walked outside to the private garden. She did not even notice.

Dismissing a serving girl who scampered after me, I sat under the cool shade of a neem tree. The neem fruits were ripening into a golden yellow, and parrots flitted in and out, picking the ripe ones and sucking the pulp out. How strange, I thought, that the fruit of the bitter neem should taste sweet as nectar! And stranger still, the parrots sucking on the sweet fruit—the same parrots that pecked at pepper corns with such relish!

Should I accept my fate too? *A fate that hundreds of princesses would kill for*, as Ambika reminded me more than once. I looked up at the parrots sucking on the sweet fruit. Amba had found her sweet fruit. Ambika had accepted the pepper corn with relish. What should I do?

The day of Amba's departure arrived. Ambika and I accompanied her as she walked happily towards a chariot loaded with gifts.

'You must be thrilled. Less competition for you now,' I whispered in Ambika's ear. She glared at me.

I turned away and looked at Amba, who glowed with the radiance of a woman in love. 'I will miss you,' I told her.

Amba smiled. 'This will help you to remember me by,' she said and removed the chudamani from her hair. She pressed the disc of gold studded with diamonds into my hands.

I was aghast! 'But … but I can't have this! This is your favourite jewel!'

She patted my cheek, the way she used to whenever I scraped my knee as a little girl. 'No silly! You are my favourite!'

I pressed the chudamani to my bosom. I would treasure it. But having a jewel was not the same as having her. I took her hand and pressed it to my cheek. My tears wet her hand. Amba stroked my head. She turned towards Vichitravirya and spoke to him with authority. She was after all an elder sister speaking to the betrothed of a younger sister.

'Brother-in-law,' she addressed him with respect, but did not call him king, 'look after my sisters well, will you?'

Vichitravirya's silks rustled closer, as he moved a step towards me. I turned to look at him and saw the kindest smile. And the imperceptible nod of an implicit promise. Ambika was blushing like a soon-to-be bride. But for the decorum expected of a future queen, she would have clasped his hand.

Should I too accept the pepper corns?

'Write to me often,' Amba said, climbing into the chariot.

I nodded.

'And we will meet soon,' she said and added, 'in … nine months?' I understood the meaning of her words only when Ambika hid her face in her hands, her toe digging into the dirt. Amba smiled, and the chariot rumbled away taking her to her destiny.

Suddenly, I realized that I was jealous of Amba.

A grand ceremony was arranged for our marriage to Vichitravirya. Throughout the elaborate rituals, he could not take his eyes off us. Ambika blushed. I had still not chosen.

Did I even have a choice?

Then as we sat in front of the holy fire, my hand was placed in his. His hand had a comforting warmth. I turned my face up and looked into his eyes. Did my eyes reflect the doubt playing in my mind? A carefree smile played on his lips, and his eyes gestured an assurance, the same assurance that he had given to Amba promising to take care of us. The tension in my hand dissipated, and my fingers relaxed. His fingers sought mine and clasped my hand gently. I didn't resist. His eyes were still locked on mine. I nodded. His smile broadened, and he gripped my hand firmly. For the first time, I felt warmth spread through my cheeks.

I was no longer envious of Amba.

One morning, soon after our wedding, Ambika rushed into my chambers. Her hair was undone, and the plaits of her long silks were not all tucked in. 'Tut-tut,' I teased, 'if you don't doll yourself up, our husband will spend the nights with me more often.'

Ambika grabbed my shoulders, and her nails dug in. 'Amba is back!' she said.

'Isn't it too soon for her to be going to Kashi? How long is she stopping here?' Spending time with Amba would be a welcome change from Ambika, who never tired of strutting the gifts our husband, the king, plied her with.

Ambika's nails dug deeper. 'You don't understand! Shalva refused to accept her!'

The room spun around me. Ambika's face became blurry and was about to disappear when she shook me violently. 'Ambalika? Ambalika!' a distant voice echoed inside my head, and the spinning room came to a stop.

'But … why?' Hadn't Shalva pledged himself to her?

'Something about her having been won by another man.'

'But that's ridiculous!' Surely our Amba would not have taken that lying down? 'What will happen now? Will our husband marry her?' I asked.

Ambika collapsed onto a low, long cushion. 'Of course not! No man will accept a woman who has rejected him.' She added, 'What need does he have for her when he has me!'

'Ambika! Surely you don't mean that?' I said sharply.

'I don't know what she intends. She is insisting that Bhishma marry her! And to push her case, she has brought Bhargava Parashurama, Bhishma's guru, along.'

'Oh! Will Bhishma marry her?' I thought they made a perfect match.

'I hope not,' Ambika was deep in thought. 'If he does, and their children are anything like him or her, then…' I understood the words that Ambika left unsaid. She nursed fond hopes of being the queen mother, hopes that had already taken deep root in her heart.

Ambika had no cause for worry. Bhishma would not break his vow, even if it was his guru commanding him to do otherwise. Angered at this insolence, Parashurama challenged Bhishma to battle. The battle raged for days. I simmered helplessly, anxiously waiting for news everyday since Satyavati, my mother-in-law, had forbidden me from meeting my own sister. The battle was inconclusive. Parashurama apologized to Amba and went away.

Bhishma begged forgiveness from Amba for refusing her but was resolute. He would rather bear the curse of a wronged woman than break his vow. Though heartbroken for Amba, my admiration for Bhishma went up a notch. How could one not admire the strength of character of a man who conceded that he had wronged? But Amba was Amba! With no one to turn to, she swore vengeance, in this life or the next, and walked away.

I watched helplessly as Amba, my Amba, left the city gates, broken and defeated. I pressed Vichitravirya to find out from the royal spies of Amba's whereabouts. The spies were able to gather little more than gossip. They said she walked into the fire, to be reborn as a warrior who would exact revenge on Bhishma.

Vichitravirya wiped my tears. 'Let bygones be bygones. Maybe it is for the good. Try to forget her,' he consoled me. But I was not consoled.

I ran to Ambika for succour. 'What happened to Amba is unfortunate,' she said, standing at the window, her face to the sun. There was a trace of sadness in her voice. 'But whatever happened was a result of her own follies.'

Is it folly to love? If it is, isn't Ambika guilty of the same foolishness? Am I not foolish too? Is it folly to stand up for oneself? If it is, isn't every one of the Kuru ancestors, right down to Satyavati and Bhishma, guilty of that folly?

'But…' I tried to say something, not sure what.

Ambika turned away from the window. 'It is good to finally be out of her shadow,' she said, smoothed her silks, and walked out of the room, maids in tow.

Ambika, the ever-practical Ambika.

Between my helplessness and Ambika's practical-mindedness, Amba was lost. Forgotten.

It was early spring, and the mid-morning sun cast pillars of light through the branches of the flower garden. The swing that Ambika and I sat on with our husband rocked gently to cooing birdsong. Ambika rested her head on his shoulder, clasping his hand on her lap.

'Arya,' I addressed him, 'don't you have to attend court?'

He patted my cheek. 'My pretty mynah, are you not happy that I am attending to you?'

With every passing day, I lost my heart to his innocent charms. I ran my fingers through his curly locks. 'But arya, you are the king! The welfare of the citizens is your responsibility.'

'How clever you are!' he said, eyes sparkling. Ambika tugged his hand and nuzzled her face into his shoulder. With his free hand, he stroked her hair but spoke to me. 'You are right, the welfare of the people is my responsibility. But tell me, dear, are they not happy? Are they not prosperous?'

'But it is elder Bhishma who…'

He put a finger to my lips. 'Shhh! You think too much, pretty parrot. What better way to fulfill my responsibility to the people than letting a person, more able than me, run my kingdom?' His innocence was at once charming and frustrating.

'And,' he said, taking off his uttariya and wrapping it around my shoulders, 'you will catch a cold if you are not careful!'

I wanted to protest, but Ambika stood up, pulling his hand. 'Arya, I am tired. Will you put me to bed?' Her lips quivered. He followed her as she led him into her apartments. I pulled his uttariya tighter around myself. It was warm, like him. It smelt of him.

I sat staring as they disappeared into the palace. Vichitravirya was a good husband, loving, caring, and attentive to our needs. He was loyal too, not taking any other women. He was more husband than a wife would want, but I wished he would be more king too.

Ambika believed that our husband loved her more. He believed that we loved him more than anything else, which was true. Seven years passed thus. But Satyavati was not happy. We dreaded that time of the month when our clothes soiled. Every month, as Ambika or I confined ourselves to isolation, she would accost us with an 'again?' How could we tell her that the soil was fertile, but the seed was not strong enough? The palace vaids had confirmed that.

The years in Vichitravirya's company were blissful but, in the absence of the pitter-patter of little feet in the palace halls, it was like a beautiful bell without a ringer. Our husband contented himself playing with the children of the servants. Every time a child rode his shoulders, gurgling with laughter, a dagger went through my heart. But my womb remained bare. The desert of my heart sucked up the spring of Vichitravirya's love. But fate eyed that spring avariciously.

A severe form of consumption afflicted Vichitravirya, and I watched helplessly as the tuberculosis wasted his lungs.

Our husband lay on a large bed, exhausted by the effort to stay alive. He was covered with white cotton sheets to keep his body cool. Serving girls constantly fanned the heat away. Ambika sat on the bed, next to him, sobbing silently, only to be shushed by Satyavati. I too stifled a sob, unable to bear the sight—my once handsome husband rasping for breath, his frame shrunken to half its former size, cheeks sunken, and eyes vacant. A cough wracked his body, the intensity half lifting him off the bed, arching his spine impossibly. Black phlegm stained the white sheet, and the attendants replaced the ruined sheet with yet another white sheet.

'Vaidji?' Satyavati turned towards the palace doctor.

The aged doctor shook his head. 'Forgive me, Queen Mother. The disease has eaten half of his lungs. The king is beyond the cure of any mortal. We can only beseech Rudra.' His words were interrupted by the ringing of the bells in the palace temple, where endless pujas were being performed for the recovery of the king.

'Beseech Rudra for what, vaidji?' Satyavati prodded, though we all knew the answer.

The old doctor stammered, 'That … that the king's passage to heaven be painless.' A tear rolled down his wrinkled cheek, as he clasped his hands in prayer and helplessness.

A low shudder passed through Satyavati, and she grabbed the bedpost to steady herself. Ambika's sobbing turned into a wail. Tears streamed down my cheeks as I wiped Vichitravirya's forehead with a wet towel. His lips quivered as he struggled to speak. Ambika and I bent close to catch his barely audible whisper.

'Madira…' he gasped, his head sinking into the cushions at the effort.

I looked at the vaid, who shook his head.

'But the alcohol will at least numb his pain a little,' I pleaded.

The vaid shook his head. 'Forgive me, my queen,' is all he would say.

Helpless, I turned back to my husband, holding his hand gently. He squeezed my hand and made an effort to lift his head. Ambika supported him, sliding his head onto her lap. Gazing fondly into her eyes, he stroked her cheek. He turned his gaze to me, a faint smile spreading over his pale lips. He let out a deep sigh and closed his eyes. His chest stopped heaving, and his hand slipped from my grip. Limp. Lifeless. The room spun around me. Everything went black.

When I came to, I was in my chambers, and the vaid was checking my pulse. Satyavati looked at him expectantly. 'Is it…?'

The vaid shook his head, 'I am afraid not. The queen passed out from shock and grief.'

Satyavati turned to leave, not caring to hide her disappointment. She had not even enquired about my well-being. The vaid had a look of disbelief. I was not surprised, this was not the first display of her stone-heartedness that I had witnessed. At that moment, it was clear what I should do.

'Mother,' I called out.

She stopped but did not turn around. 'What?'

I got off the bed, and a serving girl rushed to my side. I waved her away and walked up to Satyavati. 'I will ascend the funeral pyre with the king's mortal remains,' I said.

The bustle of the servants stopped, the guards at the entrance stared open-mouthed, and even the breeze blowing through the windows stilled, leaving the billowing curtains suspended mid-air. Everyone turned towards Satyavati. 'No!' she declared and walked away.

Long after she had walked away, I kept staring at the empty doorway, looking for something, looking for *someone*. The corridor leading from the doorway looked long, cold, empty. An icy gust blew through the latticed stone panels lining the corridor. I hugged my arms tightly to my chest, but the chill seeped into my bones. I reached out to grab Vichitravirya's arm for comfort. My hands clutched only empty air. I turned. The bed was empty beside me. *You lied to me*, I told him, certain that he was listening, whatever heaven he was in. The cold gust swirled around the room, threatening to blow out the flickering lamps that struggled to stay alive. The chill in my bones spread its icy tentacles to my heart and an unknown fear gripped me. 'Madanika!' I called out urgently to my maid of several years, not wanting to stay alone, not wanting to stay in the dark.

Madanika hurriedly shut the tall teak doors, poured oil into the lamps, and lengthened the wicks. The flames leapt higher but cast deeper, darker shadows. She wrapped a shawl around my shoulders. The shawl was cold.

We were still grieving when Satyavati summoned us to her private council hall. It was a long, pillared hall lit by lamps, with no embellishments. The council hall was cold when Ambika and I walked in, clad in widows' white. For the first time in years, Ambika held my hand.

Satyavati was seated on the only chair in the hall—high-backed, on a low pedestal. She came straight to the topic. 'A land without a king is like a doe amongst a pride of lions. We need an heir to the throne from one of you.' She pointed a finger at us.

Ambika and I looked at each other. *How is that possible?*

Satyavati left no room for doubt. 'Bhishma will do the needful!'

'No!' the word tumbled out even before my mind processed the words. I could not believe what I was hearing. We were devoted to our husband Vichitravirya. How could she suggest this to us, wives of her own son?

'Ambika,' Satyavati pointed a finger, 'you are the elder daughter-in-law. You will go first.'

I hoped Ambika would protest, but she had shut her eyes, hearing the unthinkable. Would it shut out the blasphemy that Satyavati suggested? I had to do something.

'But Mother,' I said, trying to be firm, 'we are pativratas, devoted to the memory of our departed husband, *your* son. What you are suggesting is…'

She cut me off. 'It is not a suggestion.' It was a command, to be followed without demur.

'But...'

Satyavati put up a hand and stopped me. 'You are familiar with the concept of niyoga, aren't you?'

Of course, I had heard of niyoga. The wife of a man incapable of fathering a child could beget one from, among others, the husband's brother. And Bhishma was my dead husband's brother! But, having given myself, body and soul, to Vichitravirya, even the thought of being with another man, howsoever noble the purpose might be, was revolting. I had to find a legitimate objection, and fast.

'Don't the scriptures require that niyoga be performed only when a woman so desires?' I asked.

Satyavati was not one to be flummoxed. 'What do you desire, queens of Hastinapur? That the gates of this great city be left open for plunderers to ravage her? That the ancient palaces and temples be ground to dust by marauders?' She saved her best for the last. 'Do you desire,' she hissed, 'that the citizens, who look up to us for protection, be left to the mercy of conquering hordes?'

The old woman had hit us at our most vulnerable spot. As Kshatriyas, it was our bounden duty to protect. I hung my head, defeated. My only hope was that Bhishma would refuse. Would he value his vow more than his duty?

As if in reply, Bhishma strode in. The surprise in his eyes indicated that he had not expected our presence. He bowed deeply to Satyavati. 'You summoned me, Mother?'

'May you live long, *son*,' she stressed the last word. 'Hastinapur needs a king,' she stated without preamble.

'You are right, Mother. It is time we invite my father's elder brother, King Bahlika, to take over the reins of Hastinapur.'

'Bhishma!' Satyavati thundered, startling him. 'Hastinapur belongs to the line of King Shantanu, and it is his line who will rule this realm!'

'But how is that possible?'

'Niyoga,' Satyavati said. She pointed a finger at him. 'You will do the needful!'

'Mother!' Bhishma erupted but controlled himself. 'You know it is not possible. I will not break my vow!'

'Son,' her tone turned surprisingly soft, 'by the rules of niyoga, the kshetraphala—-the fruit—belongs to the kshetrapaala, the master of the field, not the one sowing the seed. The child born of niyoga will be your brother's son, not yours. Your vow is safe.'

Bhishma's voice rose a pitch. 'I know the rules of niyoga. My vow was not that I would not beget children, my vow was that I would remain celibate! I am committed to my vow.'

Satyavati was in a quandary. It was for the sake of children to be born of her that Bhishma had been cornered into taking the terrible vow. Life indeed does come full circle. 'Son, it was for my sake that you took the terrible vow! I release you from the vow!'

'It was an act of free will on my part. What is done cannot be undone.' Bhishma brought his palms together. 'Forgive me,' he said, but his head was not bowed.

Ambika squeezed my hand. I was jubilant, too, and immensely relieved.

Satyavati pondered for a while. 'Alright then. You know my eldest son, Krishna Dwaipayana?'

Bhishma nodded. 'The revered sage Ved Vyas.'

'Send word that I have summoned him. He will perform the niyoga!'

'As you command, Mother.'

Satyavati left the council hall without another word.

My heart sank. Ambika had shut her eyes again. I wished Amba was here. She would have known what to do.

'Take me to your chambers,' Ambika asked, holding my hand as we walked back. I was surprised. She had always summoned me to her chambers, never visited mine.

We walked silently. Ambika held my hand all the way to my part of the palace. Today, the corridors seemed longer and the ceiling higher. Vichitravirya had filled my heart and life so much that without him by my side everything seemed vast in its emptiness. A tear rolled down my cheek. It reminded me of the loving hand of my husband, who would now never wipe it. The palace that I had grown accustomed to seemed alien. I tightened my grip on Ambika's hand.

My serving girls were surprised to see Ambika. They bustled about to make her welcome. 'These are your chambers?' Ambika asked, surprised.

I smiled. It was not for want of gifts that I had done up my chambers sparsely. I liked the simple, spartan decor.

Ambika flopped onto a low, long seat and buried her face in her hands. 'What do we do now, Ambalika?' she asked.

That was a question I had no answer to. But what burnt me with indignation was the way Satyavati had explained the morality of niyoga. Were we only brown farmland? Unmoving, bereft of feelings, of emotions? That anyone could plough, anyone could trample, unmindful of the hurt it caused?

The shared pain had brought us sisters together again. They say that every cloud has a silver lining. But little do they know that the clouds also rumble with thunder and rain hail.

Sage Vyas, as we had feared, acceded to his mother's request. Since Ambika was the elder wife, she would go first. All that Satyavati desired was an heir to the throne. If Ambika gave her that, I would be spared the nightmare. I felt relieved that I was not the one required to go first. I also felt guilty.

But Ambika was not so lucky. Here was a queen of one of the most powerful kingdoms in Aryavarta, yet forced to submit to another, against her will. My thoughts went back to the early days of our marriage, to Ambika's words that her son would be the king. Irony! Her words would be fulfilled and how!

I could not sleep a wink that night. A stiff breeze shook the corridors and halls, and the flames of the lamps and torches shuddered, dancing eerie patches of light and shadow on the walls. I remembered Amba now more than ever. She was unafraid of the dark, of the ghosts that dancing flames threw up. On instinct, I pulled out the family chudamani she had given me. It was a simple jewel, but I hoped that holding it in my hand would infuse a little of Amba's strength in me. 'Forgive me, Amba, I failed to stand up for myself. I failed you,' I murmured, holding the jewel. Dark shadows danced on its surface. I shuddered and locked it back in the jewellery box.

I awoke to a cloudy sky spreading gloom all around. The maids were muted as they went about their tasks. The sun rose higher in the sky, but there was no sign of Ambika. Soon, word of Ambika's ordeal reached me. Gossip travels fast within palace walls.

Ambika had shut her eyes during the act, and the sage had divined that. As a result, the son born would be blind. Before I could recover from the shock of Ambika's night of horror, Satyavati issued orders for me. The queen mother did not want a blind heir to the throne, so I was ordered to submit. I had to endure niyoga with the sage! She also sent a herbal concoction, a few drops of which I was instructed to put in my eyes so that I would not shut them.

The dreaded day arrived. I already knew the protocol: man and woman would be joined solely for the purpose of procreation, without any hint of lust or desire. Ghee would be smeared over our bodies to make us ugly, undesirable to each other. We would lie on a straw mat in a darkened room for the duration of the act, on the completion of which the man would immediately depart.

I was in a daze as the maids prepared me. I saw everything in the mirror they held up, my hideous face, my lifeless eyes, but registered nothing. Two maids led me to the small, untiled room.

One of the maids walked ahead and lifted the straw curtain at the entrance of the room. Beyond it was darkness.

I shuddered. My feet refused to walk. My hand squeezed the arm of the other maid who was leading me. 'Why is it so dark inside?'

'Those were the orders, my queen,' she stated, without emotion.

I turned to look at her. I did not recognize her. Fear filled my heart. 'Who … who are you?' I asked.

'I have been deputed by the queen mother to prepare you,' she said, tucking a lock of grey hair behind her ear. Her fingers marked a streak of ghee on her temple. I looked at her hands—they were oily with ghee. I looked at my own arms. Small lumps of the white fat blotched the smooth and glowing surface of my arms. I pulled my hands and touched my cheeks. More ghee. My hands went to the inside of my thighs. The flimsy cotton garment was sticky with ghee. I shuddered and took a step back, 'No…!'

The old maid took my hand firmly, drawing it away. I stood rooted to the spot. Is a woman only a womb? A womb for hire? Was I only a body for hire? Was *my* body for use by others?

'No!' I said, my voice barely a whisper.

'You *have* to, my queen,' she said, her voice gentle.

I shook my head. 'How would you feel if…' I could not bring myself to utter the rest of the words. A tear streaked down my cheek and was lost in the ghee on my face.

The elderly woman turned around to face me. 'I know,' she said, 'I was a body for hire too. I suckled your husband, the late king Vichitravirya. And his brother Chitrangada before him. I starved my baby boy, but the money fed him. And me. And kept us safe. That one act feeds me still.' She tugged at my hand, but I did not move.

'But … but you did it willingly!' I said.

The old maid smiled. Was it a smirk? 'Willingly? What mother willingly starves her own child to feed another?' she asked.

'But you did it to save your child,' I replied.

'My lady,' she said looking into my eyes, 'you are our queen. Are we not your children? Is it not your duty to protect us? To save us?'

Lessons on dharma and morality sound good in theory. Only in theory.

'Sometimes you have to put your dharma, your duty, above yourself,' she said as if guessing my thoughts.

'Words don't help,' I said bitterly.

'I know,' she said pulling a small pouch from the folds of her clothes, 'but this will.' She thrust the pouch into my hands. 'Ground seeds of the opium flower,' she said.

I nodded gratefully and poured the contents into my palm. She gestured with her eyes, and the other maid at the entrance to the room turned her face away. I emptied the coarse powder into my mouth and swallowed. It tasted bitter, and I suppressed a dry heave.

'Quickly now, before it takes effect,' she said and pushed me into the dark room.

I lay down on the straw mat, and an overpowering drowsiness tugged at my eyelids.

When I opened them, the room was dark, but I could see clearly. I was hovering near the ceiling, but it did not bother me. Looking down, I saw a woman, ugly and oily, lying on the straw mat, shivering. The blood had drained from her face, and she was pale with fright. I recognized her—she had my arms, my breasts, my thighs. But I felt nothing. A swarthy man, his saffron robes dripping ghee, lay on top of her, thrusting back and forth.

'Get a hold of yourself! Don't be afraid! You are only doing your dharma!' he hissed repeatedly.

Dharma! Dharma! Dharma! The word ricocheted off the walls, and my head throbbed.

I tried to think happy thoughts to shut out the pain. I tried to think of my Vichitravirya. I hoped that his smiling visage would help me endure the degradation. However, I could only see the black phlegm-covered sheet. Dirty. Filthy. Diseased.

When I came back to my senses, I was sitting up, my legs pressed close to my chest, rocking myself back and forth. I did not remember waking up. I was still groggy from the opium but recognized the room. And the straw mat on which I had lain. I looked around the darkness. It was empty. There was nothing. There was no one. I was all alone. A gust of wind blew aside the straw curtain covering the entrance, lifting it. Outside, the sky was dark, and the darkness crept into the room. I shuffled to a corner and pressed my legs closer to my chest. It was not enough. I grabbed the straw mat and wrapped it around myself. Tightly. The wind blew harder and threatened to rip the curtain and toss it into the darkness. I buried my face in my legs and crawled deeper into the corner, shivering, hoping the walls would swallow me up.

There was a soft rustle and heavy feet padded across the floor. The darkness had swallowed the curtain and was coming to get me. It peeled away the straw mat. I was shaking violently. A firm hand grasped my shoulder. I started mumbling incoherently. The hand peeled away the straw mat from around me. I sank into the corner, trying to push myself deeper, away.

'Shhhh … it's me,' the voice said.

I was still shaking and mumbling.

The voice wiped the sweat off my face with a cold towel and stroked my cheek. 'Fear not, it's me,' it said again.

It was a familiar voice. The voice settled down next to me. The heavy hand pulled my head to its bosom. I resisted, but the hand was insistent. I gave in. The hand rocked me gently, and the voice sang a soft lullaby. It was a sad song, and I sobbed. The hand continued to pat my head and nudged me into a deep sleep. A sleep where demons chased, and I ran. But there was no escape. The demons were everywhere. One of them crawled inside me.

When I awoke, morning had dawned, and I was in my bedchambers, lying on the soft cushions. I touched my face. The maids must have wiped me clean. My back ached, and I realized that a fat cushion had been placed under my hips. I reached out to pull it away. The elderly maid rushed to my side and gently, but firmly, pulled my hand away, shaking her head. Was she the voice from the night? I recognized the garment of coarse weave that she was wearing from yesterday. But the front of her dress was *not* smudged with ghee.

The guard at the entrance announced Satyavati's arrival. Satyavati visiting me—a rare occasion.

'I am disappointed,' Satyavati declared the moment she entered. 'I am told you paled with fright at the sight of my son. As a result, the son born to you will be sickly, pale.'

'Maybe you should not have sent your son to violate me!' I spat, the words tumbling out even before they formed in my head, tears clouding my vision.

'Ambalika!' Satyavati's nostrils flared, and the maid gave an audible gasp. 'You think you are the first woman to be violated?'

Her voice was cold, but there was pain in that coldness. A pain that evoked strains of a sad lullaby—a lullaby that sounded distant and familiar. And a hard truth. But I wouldn't relent and stared back coldly. I decided what I would do.

My legs felt weak, but I got off the bed. The maid tried to nudge me back onto the bed, but I pushed her away.

'Where are you off to?' Satyavati demanded.

'To have a bath,' I replied, 'to wash the filth away!'

'You will not!' Satyavati thundered.

My knees turned to jelly, and I collapsed onto the bed.

'I will have you suspended upside down all day if need be until the seed takes root!' she spat. She looked at the elderly maid and gestured with her head. The maid nodded.

The elderly maid pushed me back down on the bed. I tried to resist but was still too weak. She then pushed the fat cushion back under my hips. I tried to kick it away, but she sat at my feet and started massaging them. Her grip was firm, and she would not let me wriggle away. As if on cue, two young, swarthy maids sat on either side and started massaging my arms, pressing them down firmly on the bed. I was shackled by the iron will of the queen mother.

I looked away, helpless tears running down my face. Satyavati nodded sternly at the maids, and they bowed. Their hands would imprison me until my womb sprouted. Satyavati walked away in a huff.

Satyavati did not permit me to meet Ambika. 'I do not want her thoughts to be corrupted by your influence,' Satyavati said. 'Your sister realizes her error and is ready for penitence. She will submit to the sage once more.' I was not surprised that Ambika had begged for forgiveness.

My time of the month came, and I did not soil my clothes. The vigil around me intensified. I took out the chudamani that Amba had given me. It smelt of her. I sensed Amba's presence near me ... around me ... *with* me. I placed the chudamani back in the box. Vigil or no vigil. I would *not* submit.

From that moment, I stopped eating. I would kill myself if need be to extinguish the filth growing in me. The maids cajoled and coerced, but I did not relent. Word reached Satyavati, and she walked into my chambers. With a wave of her hand, she dismissed the maids. She sat next to me on the bed and took my hand in hers. I jerked my hand away.

She smiled and took my hand in hers again. Again, I jerked it away. Without reproach, she took my hand in hers yet again and held it with a firmer grip. There was something familiar about that touch. I put up a token resistance.

She stroked my hand as she spoke. 'You know my son Krishna?'

'You mean Maharishi Vyas?' I asked, the bile rising in my throat at the very mention of the name.

'Yes,' she nodded, 'Krishna is the name *I* gave him.'

I nodded.

Satyavati's gaze focused on the distance, beyond the window in the far wall. 'Do you know how he was born?'

I had heard vague stories but was not certain. Right now, I was not interested in Satyavati or *her* Vyas. I was about to make a nasty remark, but Satyavati spoke, her voice distant.

'I was ferrying the sage Parashara across the river in a little canoe. He was the lone passenger when he took me.'

I remembered. The story went that the sage took Satyavati with her consent and, in return, bestowed exotic boons on her. I had believed it. But after my ordeal, I was not so sure about the consent. 'Did you…?' I could not bring myself to complete the sentence.

Satyavati turned to look at me. 'Consent?'

I nodded, feeling uncertain and awkward.

'What do you think?'

I wanted to believe the story that the moist eyes of this woman told—the same story that the moist eyes of all women tell. But the stories that men told pulled a veil over pleading eyes. I kept quiet.

'I was all of fifteen years old. Do you think my consent mattered?'

I *wanted* to believe her.

Neither of us spoke. The image of a fifteen-year-old girl, her lips quivering with fright, with confusion, filled the empty silence between us. Did she cry then? Did she cry afterwards, as the unwanted seed grew in her, sucking her blood … her life … her soul? Was she crying now?

I turned to look at Satyavati's face. Not a tear rolled down her cheek. I felt foolish and wiped away the tears that rolled down my cheek before she could notice. 'And yet, here you are … the empress of Hastinapur and now the queen mother,' I said.

Satyavati sighed. 'And yet, here I am.'

She had not stopped stroking my hand. She turned my palm over and smoothed the lines. 'I have been in your position many years ago, but … I cannot … will not force you. But just think about your son growing inside you. Is it his fault that he was conceived thus? Should you starve him for no fault of his? Should you squeeze the life out of him for no mistake of his?'

I had made the mistake of succumbing to emotional blackmail before. I was not going to repeat that mistake. 'I am not going to lis…' I started to protest when Satyavati put up a hand.

'Do not protest now. If you feel the same way after nine months, I will not stop you from doing whatever you want. In any case, there is a precedent in the family of a mother killing her newborn infants.' She was referring to Ganga. She continued, 'Would my son have wanted you to terminate the pregnancy?'

Satyavati's parting question bothered me long after she left. What would my husband have wanted? I remembered his smiling face, his hearty laughter when he played with the children of servants and maids. Would he have approved of my snuffing out a life? Of my preventing a baby from coming into the world?

But my husband was dead. He had always done that which his heart desired, not what his queens wanted, not what his dharma as king demanded. Why should *his* memory come in the way of my honour?

Vichitravirya's hearty laugh faded away and another voice replaced it. *And yet, here I am, empress of Hastinapur and the queen mother,* it said.

I took out Amba's chudamani. Its face glowed with jumping flames. The jewel exuded power. It belonged in the company of power. Amba was destined to be empress, but she chose otherwise. So, the chudamani left. It came into my hands. I wore it in my hair and looked into the mirror. The woman in the mirror smiled.

I looked down at my swelling belly and stroked it. I felt a tiny kick.

My son!

He was coming into this world guileless, faultless, trusting. Who but I would shield him? Who but I would care for him? He came from me. He was a part of me. But for one tiny seed, he was all me—made of me, made *by* me, made with *my blood, my flesh*. He was *me!*

I stroked my belly. He kicked again.

I walked into Ambika's apartments. Satyavati was there, tending my sister, whose swollen belly indicated a strong strapping boy. Ambika looked at the chudamani in my hair. Her eyes widened with horror.

'Ambalika! You are a widow! You cannot wear a chudamani!' she said.

I turned to Satyavati and raised an eyebrow. Satyavati nodded, a faint smile spreading on her lips. I nodded back.

Ambika's serving girls, some carrying trays, some fanning Ambika, some guarding her apartments, some lighting lamps, all stopped whatever they were doing. Every one of them turned to me. And bowed deeply. I acknowledged them with a nod, turned, and walked back to my apartments. Two of

Ambika's guards left their place by the door and ran behind me, to escort me.

Walking back to my apartments, the walls and the painted ceilings of the corridor sprang to life, the carved images shimmering in the bright sun. I smiled. I was familiar with the patterns on the tiled floor but had never noticed the walls or the ceiling. Taking slow steps, I patted my belly. 'Chakravartin!' I said softly.

Nine months later they handed him to me, my baby, swaddled in white: tiny, pale, and helpless. He opened his little pink mouth and wailed.

At that moment, it did not matter that I would be empress. Or the queen mother. It did not matter whether he would be emperor. All that mattered was that he was mine … *he was me.*

I pressed him to my bosom and bathed him in tears. The old maid gently moved aside my uttariya and put his tiny mouth on my breast. I felt a squeeze in my chest and was wracked by sobs.

Pandu, I called him.

The room erupted with cries of victory to Emperor Pandu. And to Queen Mother Ambalika.

4

Brave Barbareek: The Story of Ghatotkach's Son

Kavitha Sankaranarayanan and Paras Artwani

> 'Know that the origin of sacrificial action is the Almighty Lord and, therefore, the Almighty all-pervading Lord is ever present in sacrifice.'
>
> —Bhagavad Gita

Etched in the annals of the epic Mahabharata is the sacrifice of a young lad, Barbareek, who, in his unique way, under the guidance of none other than the Almighty Lord Sri Krishna Himself wholeheartedly joined the battle of righteousness.

This is the story of a hero who was the mightiest warrior in the Kurukshetra battle, one who climbed the rungs of valour by virtue of his ethics and principles. His tale is unique since untold honour was bestowed upon the valiant hero without him even physically fighting in the battle.

The hillocks near the Kurukshetra battlefield were bathed in the golden hues of the rising sun on this morning as it did on any other day. But something had changed.

Today, there was another source of radiance on the hill—the head of Barbareek, impaled on a spear, alive and in silent meditation, radiating an aura of peace and calm. A gentle smile playing upon his lips, the gentle breeze ruffling his black curly locks, Barbareek's head remembered his ancestors in gratitude for having blessed him with attaining his current state. Grandson of Hidimbi and the mighty Pandava Bhim, and the son of Ghatotkach and Maurvi, Barbareek was no stranger to bravery and courage. However, it was this lad who brought glory beyond dreams to his family by doing what he had done the previous day. As the rays of the sun caressed his face, Barbareek's thoughts flew to his childhood days.

'Tell me a story, Dadima,' crooned little Barbareek to his grandmother Hidimbi, as he jumped up and down on the pile of leaves in the garden of their tidy little hut deep in the jungle.

'Okay, okay. You don't have to mess up the swept pile of leaves. Sit quietly on that rock there. Only then I shall tell you a story.' Jumping in glee, Barbareek climbed up the rock and sat cross-legged in a manner of utmost obedience as he eagerly waited for Hidimbi.

Barbareek was the apple of her eye. After all, she not only had to lavish her affection on her only grandson but also had to step into his grandfather's shoes as well in pampering the little boy. Bhim, with the duties he had to execute being a Pandava, rarely visited them and missed spending time with his grandson. She smiled to herself as she sat and pulled him onto her lap and, with a kiss on his lovely black curls, she asked him, 'What story would you like to hear today little one?'

Barbareek promptly replied, 'Tell me the story of how Matashri and Pitashri married and I was born.' This was a story Barbareek never tired of hearing, and Hidimbi started narrating the tale of her wedding to Bhim when the Pandavas were in exile and how she had helped them escape the clutches of her rakshasa brother, Hidimba. She proudly narrated how she had raised her son Ghatotkach in the forest and tutored him, not only in physical prowess but also in leading a righteous way of life. She never missed this opportunity to reiterate to Barbareek that the immense strength bestowed on their family due to the Rakshasa blood flowing in their veins was something to be used for the benefit of people and not for abusing the weak. Barbareek nodded solemnly. This was a lesson he had heard many times and understood well too.

Hidimbi continued the story. 'Your father Ghatotkach learnt everything so quickly just like you do. He is a very mighty but just person and knows that the powers he possesses are to be kept in check to be harnessed only to serve the weak. He never allowed his rakshasa instincts to run wild. Would you not be like that too, Barbareek?'

'Yes, yes, yes. I would be just like Pitashri, Dadima. I would be brave, mighty, and powerful, and a very good person too, just like him. But tell me what happened after he got his training, Dadima,' cooed little Barbareek.

Hidimbi laughed as she tousled his hair. 'Have patience, little one. So, this was the time when Lord Krishna, with his consort Satyabhama, reached the abode of Narakasura to slay him. Narakasura was a powerful demon, and your nanaji, Danav Mur, was his commander-in-chief. But they were no match for the Lord and attained moksha at his hands. Your brave mother, Maurvi, stood shaking with sorrow and rage and tried to accost Krishna. She was no less than her father in prowess and was blessed by the Goddess Kamakhya with many boons. Fuming with rage, she tried to attack Krishna, but her attempts were thwarted by the appearance of Goddess Kamakhya, who forbade her from fighting the creator of the world. Your mother understood the power of Lord Krishna and bowed coyly as the goddess told her that Krishna is the only one who can guide her in finding a suitable groom.'

Not far from where they sat, Maurvi, who was plucking flowers for the daily puja, blushed as she remembered the events.

Hidimbi continued, 'Your mother was a very brave and mighty warrior, Barbareek. She possessed supreme skills not only in matters of war and governance of a kingdom but was also a revered scholar. She desired to wed a person who surpassed her in both these aspects, which was difficult since such men were not very common. As time passed, your Nanaji, as well as your mother, lost hope of finding someone who could defeat her in brains and brawns, and the very possibility of her marriage seemed to be fading away. It was at this point that Krishna blessed your mother and assured her that it was his responsibility to find a glorious and worthy husband for her. Krishna had your father in mind as he blessed your mother and, hence, came straight to meet me. He instructed me to send your father to Pragjyotisha and seek Maurvi's hand.'

Nearby, Maurvi's fair cheeks became redder as she recollected how, upon reaching Pragjyotisha, Ghatotkach was treated by her with scorn just as the other suitors before him had been. How was she to know that he was the one chosen by Krishna? With Krishna's blessings as his armour, Ghatotkach was undaunted and accepted Maurvi's challenge to defeat her in intelligence by asking her a question that she could not answer. Invoking Sri Krishna, Ghatotkach narrated the following story to Maurvi.

'Long ago, there lived a lecherous man who was in a relationship with an immoral girl, and they begot a child out of wedlock. As this baby girl grew up into a pretty woman, the man's vile eyes started coveting her as well, and, in his lust, he lied to her saying that she was not his biological daughter, but he had merely brought her up. The poor girl, believing in this story, ended up in a relationship with the evil man much against the moral ethics of mankind. They begot a child as well.'

Ghatotkach then asked Maurvi about the nature of the relationship the man had with the newborn baby. Was it his daughter since he had sired her, or was it his granddaughter since the baby was born to his daughter? Maurvi, baffled by this question, realized that she had finally met her match in brains. She, however, did not concede and challenged him to a duel to test his strength and valour. Ghatotkach overcame Maurvi with ease; Maurvi accepted her defeat gracefully and surrendered by touching the feet of her would-be husband, Ghatotkach.

'Matashri and Pitashri both fought each other, right Dadima?' Barbareek asked Hidimbi, urging her to continue the story. 'Yes, little one, and your father won her with both his might and his brains. Your grandfather and granduncles all rejoiced at this news, and we had a grand wedding with all their blessings.'

Little Barbareek, at this point in the story, clapped his tiny hands in glee, as Hidimbi and Maurvi both looked lovingly at his cherubic face.

Maurvi walked over to the grandmother-grandson duo and pulled little Barbareek to her lap. 'Now, let me tell you what happened after that. In due time, we all came to know that the Lord had blessed us, and you were soon to be born. Your Dadima was so excited and happy that she ran around telling everyone about this and distributed sweets to everyone in the tribe. The news was sent to your grandfather, Bhim, and your granduncles too. Everyone rejoiced at the news. Your father loved to talk to you when you were in my stomach and, on hearing his voice, you would kick me with your tiny little legs. How we used to rejoice on feeling that tiny kick!' Maurvi fondly recollected. 'You were so naughty even then,' she jocularly told Barbareek, patting him on his cheek. 'Dadima and I saw many good omens in the forest before your birth, and even the high priest thought the signs foretold the birth of a great personality.'

'And that is me. That is me. That is me...!' squealed little Barbareek.

'Yes, yes, you were so eager to come out and see the world that you did not even have the patience to spend the customary nine months in my womb,' said Maurvi fondly.

Barely seven months into pregnancy, Maurvi had entered into labour much to the surprise of the family and the midwives treating her. They had attributed this to the Naga blood flowing in Maurvi's veins. Her eyes welled with tears of joy while she recollected Barbareek's birth as the heavens rejoiced.

Little Barbareek used to love this part of the tale since Hidimbi's face used to light up with joy and pride as she stroked her grandchild while fondly remembering the first time she had lifted Barbareek in her arms. She had proudly christened the baby Barbareek, a name to match his pretty curls. She told Barbareek, 'Your black curls were what first caught my eye as I held you in my arms. Well, that is in stark contrast to your father's head, right? The baldie that Ghatotkach is!' At this, both grandmother and grandson broke into peals of laughter as they visualized the shiny bald head of Ghatotkach. However, the difference between the father and son ended there for they were much alike in every other aspect. Barbareek, like his father, grew up magically, and within hours of his birth, attained the physique of a young lad. Back then, Hidimbi had explained to an astonished Maurvi that Ghatotkach had also grown this fast right after he was born. At just a few hours old, Barbareek was able to stand confidently on his feet and greet his mother with folded hands.

Ghatotkach, meanwhile, came back with a bunch of fruits in his hands for his little lad and threw them up for Barbareek to catch. Jumping to his feet, Barbareek ran and caught all of them effortlessly as his parents and grandmother beamed with pride at his agility. The happy family then proceeded to the altar beneath the peepal tree in front of their hut and offered their prayers as dusk approached. They folded hands in gratitude in front of the idol of Kali Ma as they sang her praises.

Barbareek was a very ambitious lad and possessed all the traits one could wish for in a child. He was righteous, ambitious, hardworking, well-mannered, and forever eager to acquire more knowledge and skills. Hidimbi devoted her entire time to the upbringing of her grandson, and they both shared a strong bond, much to the joy of Ghatotkach and Maurvi.

Hidimbi had once asked the revered sage Vyas about Barbareek's future, to which the sage replied that his childhood would bring untold joy to his family. When questioned about his youth, the sage remained silent. When a worried Hidimbi enquired further about what was in the future for her grandson, Sage Vyas wisely told her that knowledge of the future may not always be desirable and, to reassure her, he predicted that Barbareek would carve his name eternally in the books of time and bring glory to the family. Hidimbi, thus comforted, had sought the sage's blessings for Barbareek.

Under the able tutoring of Ghatotkach, Maurvi, and Hidimbi, Barbareek soon mastered all the skills needed to be a good warrior but was forever eager to learn more. Hidimbi then realized that the time had arrived for the bird to leave the cosy nest it was sheltered in. She summoned Barbareek one fine evening and said, 'Barbareek, you have been a very good student, and I have taught you whatever I can. However, a wise person should never stop learning. Life is full of lessons, and if you are observant and adaptable enough, you can attain more knowledge. You should have the best possible education, and for that, I want you to go to Sri Krishna and be tutored by him. He is the divine Lord, and just being with him would elevate your consciousness significantly. He is the best teacher one can ever have. I wish for you to seek his mentorship now.'

Young Barbareek was thrilled to hear this. The very next day, taking his bow and arrow and with a sword dangling at his side, he set out to meet Krishna, a name much revered by everyone in Barbareek's family. Not a day would pass without a mention of the Lord, his benevolence, or his powers. Not a day would pass without singing his glory. An image had formed in young Barbareek's mind, and he was suffused with nervous joy as he reached Krishna's abode and sought him out. This was his first meeting with the Lord, and the very sight of Sri Krishna's face lightened his heart and set him at ease. After introducing himself, he prostrated himself at his feet, offering his obeisance. Krishna, delighted to see Barbareek, blessed him and embraced the young lad. 'How time flies, Barbareek. It seems like just yesterday that I met Maurvi in Pragjyotisha, followed by her marriage with Ghatotkach, and now here I behold you, a fine young lad. Pray, tell me what brings you here to see me, my child.'

Enthralled by Krishna's loving query, Barbareek folded his hands as he beseeched the Lord thus, 'Sri Krishna, my grandmother Hidimbi has left no stone unturned in tutoring me on the various techniques a warrior should learn. I believe I have mastered them to a certain extent. She now wishes for me to be tutored by you. It would be my greatest honour if I could continue my education with you. Kindly accept me as your disciple, my Lord.'

Krishna was impressed by this ambitious little boy who possessed a very charming style of speech. Despite this favourable impression, Krishna tested Barbareek further, by asking him many questions of wit and wisdom, which the lad answered with ease.

Krishna then asked Barbareek, 'My boy, tell me, what are your ambitions?'

Barbareek, with an animated look on his face, replied, 'My Lord, having been born in the lineage of the mighty Pandavas with Bhim as my grandfather and Hidimbi as my grandmother, I wish to possess at least a fraction of the valour that my ancestors possess. I have only heard of my grandfather Bhim but have not had an opportunity to meet him. I wish to have enough strength and power to make him proud of me. My granduncles, Yudhishtir, Arjun, Nakul, and Sahadev, all possess exemplary qualities making them mighty warriors. I wish to impress upon them with my strength. My father is a mighty warrior too and strikes terror in the hearts of wrongdoers. My mother, Maurvi, has also, as you know, been a strong woman. With such a lineage, I wish to live up to the name I have inherited and make my mark in this world too.'

Impressed by the young boy's enthusiasm, Krishna patted his head before advising him, 'Barbareek, power and valour alone do not make one strong. Physical prowess is important, but wisdom is the tool that can harness immense strength and put it to good use. Hence, you should also strive to acquire the appropriate wisdom to use your strength wisely.' Barbareek nodded his head as he bowed down to Krishna in gratitude for this piece of wisdom.

In the following days, Krishna personally trained Barbareek in archery, mace fighting, wrestling, and sword fighting, skills that the young lad mastered in no time. Satisfied with the progress Barbareek had made in a short span of time, Krishna told him, 'Barbareek, my child, you have mastered the physical techniques needed for a warrior. I hope that these skills will be put to good use by you. However, there are certain hallmarks of a fine warrior, and I think Sage Vijaysiddhisen would be the right person to teach you that. You should now seek him out and request him to guide you further as a guru. My blessings go with you, my child.'

Armed with Krishna's blessings, Barbareek set out on this quest to further his skills under the guidance of Vijaysiddhisen. With a bow and a quiver of arrows slung on his broad shoulders, he moved from forest to forest in search of his guru-to-be. Soon, he arrived upon a plain, where he noticed a mendicant deep in meditation in a small shrine of Kamakhya Devi. Barbareek stood there in silence, absorbing the positive vibrations emanating from the face of the sage. It was at this time that he had noticed a few demons approaching the shrine, apparently intent on killing the sage. With his enhanced hearing skills, Barbareek managed to learn that the demons were afraid to let the sage complete his penance since it would mean that they would have one more powerful enemy who could vanquish them. They had thus decided to kill the sage while he was engaged in penance. With their swords drawn out, they stealthily approached the shrine where the sage remained deeply absorbed in meditation.

As the biggest of the rakshasas, who looked like their leader, raised his sword to behead the sage, an arrow flew and knocked the sword out of his hand. Barbareek, very quick in reflexes, had not wasted much time as he shot the arrow that saved the sage. Seething with rage, he admonished the rakshasa thus, 'O stupid rakshasa, are you not aware of the sin you were about to commit? Attacking an unarmed person sitting absorbed in prayer is a deadly sin. You would have found a place in hell if you had continued this path. Bow down at the sage's feet and seek his forgiveness.'

The stunned rakshasa looked around to see who had the audacity to speak to him like this. Seeing Barbareek, he started laughing out loud. 'You puny little boy, do you even know whom you are talking to? You are but a speck of dust in my path. Run away before I kill you.'

Barbareek, though angered, remembered Guru Sri Krishna's words and decided to give the rakshasa another chance. 'Hey rakshas, I am not a coward to run away. I may be younger than you, but don't underestimate me. It is not right of you to use your power to harm the weak. It is time you used it to protect them instead of going on a rampage like this. Mend your ways before it is too late.'

Enraged on hearing these words from a small lad, the rakshasas turned their attention to Barbareek to get rid of him first before proceeding to kill the sage. Little did they know what lay in store for them. Seeing his youthful, innocent looks, they underestimated the power of Barbareek but soon realized their folly as he felled them like feeble trees in the direct path of a massive cyclone. In no time, the ground was strewn with the bodies of the demons and, as the sage opened his eyes, he understood that his life had just been saved by the charming boy who stood in the midst, resplendent like the rising sun.

Sage Vijaysiddhisen rose gently from his seat as Barbareek bowed in front of him, seeking his blessings. Touching Barbareek's head, he said, 'My gratitude to you for having saved my life. Who are you, my boy? What brings you to this jungle?'

Barbareek replied, 'Pranam Rishivar, I am Barbareek, son of Ghatotkach and grandson of the mighty Pandava, Bhim. I am here on a quest to seek Sage Vijaysiddhisen as my Guru Sri Krishna has advised. I was on my way when I noticed these rakshasas trying to attack you, and, having been taught to use my power to protect others, I could not pass on leaving you thus. I just did my duty.'

The sage now revealed to Barbareek that he was none other than the person being sought. Barbareek's joy knew no bounds on hearing this, and he prostrated before the sage beseeching him, 'Guruji, it is my good fortune to meet you thus. Please grant me the honour of becoming your disciple. I vow to abide by what you say and will do my utmost to be a good pupil.'

Vijaysiddhisen bent down to lift Barbareek up and replied, 'I would love to teach you the little I know, my son. You have been tutored by Sri Krishna, so I am not sure what else remains to be taught by an ordinary man like me. However, I am midway through a ritual of penance to appease the goddess, which is to last another seven nights. This phase of the penance is very rigorous, during which I am to be disturbed on no account. It is for this reason that the rakshasas sought to disturb me, and I am sure there will be more of them who will continue to pursue their mission of destroying me. If you can stand guard and ensure that I am not disturbed for the next seven nights, I can complete this ritual and then guide you in the pursuit of the power that you seek. Would you be able to do this, Barbareek?'

Barbareek humbly bowed down to the venerable sage and said, 'With your blessings Guruji, I can vanquish not just these rakshasas but any huge army too. Please continue your penance, and be assured that as long as there is even a bit of life in me no one will disturb your penance.' Saying this, he sought the sage's blessings. Vijaysiddhisen then proceeded to continue his penance, his mind now at ease with Barbareek standing guard, for he too had sensed that this was no ordinary lad but a divine child.

Barbareek circled the shrine incessantly, his senses alert, picking up the faintest of sounds from far away. As the days passed, the asuras had come in hordes to attack the sage and his guard. However, even the mightiest of them were no match for brave Barbareek. He held his ground and wreaked havoc among the asuras, and the remaining frightened rakshasas fled away from the place, realizing that they stood no chance against this brave young boy. It was an exhausted but undaunted Barbareek who, after seven days of constant vigil without food, water, or sleep, still stood alert, protecting Vijaysiddhisen as the last day of the penance had dawned.

The penance bore fruit towards twilight as Kamakhya Devi appeared in front of the sage and bestowed her blessings upon him. Having thus successfully completed his penance, Vijaysiddhisen stepped out from the shrine just in time to see Barbareek on the verge of collapsing with fatigue. Filled with immense gratitude towards the young boy who had unflinchingly kept his word, the sage lovingly blessed Barbareek.

An exhausted but exhilarated Barbareek was overjoyed since he would now be accepted as a disciple by Vijaysiddhisen. The sage then whispered a sacred mantra in Barbareek's ears and told him, 'Barbareek my child, this is the divine mantra that you need to chant to invoke Maa Kamakhya. This is a very powerful mantra to be chanted non-stop standing waist-deep in water. The power of the mantra is so high that even the elements of nature will undergo an upheaval and try to disrupt your penance. You should be focused and not let anything disturb you. It is very hard, but if you remain resolute and courageous then the divine goddess, Kamakhya Devi, will bestow on you powers that you cannot even imagine. With them, you can become an invincible warrior and achieve your dreams, Barbareek. May the Divine Mother protect you and help you attain this siddhi.' Vijaysiddhisen then proceeded to pray for his disciple's success in this quest. Barbareek wasted not a single moment in relaxing and immediately proceeded to the middle of the river where, with closed eyes, he invoked the goddess by chanting the mantra.

As Barbareek chanted the mantra, every element of nature underwent an upheaval as the sage had predicted. Scores of wild animals and crocodiles swarmed around the meditating Barbareek and attempted to harm him. Barbareek, however, immersed in penance, was protected by the shield of his concentration and successfully overcame all the hurdles. His determination was evident as he remained fixed on the goal even amid grave danger. Powerful, howling winds, strong currents, balls of fire, and earthquakes did not daunt Barbareek as he finished the penance. A luminance from the sky descended, and Goddess Kamakhya appeared before Barbareek and awakened him.

'Open your eyes, Barbareek. You have pleased me immensely with your power of concentration and rigorous penance. This is something even mighty sages and warriors have not been able to attain. I bestow upon you these arrows with which you will remain undefeated in any battle you participate in.' She then presented him with three arrows and a vial of vermilion with which he could destroy even the strongest army. Having blessed him thus, she disappeared as Vijaysiddhisen rushed in to congratulate him.

Beaming with pride at Barbareek's achievement, the sage proceeded to explain to him the special powers that he now possessed. 'Barbareek, you have achieved something that anyone in this world would vie for. I am proud of you, my boy! These three arrows can help you conquer anyone, however mighty they may be. If you were to invoke Mother Kamakhya and dip the first arrow in vermilion and shoot it, it would mark the enemies whom you wish to destroy. The second arrow can be used in a similar manner if you wish to mark the friends you want to protect. The third arrow could then be fired to either save or destroy the ones marked by the first or second arrow. In short, you could wipe out the entire creation if you wished to in a matter of minutes. But when possessing such great powers, one should also remember that with them, one also acquires a great responsibility. The powers should only be used to protect the weak and not for personal gains or for matters of the ego. Strength is something even asuras possess in abundance, but what makes a true hero or warrior is the ability to control or keep these strengths in check and not let them run amuck. I want you to promise me that you will use these powers only while fighting for the weak, and not misuse them. Always strive to protect and fight for the weak and the oppressed.'

Barbareek, who had been listening with rapt attention, could understand the importance of these words and readily vowed that these arrows would be used by him only to fight for the weak. This vow, made in all earnestness, would soon prove to be a decisive and turning point in young Barbareek's life.

At the very moment Barbareek was climbing the pinnacles of glory, his grandfather Bhim and the other Pandavas were roaming in the forest incognito and in exile having lost their kingdom and all their possessions to the Kauravas.

The homeward-bound Barbareek worshipped Goddess Kamakhya in gratitude every morning in all reverence and austerity. One day, as he went to fetch water from the river for his prayers, he was angered to see a tall, well-built man washing his feet in the very place he took water from. Furious on seeing the water he used for worship defiled thus, he admonished the intruder, 'You silly man, don't you have any reverence for the gods? This is a place of worship, and you desecrate it thus by washing your legs in the very water used for offering to the gods.'

Startled by the sudden rebuke, the man turned around and was astonished to see just a young lad fuming with anger. He found the scene hilarious and laughed out aloud before saying, 'I am amused by your remarks, little boy. However, I am also surprised that your parents have not taught you how to speak to elders with respect. This is not the tone to adopt when addressing people older than you.'

This angered Barbareek even further. He drew his sword out as he shouted, 'Enough of your impudence. I can shred you to pieces in no time. However, I see that you possess no weapons, and, hence, let me vanquish you with my bare hands and make you see reason instead of spewing words like this.' Throwing his sword aside, Barbareek jumped on the huge man who was none other than his grandfather Bhim. Not having met his grandfather before, Barbareek could not recognize him, and Bhim too failed to recognize his own grandson. A duel ensued, with both remaining undefeatable. Bhim realized that this was no ordinary child as any other would have been defeated in a matter of minutes. Barbareek also realized that this was no ordinary man that he was duelling. As both the mighty warriors fought on, even though they were weakened, Sage Vyas appeared before them and revealed each other's identity.

Bhim was overjoyed to meet his grandson and embraced him even as tears of remorse and shame flowed down Barbareek's face. Barbareek, ashamed of his inability to control his anger, sought Bhim's forgiveness.

'Please forgive me, Dadashri. I have exhibited a behaviour to be ashamed of and with these very hands fought against the one I should have worshipped and served. I have sinned. Please forgive me, Dadashri. I vow to never let my anger take the better of me and to keep myself disciplined before reacting to situations.'

Bhim lovingly embraced him, and the grandfather-grandson duo spent some joyous moments together before Bhim proceeded on his journey. This was one of the very few times Barbareek had spent with his grandfather, and he mentally made a note to make Bhim proud of him someday to atone for what he thought was an embarrassing display of his anger.

Hidimbi, meanwhile, was anxiously awaiting the return of her grandson whose absence had created a large void in her life. The bond between the grandmother and grandson was so strong, and she had to exert huge control to restrain herself from being overprotective of the child and thus hampering his progress.

On his return, Barbareek was greeted with much joy by his parents, Hidimbi, and the entire tribe. He proudly described to them the powers of the arrows and how he could defeat even the strongest in no time with these weapons. Hidimbi and Ghatotkach again reminded that such gifts from the divine should be put to good use. Hidimbi said, 'Barbareek, you have now attained powers and celestial weapons that could make you one of the mightiest warriors. However, let this not tempt you to harm the weak and poor. Power is a two-edged dagger; it should be used wisely to protect truth and righteousness and remember never to sway from the path of dharma. You have these weapons at your disposal to protect the weak and downtrodden. Remember this always, Barbareek.'

Hidimbi and Ghatotkach, despite the rakshasa blood running in their veins, were redeemed souls. Unlike the rest of the Asura clan, they could distinguish between right and wrong and had the aspiration to use their might for good and not to wield their power to terrorize the weak.

Meanwhile, not too far away, in Hastinapur, a war was brewing. The battle of Kurukshetra was soon to commence. It was an event that would mark the clash of the titans—the Pandavas and Kauravas. Despite the efforts of many to establish a truce between the cousins, the battle could not be averted, and now war seemed imminent. Even after having completed the exile, in accordance with the conditions laid out by Duryodhana and Shakuni, the Pandavas were denied their kingdom and forced to face their cousins on the battlefield. Krishna himself could not manage to convince the Kauravas to adopt a path of peace, and, hence, with no other recourse, the Pandavas started gearing up for the war. The Pandavas, though powerful with Krishna on their side, were lesser in number in comparison to the massive army of the Kauravas and their allies.

Early the next morning, the peaceful ambience of the jungle where Barbareek lived was disturbed as the birds flew helter-skelter, heralding an intrusion in their midst. Soon, the sound of hooves was heard, and shortly a soldier alighted from a horse seeking Ghatotkach. 'Pranam Yuvraj Ghatotkach, your father, Pandu Putra Bhim, and your uncles have sent me here to inform you that the battle of Kurukshetra will soon commence. They have conveyed the message that when the time is right and your presence is needed in the war, you will be summoned. They want you to be prepared in any case.'

Young Barbareek stood near Maurvi, listening to the news the messenger had just conveyed. It sent a thrill down his spine. The battle of the century, warriors whom everyone revered, clashing against each other, his relatives on both sides, and, most importantly, his grandfather Pandav Bhim. He had not spent much time with him, at least not as much as he would have wished. He longed not only to meet him but also to impress upon Bhim his own prowess. After all, Bhim had missed out on his grandson's growing up years in the forest and had no inkling of his might other than the embarrassing event near the river.

As the preparations for the epic battle of Kurukshetra were in full swing, young Barbareek longed to participate in the war. It would be an epic battle and what better way to test his strength after acquiring his special skills than to participate in the Kurukshetra battle and prove his valour. He did not want to miss this golden opportunity.

When he expressed this desire to his parents and grandmother they consented. Invoking Devi Kali's grace, Barbareek set off armed with the three arrows and a special bow, which was said to have been gifted to him by Agni Dev. Before starting on his journey to the Pandava camp, Barbareek sought their blessings and once again promised Hidimbi and Maurvi that he would be in perfect control of his powers and would use them only to fight for the weak. Maurvi and Hidimbi prayed to Devi Kali for Barbareek and sought for him a life of glory and valour as he set off to participate in the Dharma Yudh.

Mounting his blue horse, Leela, the brave warrior sped like the wind through hills and plains and soon reached his destination. He was greeted with joy by his grandfather, granduncles, and other elders, along with Krishna, and welcomed in their midst. In accordance with the ethics of the battlefield, Barbareek chose to camp at a distance since he had not yet fully gauged the situation and ascertained his allegiance to either of the sides. Bound by his vow, Barbareek could only fight on the weaker side and hence wanted a thorough understanding of the situation in the war camps.

As the war became unavoidable, Krishna, in his mystical way, posed a question to each of the mighty warriors, asking how many days they would require to finish the battle if they were to fight alone. This question was answered by Bhishma Pitamah, Dronacharya, Arjun, Bhim, Karna, and many others. Each one according to their might anticipated the war to be completed by them single-handedly in around twenty to thirty days.

When this question was jocularly posed to Barbareek by Krishna, he confidently replied, 'Prabhu, I can finish the war in just one day or, rather, in a matter of minutes if I were to fight single-handedly.'

The Pandavas admired Barbareek's confidence but also wondered why he was bragging when even mighty warriors like Bhishma Pitamah had been more realistic about their answer. Seeing the looks of bewilderment on their faces, Barbareek then revealed to them the power of the three arrows in his possession.

It was then that the Pandavas realized with joy that their grandson would remain invincible. Rejoicing thus the strength they now had on their side, they returned to their camps. Barbareek was glad to see his elders pleased. Finally, he would get a chance to impress them with his valour. As the Pandavas walked back to their tents, Krishna, however, lingered around to talk to Barbareek. During the conversation, Krishna asked him about his training with Vijaysiddhisen and listened with rapt attention as Barbareek recounted his experiences. Barbareek proudly gave him the details of the weapon Maa Kamakhya had blessed him with and the promises he had made to his guru and grandmother after receiving this power.

A cloud of concern passed over Krishna's face on hearing that Barbareek was bound by this vow to use his powers to fight only for the weaker side. Barbareek was quick to sense this transition and addressed Sri Krishna thus, 'Prabhu, I gather now that the might of the Pandava army is significantly weaker than that of the Kauravas. That means I can fight for the Pandavas and abide by the promise. Why, then, do I see this cloud over your ever-smiling face, my Lord?'

Deep in thought, pacing up and down in the shadow of the huge peepal tree near the camp, Krishna replied, 'Barbareek, my child. Promises are a sacred string of words threaded together by conviction and devotion. They are not meant to be used casually and never in haste without much thought. Often, promises made thus, end up causing an outcome that beats the intention with which it was made.'

Barbareek innocently replied, 'Guruji, if one were to think and analyze before making a promise, then it would no longer be a promise but a deal. Promises come from the heart that encourages the individual to commit to a particular action. What thought is needed then?'

Having been raised by Hidimbi, who had been the epitome of all virtues, Barbareek understood the importance of a given word by a true warrior, and he intended to stick to it whatever the outcome may be.

If it had been any other moment, Krishna might have appreciated Barbareek's words. But he was the only one who seemed to understand the gravity of the situation and the danger Barbareek's invincibility posed to the Pandavas. Having realized that Barbareek would adhere to his promise no matter what, Krishna asked Barbareek to demonstrate the usage of the powerful arrows. He challenged Barbareek to consider the big peepal tree under which they both stood as a battlefield and each of the green leaves on the tree as soldiers of the enemy to be vanquished and make a hole in each of them with his arrows. Barbareek enthusiastically accepted the challenge and invoked Maa Kamakhya as he dipped the first arrow in vermillion and mentally marked each leaf in the tree for the arrow to pierce.

Barbareek, having targeted the leaves in his mind, proceeded to shoot the first arrow directed against the peepal tree. As the arrow encircled the tree, it marked each of the leaves of the tree in the process readying for the next arrow to do its work. Quick as lightning and unseen by Barbareek, Krishna removed one leaf from the tree and hid it under his foot. His mind was racing to find ways to protect the righteous Pandavas in the event of them having to face these arrows. There had to be a loophole somewhere. He had to identify it and use it to protect them. If only he could protect this leaf, there still remained a chance—a chance that Barbareek could be fought against on the battlefield while fighting alongside the Kauravas without losing any of the Pandavas.

As Krishna ruminated thus, the first arrow returned to Barbareek after completing its work, and he shot the third arrow that proceeded to make a hole in each of the leaves on the tree. However, instead of returning to the quiver after doing so, the second arrow hovered around Krishna's foot. Mystified by this, Barbareek looked at Krishna who then removed his foot, letting the arrow complete its mission of making a hole in the last leaf which had been stealthily removed from the tree by Krishna.

Appalled by this, Barbareek cautioned Krishna thus, 'Prabhu, why did you take this risk? That spot on your feet marked by this arrow would now be a vulnerable point in your body. Why did you have to do thus, Prabhu?' (Ironically, a good many years after the time of this incident, it was this point marked by Barbareek's arrow on Sri Krishna's foot that got pierced by a hunter's arrow when he decided to give up his physical being.)

Krishna pondered, 'If even a small leaf could not be protected from the arrow by me, how then could I save the Pandavas from these arrows if Barbareek fights on the side of the Kauravas? Everything seems fine if he remains on the side of the Pandavas. But would that be the case? The promise he made … that remains the weak spot.'

Barbareek did not fail to notice Krishna lost in a whirlpool of thoughts with confusion writ large on his face. He ventured to ask him the reason, and the Lord disclosed it to Barbareek thus. 'Barbareek, you are not aware of the consequences of the promise that you made and the disaster it may result in. At this point in time, the Pandava army is weaker in strength of number, so you will fight for them. With weapons like these and your infallible strength, whichever side you take will become the stronger one. In no time, it will be the Kaurava army that will be weaker. Bound by your promise, you will have no choice but to switch sides and fight against the Pandavas. Once again, the Pandavas would become weaker, and you would have to switch sides once more. You would thus keep shifting sides till the entire armies on both sides, including your own clan, the Pandavas, are destroyed, and it would only be infallible you, standing alone. The promise you made was not thought about properly. This is a huge predicament that cannot be dealt with in any manner if you fight. The truth must triumph, Barbareek… At any cost,' he added in a whisper.

Having understood the situation and watching with sorrow the confusion on Krishna's face due to the promise he had committed himself to, young Barbareek stood rooted to the spot. He did not know what to do or how to overcome this predicament. All he knew was that this was one chance for him to prove his mettle as a warrior, one chance for him to make his elders proud of his valour, the one chance for him to do something worthy enough to be part of the lineage he had been born into. He promised Krishna, 'My Lord, I now understand the gravity of the situation. However, as much as I would stick to the promise of fighting for the weaker side, I also make a vow to abide by whatever you decide on the path to be taken by me. I shall not flinch from it under any circumstance. May the truth triumph, my Lord.'

Meanwhile, the Pandavas, who had walked back on seeing the display of Barbareek's arrows tried to dissuade him from making such a commitment. However, the young lad was determined and proceeded to give his word. Barbareek thought, 'When the creator of the universe is the one making the decision, it would be for the greater good, and what better way to contribute to the war than by abiding with his decision.' Fame and glory did not seem important then.

'The greater good—that was what was important,' thought Krishna, as he told Barbareek that it was customary before any war to sacrifice a mighty warrior to appease the deities. He said that only three warriors qualified for this honour—Arjun, Barbareek, and Krishna himself. Hearing this, Arjun offered to give his life up as a sacrifice for the victory of the Pandavas. Krishna admonished him, saying, 'Arjun! This is a war of dharma, and it can retain that name only as long as you five Pandava brothers who represent truth emerge unscathed at the end of the war. How would that be possible if you were to offer yourself for this sacrifice? It is out of the question that you volunteer for this. I am just a charioteer in this battle, and, hence, it is better that I sacrifice myself for the victory of the Pandavas.'

Barbareek shuddered and covered his ears upon hearing this. He could bear this no more. He knew that this was the moment he could make a difference in the war. It may not be in the valiant way he had imagined it to be, but it would still be a sacrifice for truth. He would miss fighting alongside his grandfather and granduncles, but this needed to be done to save them. 'How I wish to make them proud of my valour, but alas that is not going to happen now.' Promises are indeed to be made thoughtfully, Barbareek reflected, as he knelt at Lord Krishna's feet and said, 'My Lord, you are my guide and guru. You are the creator of the universe. How could there be a world without you? It is hence appropriate that I offer myself in sacrifice before the war. It is my privilege to be offered this opportunity to participate in this battle for Dharma. Kindly behead me and grant me this fortune.'

Krishna touched Barbareek's head gently and replied, 'Barbareek, you are a very brave warrior and have proved it now by being ready to make this sacrificc. However, I cannot behead you since an offering to be made as a sacrifice should be done by the person himself.'

On hearing this, brave Barbareek then unsheathed his sharp sword, bowed down in reverence to the Lord, and then, with a quick flash, boldly cut off his head and offered it to Krishna. Petals showered from the heavens as Krishna accepted the offered head and, with immense gratitude and joy, addressed Barbareek thus, 'Brave Barbareek, you have made the ultimate sacrifice without any hesitation and have now risen to the ranks of the supreme warriors in war. I bless you with a title nothing less than my own name—Shyam—the one given to me by my mother, Yashodha, herself. With this, you also get my powers, and you will be worshipped as Shyam in Kali Yug where you will be hailed as the protector of the weak, the one who offered his head in sacrifice for upholding the righteous. I bestow immortality on this head in my hands. Tell me what it is you wish for, and I shall ensure it is fulfilled.'

Barbareek, whose severed head had remained conscious with the blessings of the Lord, closed his eyes as a mark of respect to Krishna. His articulated the two wishes in his mind. 'My Lord, it is my honour to be part of this war in this way and ensure that my clan is assured of victory. I have two small wishes I would request you to grant. I have long aspired to be a part of this war and experience the battle by being at the forefront. However, even though I cannot participate in the war given my current condition, I wish to witness the battle since it is one that will be marked down in history, and I do not wish to miss it. Kindly help me to at least watch the battle. My second wish is that I want my headless body to be consigned to the flames with your hands.'

Krishna raised his hands in blessings as he granted both these wishes and arranged for Barbareek's head to be placed on top of a hillock facing the battlefield from where he could witness everything happening in the war.

Hidimbi and Maurvi rushed to the place when they heard the news. Maurvi accosted Krishna harshly, accusing him of taking her boy's life to ensure his own plans for success. A patient Krishna let her vent her sorrow and even stopped others from restraining the wailing Maurvi. Barbareek addressed his mother and comforted her saying that he was still alive, and it was he who had willingly sacrificed himself, and that Sri Krishna did not kill him as she had thought. With these words, there was a voice from the heavens that proceeded to explain a story hitherto unknown about Barbareek's earlier birth.

'Barbareek was a yaksha in the heavens before being born on earth as Ghatotkach's son. It was a time when asuric forces were prevalent on earth, and all the devas proceeded to Lord Vishnu asking him to redeem earth from the clutches of evil. The yaksha, on hearing this, proudly declared that he alone was sufficient to do this task and Vishnu need not bother to come to earth for this job that he could handle alone in no time. Infuriated by his arrogance, Brahma cursed the yaksha to be reborn as a mighty warrior on earth and that, in the battle of good and evil, he would be the first to be killed by the Lord. It was this yaksha who was born as Barbareek, and, true to the curse, it was his blood that was first shed in the battle of Kurukshetra.'

Hearing this, Maurvi was consoled and sought Krishna's forgiveness for having uttered ignorant words in her anger on losing Barbareek.

Hidimbi, for her part, knew now that her grandson was on the verge of carving his name in the annals of history as he unflinchingly gave all that he had to protect the right. Now, even as his severed head lay impaled upon the spear, Barbareek was proud of his determination to keep promises made by him and did not regret for a minute what had transpired after that.

The sun rose steadily across the sky and Barbareek was shaken out of his reverie. The epic battle of Kurukshetra began with losses on both sides but, with the able guidance of Sri Krishna, the Pandavas emerged unscathed and victorious in the end. Barbareek followed every minute of the war with his astute eyes. He witnessed the Bhagavad Gita being narrated by Lord Krishna himself; he witnessed warriors falling defeated; he witnessed his cousin Abhimanyu being cruelly killed; and he witnessed the death of his father, Ghatotkach, as he too sacrificed his life to protect Arjun. He remained calm and composed as the events of the war unfolded before his eyes. He felt equally for the losses suffered by the Pandava as well as the Kaurava sides. He witnessed the triumph of truth as the Pandavas won the battle.

One evening, not long after the battle of Kurukshetra had ended, the Pandavas sat together, reminiscing about the events of the war. A debate then ensued over the person most responsible for the Pandavas' victory in the battle. Brave Arjun, who had killed Karna, Bhishma, and many other Kaurava warriors; or mighty Bhim, who had killed Duryodhana and Dushasana; or Abhimanyu, who fought bravely despite being cornered mercilessly by the Kauravas; or Ghatotkach, who instigated Karna to use the invincible Shakti weapon on himself, thus saving Arjun's life. Unable to decide, they asked Krishna what he thought about this. Krishna humbly replied that he had been just a charioteer and was unable to give an opinion on this, but the entire battle had been watched by the mighty warrior, Barbareek, who could offer his unbiased view on this topic. They walked towards the place where Barbareek's head lay to ask him about this matter.

Barbareek watched them approach the hillock and, bereft of hands with which to salute his elders, he closed his eyelids in respect. How he wished to touch their feet with his hands and to fold his hands in obeisance. But he had to remain content to offer his respect thus.

Krishna, along with the Pandavas, then posed this question to Barbareek. Barbareek pondered for a moment as he replayed the events of the war as it had played out from the start to the finish. He reminded Bhim that he had bypassed the rules of war ethics in the mace fight with Duryodhana and that Arjun had used Shikhandi as a shield while fighting Bhishma, thus highlighting the flaws in each of their victories. Humbled, the mighty Pandavas hung their heads in shame for having been so arrogant and proud as to consider themselves the cause of the victory of dharma. Barbareek then proclaimed, 'I have witnessed the entire battle and have seen who was responsible for the victory. Wherever I turned, I saw Vasudev Sri Krishna wielding his Sudharshan Chakra, killing the evil. At every nook and corner of the battlefield, it was his presence that was annihilating adharma. It was the Sudharshana Chakra rotating over the entire area, weeding out the bad and supporting dharma. It is just Sri Krishna alone who is responsible for the victory of the truth. He alone pervades the universe. He is the beginning. He is the end. Without him, nothing manifests. He is the supreme power behind everything.' Saying thus, he closed his eyes in obeisance to Sri Krishna and continued, 'I also saw Mother Draupadi drinking the blood of the enemies. With her dishevelled hair flying around, she tore at the chests of the evil and drank their blood. When I looked closer, I realized that it was Mother Kali in her terrifying form, striking out the enemies. I recognized it as the wrath and vengeance of the thousands of women who have been disrespected in the world. Mother Draupadi and many women being dishonoured and ill-treated were seeking their vengeance in this form. They are appeased now but will rise again if the shakti of women is not respected anywhere.'

Barbareek ended this discussion by quoting Sri Krishna himself, as he explained in the Bhagavad Gita:

> tasmāt tvam uttiṣhṭha yaśho labhasva
> jitvā śhatrūn bhuṅkṣhva rājyaṁ samṛiddham
> mayaivaite nihatāḥ pūrvam eva
> nimitta-mātraṁ bhava savya-sāchin

'The annihilation of the wicked and victory of the righteous,' Barbareek continued, 'is something preordained by the divine. It cannot be altered in any way, and mortals are just instruments for executing the divine will. Being chosen as an instrument of the divine is a huge privilege, but one ought to remember that our role is just to be the instrument since the annihilation has already been decided and even executed by the divine.' Hearing this, Arjun, to whom the Gita was directly explained by Sri Krishna, felt ashamed of having forgotten the teachings imparted to him and having been part of the foolish argument on who among these mortal warriors was instrumental in ensuring the victory of the Pandavas.

With Barbareek explaining the reality behind the Kurukshetra battle, the assembled Pandavas felt chastised as they realized that the supreme truth is Lord Krishna, and they were just his instruments to execute the divine will. Bowing down again at the feet of the divine, they sought pardon for their pride and hailed Barbareek, the unsung hero in the battle.

Krishna praised Barbareek's sacrifice in the battle, that ensured that the Pandavas regained the kingdom and dharma won. He hailed him as the righteous one who had sacrificed his life to keep up his promises.

Many years later, in Kaliyug, in a village called Khatu, in Rajasthan, a cowherd noticed an unusual phenomenon as his cow grazed on a small hillock. As the cow neared a small mound, the cowherd watched in astonishment as milk started flowing automatically out of the udder. Reporting this to the local village elders, they decided to dig the place up. Much to their amazement, the head of Barbareek was found there and was installed in a temple for worship. The ruler of the place at that time, Maharaj Roopsingh Chauhan, and his consort, Narmada Kanwar, built the original temple in 1027 AD; it was then renovated in 1720 AD by a nobleman, Diwan Abhaisingh, under the instructions of the then ruler of Marwar. Devotees throng to the shrine to get their wishes fulfilled by their Shyam Baba, the supporter of the weak.

To this day, Shyam Baba is worshipped as Khatushyam, Baliya Dev, and under many other names in various parts of the country. His life, though short, bloomed with full intensity, spreading the fragrance of devotion, dedication, sacrifice, nobility, and other virtues. Had he wished, he could have attained glory as the one who was invincible and, true to his word, ended the Kurukshetra war in one day and emerged the sole winner. He could have broken his promises and fought for the Pandavas alone, but brave Barbareek chose to lead a life based on the examples his grandmother Hidimbi, father Ghatotkach, and mother Maurvi had set for him. He chose to live true to the lessons he had learnt from his gurus. This made him shine as one of the brightest stars in the Mahabharat. He was one of the fortunate four who could not only witness the entire battle of Kurukshetra but also beheld Sri Krishna's Vishvaroop and heard the Bhagavad Gita from him directly.

'Whatever action a great man performs, common men follow, whatever standards a great man sets through example, all the world pursues' (Bhagavad Gita).

His name etched in the books of our culture inspires the young and old alike on thc importance of making the right choices in life, the fine line that can make them god-like or rakshas-like.

Haare ka sahaara, Baba Shyam hamaara (Hail our Baba Shyam, the protector of the weak).

5

Madri: The Passage of Dharma

Neena Mukherjee

Madri stroked her long braid, embellished with white and red flowers, and thought about her brother Shalya, the king of Madra Pradesh, with whom she had shared a strong bond since childhood. Her eyes moistened at the thought of leaving all that had been hers till now—the majestic Madra palace, her artistically decorated quarters, and her most precious garden that she had nurtured with utmost care and love. A stroke of her forefinger on the strings of the veena lying next to her made a familiar, comforting sound. The sense of relief Madri felt at touching it brought back memories of the hours spent at music lessons with her mother, her guru. She wiped a stray tear rolling down her cheek with her golden shawl and tried to focus on what lay ahead. She had just been betrothed to Pandu, who had gained fame in the entire Bharat Varsh for his valour and was the proud heir of the Kuru clan legacy. As she journeyed to Hastinapur, the capital of the Kuru empire, her heart fluttered with a blend of anticipation and excitement.

Madri bent her head to look out of the palanquin at the entire entourage—horses, elephants, carts loaded with precious wedding gifts, and a troop of companions to accompany her on her way. Leading the entourage was the grandsire of the Kuru clan, Ganga Putra Bhishma, known and respected in the entire Arya land for his vow of celibacy to fulfil his father King Shantanu's desire to marry Satyavati. He looked magnificent in his flowing white attire, and his proud head was held high. She was in awe of his personality. As her thoughts diverted towards Pandu, she felt blood rushing to her cheeks, turning her celestial complexion a rosy shade of pink. Pandu, her husband. Pandu, whom she had only seen once while accompanying her brother during one of his expeditions. Pandu, who had married Kunti in a swayamvar a year ago, when the princess Kunti had selected him as her life partner from among many kings and princes in a ceremony organized by her father. She winced at that last thought, and the veins tightened around her forehead.

Didn't that mean she would be the second wife of Pandu?

Although it was a common practice to have multiple wives amongst the royals of Aryavart, Madri was finding it hard to adjust to the idea of being second to anyone. She had heard that Kunti was the daughter of the yadav chieftain Shoor and was adopted and raised by the noble Raja Kuntibhoja. Madri glanced at her sapphire-studded hand mirror and raised her chin. Surely, she, with her beguiling beauty and royal blood, had nothing to worry about.

She tried to brush away the thought and immediately looked out.

The tall trees and lush green surroundings offered some peace to her fluttering heart. She rested her gaze on them and soaked in the beauty of the mountainous region of the Madra kingdom. It was a pleasant morning, complete with grazing sheep, camels in every imaginable shade of brown, show-quality horses trotting around, tall trees, and green pastures on the riverside where she had played with her cousins during summers. She took a long look, soaking in every inch of her home, as if for the very last time.

Madri's heart leapt as they crossed the Iravati River into the Saraswati Valley. She flinched at the first whiff of humidity and the stark, bright sun and drew her face into her palanquin. It would take days to arrive in Hastinapur.

When, finally, the entourage entered the city of Hastinapur, Madri's heart skipped a beat as she looked around at the massive gateway and the vast row of impressive houses on both sides of the pathway to the royal palace. Festivities had begun with the announcement of Bhishma's arrival by the messengers. The palace was embellished with fineries, and the royal family was preparing for the big event of Pandu's wedding. The citizens sang merrily and welcomed the new queen of Prince Pandu.

In contrast, the marriage itself was a formal, sombre affair.

Once the marriage celebrations were over, the ladies of the Kuru clan took the new bride towards the inner chambers of the palace. Madri's eyes followed the embellished arches into a huge hall that seemed to have been decorated specially for the new bride—a fancy chair in the middle for her to sit on and other chairs on both sides for the guest ladies and family members.

Madri looked around and immediately recognized Gandhari by the band she had tied to her eyes. Madri had heard many stories about the people of Hastinapur, each unique in their own way. Despite her lowered head, she stole admiring glances at Gandhari's resolve to keep her eyes tied for her entire life as she was married to the elder prince, the powerful but blind Dhritarashtra. Mothers Ambika and Ambalika, who looked alike and were inseparable, welcomed her with open arms as she bent down to seek their blessings.

Suddenly, she became aware of a very strong but pleasant fragrance in the air.

Was it a special oil from exotic herbs, perhaps agarwood? Or a perfume sprayed by one of the girls dressed in shades of bright blue and yellow?

Many of them were constantly bustling by with either baskets of flowers or a silver pot resting on their waists.

She looked around and saw a towering figure standing in the doorway on her left, adorned in a white silk shawl and with shiny white hair, and strings of expensive white pearls around her proud neck. The figure stood there, surveying the activities and seemingly judging the new bride. Madri shifted uneasily in her chair. As the lady entered, wearing a faint smile that contrasted with sharp observing eyes, Madri noticed mothers Ambika and Ambalika getting up from their chairs in respect, and suddenly she realized who this lady was.

Oh, she is the grandmother Satyavati, the daughter of the chief of fishermen, with whom the great King Shantanu had fallen in love—the reason for Bhishma's famous vow and celibacy! The renowned Kuru Vansha, every personality carries a legendary story to tell!

She quickly lowered her widened eyes.

Satyavati came nearer and raised her hand lovingly to bless Madri as the latter bent down in veneration.

Throughout the celebrations, Madri's mind wandered. She had seen Pandu during the wedding rituals. He had a pale complexion, just as his name suggested. With that golden hue around him and a well-built muscular body, he struck a majestic figure even in a sea of royals. Pandu also seemed bewitched by his new bride's extraordinary beauty. His pursed lips, curved in a smile, assured Madri of that fact.

Madri restlessly fiddled with her rings. The only thing that was bothering her now was meeting Pandu's first wife, Kunti. She didn't know what to look for exactly. Her eyes darted around, trying to spot a distinguished lady who could be Kunti.

Where was Kunti? Was she upset? Upset enough to ignore all the wedding festivities?

Finally, all the rituals were over. Madri was tired, having travelled for many days in a palanquin. She was happy to comply when she was taken towards the left wing of the palace, towards Pandu's inner chambers. She walked slowly on the rose petals through the corridors with lowered eyes, shy and demure, as a new bride should be.

There, at the entrance, stood the calm and composed Kunti, looking ravishing in her pale pink attire and smiling brightly with her amiable demeanour. Madri was taken aback for a second.

Wasn't her behaviour a little incongruent given the situation?

Madri smiled politely and accepted her welcome gracefully. But she discreetly stole glances at Kunti's expressions, looking for signs of jealousy. There were none; instead, the self-assured smile and large kind eyes seemed welcoming.

Madri slowly entered their private chambers, accompanied by her two companions, Dhara and Chhaya, who had travelled with her from the Madra kingdom. She looked around at the room and her wedding bed, adorned with flowers. The aroma of the burning oil lamp filled the ambience with its pleasantness. Her heart was beating rapidly as she waited for her groom to enter the room.

Just then, the guard announced Pandu's arrival in the inner quarters. Madri held her breath. A few minutes passed, and there was still no trace of Pandu. Madri felt queasy.

Had he gone to Kunti's chamber? Where was he? Was he ignoring her?

The thought pricked Madri sharply in her heart, and suddenly tears welled up in her eyes. She would have to understand the meaning of being a second wife. She was in the habit of being next to no one, so this was new, and it was making her extremely uncomfortable. A few more insufferable minutes passed by before Pandu walked in majestically. Madri did not lift her head, wishing to hide her tears. But as Pandu came near, she forgot her complaints and eagerly waited for him to come and sit by her side. She was enthralled to see her reflection in his large eyes as he held her hands and gently kissed them.

Madri smiled at her husband as she sat in the soft, sunlit oriel window in the northeast corner of her chamber, playing Raag Bhairav on her veena. Pandu, reclining on a silk cushion with his eyes closed, palpably savoured the musical notes floating in the air. Such were the most glorious moments. With romance very much in the air, Madri immersed herself in her love for Pandu, who had left no stone unturned to please his new bride. Pandu was enamoured by both his wives, but it was gratifying for Madri that he showed special affection towards her.

A sudden intervention broke the spell, as the doorman brought a message from Bhishma Pitamah. The grandsire had summoned Pandu, Dhritarashtra, and Vidura to discuss royal matters.

Madri waited impatiently for Pandu to return, toying with the strings of the musical instrument while lost in her thoughts. She could feel her heart beating fast with apprehension when, an hour later, Pandu returned to his chamber and wished to be in the presence of both his wives.

As the women listened, Madri's worst fear came true when Pandu announced that he would be going on a military expedition to establish his supremacy in Bharatvarsh. Her heart sank, and she tried to blank out the conversation.

Bhishma, Dhritarashtra, and Vidura had expressed their view that now was the time for Pandu to start his Digvijay yatra—the much-expected military expedition to uphold dharma—to expand his kingdom and take its glory to new heights. Together, they had formulated a plan, decided the route of the expedition, and chosen an auspicious date and time.

Kunti showed interest and even asked a few questions before agreeing with Pandu's plan. Her understanding of the needs and aspirations of kings, backed by her upbringing, intimidated Madri, who had been exceptionally quiet. Pandu, noticing this, addressed her and asked for her opinion.

After much cajoling, she spoke, 'O Lord, I do understand the requirements of the kingdom. All my life, I have seen my father and later my brother engage in expeditions to expand the kingdom. But after becoming your consort and living in your company, I am terrified by the separation that this expedition of yours will mean. I am too much in love with you and will not be able to bear your absence.'

Pandu's eyes softened, his heart no doubt melting like a candle at her impassioned words and moist eyes. 'I too will miss you, my dear,' he said, 'but it is my prime duty to bring glory to my kingdom. I need to attain that stature for Hastinapur, which a powerful king is supposed to acquire by his karma.' He further explained that as a king, it was his duty to fulfil his Purushartha—his objective—by getting artha, riches for his kingdom, and bring glory to its name. Madri, deeply soaked in self-pity, nodded her head in consent but did not try and understand the essence of his words. She did not get a wink of sleep that night.

From the next day on, the preparations began. Pandu, with the help of his brothers and under the able guidance of Bhishma, got an invincible four-winged chaturangini army ready. Kunti actively participated in getting Pandu ready for the long haul and helped however she could. Madri remained withdrawn.

Finally, the auspicious day of departure arrived. Pandu looked stately and handsome in his war attire. After seeking blessings from the mothers, brothers, and all elders in the family, he took leave from his beloved wives, assuring them that he would be well and come back victorious. Kunti performed the auspicious prayers with a lit silver lamp on a plate embellished with yellow flowers and gestured for Madri to come forward. Lowering her heavy eyelids, Madri took the plate from Kunti. She carefully dipped her finger in the little bowl of saffron and rice, hesitantly looked up, and put a tilak on Pandu's broad forehead as a mark of the auspices of being victorious. However, she quickly looked away to hide her moist eyes.

Pandu, in his excitement, did not notice this. He smiled at everyone with folded hands and turned to leave. Madri watched him descend the steps of the palace ceremoniously and stand proudly in his chariot before leaving with his army to win over kingdoms from all corners of Bharatvarsh.

Days passed and became months. Pandu's departure had left a deep void in Madri's life. She felt very uncomfortable amongst the formidable, upright ladies of the Kuru clan. In her home kingdom, she had always been the centre of attention—the protective and loving atmosphere had not prepared her to face life outside her comfort zone. With each passing moment, she felt lonelier and more depressed. Her only comfort was her veena, which she played every evening. Those moments transported Madri back to her parental home.

It didn't help that Madri still felt intimidated by Kunti, who had gone the extra mile to make her feel comfortable in her presence. Kunti was, after all, a year older than her and seemed quite well-read too.

What did Kunti do all day?

She didn't seem lonely, and she always had a calm smile on her face.

Should she go and talk to Kunti? What if she does not respond well?

One fine morning, when Madri was sitting in her garden with a basket of fresh flowers in her lap, Kunti came by and sat next to Madri. Madri looked up in surprise and smiled, wondering what she had in mind.

Kunti put her hand on Madri's shoulder and said, 'I can see you are feeling very lonely. You can come to my room any time if you need to talk.'

'Isn't it natural?' replied Madri. 'I do not know anyone here except my two childhood companions who came with me. I do want to ask you how you pass your time. I do not see you outside your chambers much.'

'Alright, then I invite you to come to my chambers tomorrow morning, and we can share our thoughts.'

Madri, pleased at the idea, instantly nodded in the affirmative.

The next morning, after many days, Madri put flowers in her hair and darkened her eyelids with kohl. She waited for the sun to come overhead, not wanting to seem too desperate. As she stylishly entered Kunti's quarters with her head held high, she was immediately overcome by surprise at the simplicity of Kunti's room. It was as big and well-maintained as hers, yet the element of sobriety was noticeable. On one side, there was a desk with some scriptures, inscribed copper plates, palm leaves neatly arranged, and a fine feather tip to write with. In the other corner was a beautiful idol of Lord Rudra carved out of a single log of sandalwood, a brass oil lamp, and an incense stick burning in front of it. The entire room had a tranquil ambience.

Charmed by Kunti's warmth, Madri dropped her guard. They chatted effortlessly, munching on the nuts served on the silver platter. As the conversation became more intimate, Madri felt as if her quest for knowledge could be satiated by Kunti.

A few days later, after a walk on the banks of the river Ganga, Kunti and Madri sat chatting on the marble seats in the garden. Madri asked Kunti about the palm leaves. She had been curious about what Kunti studied in her free time since the day she had seen them on her desk.

Kunti smiled at her and said, 'When I was a young girl, Sage Durvasa visited our kingdom. He was our guest for quite a few days. Now, Sage Durvasa is as famous for his uncontrollable anger as he is for his scholarly wisdom. So, my father, Raja Kuntibhoj, entrusted me with the responsibility to take care of his hospitality and his temper. I served him with all my heart and made sure he didn't find a reason to be upset. Pleased with my efforts, he started teaching me the *Atharva Veda* and initiated me into Vedic studies. Since then, I have made it my routine to study the Vedas regularly and make my own notes. It has guided me in my weaker moments.'

Madri pondered intently for a second. Then she said, 'I would also like to learn from your knowledge, Kunti didi.'

Kunti, visibly touched by the fact that Madri had addressed her as an elder sister for the first time, held her hands and said, 'Sure, why not! But I usually study at dawn. If you wish, you can come tomorrow morning after your bath. We shall study together.'

That night, Madri could not sleep; this time, however, it was not melancholy but excitement. She had not been introduced to the serious questions of life. Her parents and later her brother, King Shalya, had always kept her in a harmonious bubble, focused only on the comforts of life. After leaving home, she realized that her mind had started asking questions to which she did not have answers. She lay awake, waiting for the dawn to lighten up her dark sky.

At the crack of dawn, after bathing, she dressed up in sober clothes, looked at the early morning sky that was turning pink in the east, and happily walked towards Kunti's chambers.

This time, she entered the room quietly. The faint aroma of a burning oil lamp in the half-lit corner and the meditating calm figure of Kunti in front of Lord Rudra gave immense peace to Madri's agitated mind. There was no hustle-bustle of the maids, only the faint chirping of morning birds in the distance. She sat on the other mat that lay ready for her and tried to breathe in the purity of the ambience. A few seconds later, Kunti opened her eyes and acknowledged her presence with a soft smile.

Kunti turned towards Madri and spoke.

'O Madri, you are like the younger sister I never had. Fate has bound us together, and henceforth, our lives will be interlinked with each other. Please feel free to discuss with me anything that plagues your troubled mind.'

'Kunti didi, I am thankful to you for your kind gesture. I have been very lonely since Maharaj Pandu left on his military expedition. I have experienced a kind of love from him that was very new to me. I totally devoted myself to him and feel like I have become an inseparable part of him. Yet, he left me and you. The purpose of his excursion, as I understand it, was to earn accolades for his kingdom. He said that to fulfil his purushartha, the ultimate goal of life, he had to undertake this expedition. It was his royal duty.'

'As it certainly is, Madri. For every person, the Purushartha, or the objective of life, is in accordance with one's aspirations, potential needs, and desires. Each person aspires to achieve what their inner personality guides them to achieve. As a king, it is his dharma to work towards the betterment of the kingdom and acquire more artha, more money, and, along with it, replenish the lost glory of Hastinapur kingdom.'

'But why is artha required if he has many riches already?'

'The pursuit of wealth or material advantage is one of the aims of life. It includes wealth, financial security, and economic prosperity for all to have a good life. It is a king's duty to take cognizance of the entire ecosystem and not only his personal selfish needs.'

'But does he not have a duty towards us? Is it appropriate to leave your young bride alone while she is so much in love with you?'

Kunti laughed lightly. 'Madri, my sister, it is the kama, the lust within you, that speaks thus. It is an important part of life. What you seek is passion, the pleasure of the senses, but do understand that pure love can be with or without sensual pleasure. It is associated with mutual love and respect for each other. When it is experienced with religious values, it purifies and elevates the soul. It is his dharma to fulfil his royal duties.'

'Dharma? What is dharma? Is it not praying to God? How can dharma be different for different people?'

'Dharma is the soul of an individual. It is the principle that governs the universe, prescribing the concepts of duty, selfless service, and the right way of living.'

At this, Madri looked confused, but Kunti went on:

'There are three kinds of dharma that help one overcome the perils of life that cause dukkha, or suffering. Adi Daivika is the one you are referring to. It is the veneration of one's presiding deity, which includes prayers and following prescribed rules and restrictions. Adi Bhautika is the social dharma that one should follow as part of the ecosystem. And then there is Adhyatmika, or one's personal religion, which is for self-elevation, where one gives up their identity to merge with the super-consciousness. All these three have to be in harmony with each other for a person to live a dharmic life.'

'I do understand my personal dharma, but what is my social dharma?'

'Your dharma as the queen is to support your king's actions in enhancing his kingdom and be a wife by his side in need of the hour with all your heart.'

Madri pondered this for a moment.

'So, this entire life is bound by dharma?'

'One must lead one's life in accordance with purushartha. According to this, the aim of every person is to attain four noble ends, which are Artha, Kama, Dharma, and Moksha.'

'Moksha? Isn't that salvation, the end of life? What can one do to get moksha?'

Madri felt overwhelmed.

Kunti put a hand on her shoulder. 'You do not need to think about moksha right now. You will know when your moment arrives. Come, let us go out and enjoy the rising sun together.' She smiled and helped Madri get up from her seat. They both walked into the garden hand-in-hand, even as Madri remained lost in her thoughts. These few moments had suddenly bound the two with a combined sense of duty and dharma.

The arrival of the monsoon was announced by the change in the wind direction. The dark clouds that gathered on the distant hills seemed to rush towards the plains to quench the thirst of the parched earth. Madri's first summer in Hastinapur was too hot and humid for her. She was also hoping that Pandu, who had earned many war accolades and gathered much wealth from the kingdoms that accepted his supremacy, would now turn homewards. These months had passed in much anticipation, but her acclimatization to the Kuru clan was one important thing that had happened during this period. Pandu's absence had given her the opportunity to have close interaction with the other ladies of the palace. She finally felt like one of them, although she still missed her homeland, its chilly winds, and the mountainous terrain.

As the chariot halted in front of the palace, Madri's heart skipped a beat. She was about to see him again after almost eighteen months. Bhishma Pitamah himself went down the stairs to give the victorious king a warm embrace. Disembarking the chariot, Pandu bent down to take his blessings. The past glory of Hastinapur from Maharaj Shantanu's reign had been restored. Dhritarashtra, Vidura, the mothers, and Satyavati all came forward to give him a warm welcome. The wives were just behind them. Pandu greeted all in the family before moving towards his wives. Madri could not wait to see Pandu in the privacy of her chambers. She was eager to hear stories of his heroic adventures. She had waited patiently long enough, and now she was eager to have her husband all to herself. Just then, from the corner of her eye, she saw Kunti, who seemed just as eager without losing her composure. Madri heaved a sigh.

Once the celebrations were over, Dhritarashtra suggested that they should perform the Ashvamedha yagna, the horse sacrifice ritual, to announce their supremacy to the surrounding kingdoms. But Pandu had other plans. He wanted to be in the forest, far away from the activities of the kingdom, to spend some peaceful, exclusive time with his wives.

After a few days, Pandu, Kunti, and Madri left for the forest. Madri inhaled deeply as she stepped off the chariot. The memories of visiting this place a few days after her wedding were still fresh in her memory. Pandu had not forgotten his promise to come and stay here, right next to the lake blooming with lilies. The lavish set-up—many maids and servants to look after their daily needs and a fleet of armed men for security—and the provisions regularly supplied from the capital made their lives very comfortable. It looked like a little town in its own right.

Their personal abode, the two adjoining cottages facing the lake, was in a secluded place. The monsoon had turned the entire forest lush green. The freshly washed trees, the soft new leaves erupting from withering plants, and the green carpet of grass, all inspired romance. The three of them leisurely spent time together, indulging in various activities while relishing the resplendent natural surroundings.

Weeks passed by. One day, Pandu expressed his wish to go hunting in the deep forest. With a few of his trusted men, he got his favourite horse, Vidyut, ready and rode down the narrow paths with huge trees on both sides.

It had been a few hours, and the sun was about to set. Dark clouds were gathering in the sky, and Pandu had not yet returned. The thought bothered Madri. Her impatience defied logic. She waited outside her cottage, looking in the direction of the forest.

After a while, she saw the men coming back without Pandu. She ran towards them and asked where Pandu was. They didn't reveal much—only that Pandu had asked them to go back and take the horse. He would come back on foot. Hearing the commotion, Kunti also came out. Both the wives waited restlessly for Pandu to return.

An hour passed, and then they saw a glimpse of a dishevelled Pandu, walking distractedly in their direction with drooped shoulders, like a man who had lost everything. He came nearer and fell on his knees, sobbing uncontrollably. Madri ran to him and sat beside him. Kunti followed, brows furrowed and put her palm on his forehead as he narrated his ill-fated experience in between his sobs.

His voice trembled as he spoke: 'After waiting in the forest for hours in silence, I finally spotted a deer couple mating behind a dense bush. Not one to miss such a chance, I shot five arrows, one after the other, at them. The doe died instantly, but to my horror, the stag, fatally injured, changed form … It was Sage Kindam and his wife, mating in the form of deer.'

'The sage, distraught at seeing his wife dead, accused me of being unfair in my hunting … of committing a thoughtless act. I realized my mistake and apologized profusely. But the dying sage was in no mood to forgive. He cursed me … He cursed me that if I ever tried to mate with anyone, I would die instantly.'

'With those words, he breathed his last … leaving his lifeless body to unite with his consort. I sat there for a long time, blaming myself for my hasty act. I … I don't know how to face you two … I failed you both as a husband.'

The regret in his voice was unmistakable.

Madri's heart melted with compassion at Pandu's story. She found it hard to console her distraught husband, knowing too well how difficult it would be for him to live a life of celibacy because of the curse. She would still love him deeply and be with him in all circumstances, she thought. She fondly remembered all the loving moments she had shared with her husband. She raised her hand to wipe the sweat from his forehead, forgetting that there were more people around them. Pandu pushed her hand away and kept blabbering, soaked deeply in self-pity. Kunti sat by him, patiently letting him vent his grief.

After Pandu calmed down, he declared that he did not want to go back to his kingdom. He had committed a grave sin, and he would go to the Himalayas and spend the life of an ascetic. He beseeched his wives to go back to Hastinapur with the entourage and leave him to take sannyasa. He would become a recluse and seek penance for the sin he had involuntarily committed.

Madri was taken aback by Pandu's decision and his cold behaviour. She looked at Kunti with discomfiture. At such times, the decision-maker had always been Kunti. Kunti took a deep breath and said, 'O Lord, we are your wives and have pledged to be with you in good times or bad. We cannot leave you alone in such a trying time. If you wish to live the life of an ascetic and not go back to your royal duties, we too shall follow suit. You do not need to take sannyasa; instead, you could be in vanaprastha ashram and take your wives along with you on the same path.'

Madri gestured thankfully to Kunti. Pandu too sighed with relief at Kunti's idea. It was surely comforting for him to know that his wives had not discarded him because of his unwarranted mistake. All the people serving them were ordered to go back to Hastinapur and convey their decision to the royal family.

The next dawn saw the three of them leaving the cottages with minimal belongings and simple clothing, walking northwards before the morning broke. They had donated all their jewels, expensive clothes, and other personal belongings the previous evening to the poor Brahmins and little urchins residing in the nearby villages. Firm in their decision to live a reclusive life, the two queens and their king decided to follow the upward course of river Ganga to reach the mighty Himalayas.

The path was rough, the terrain unfamiliar, but with steadfast resolve, they moved on. Their life was tough—every day they had to go in search of food and shelter. Pandu had given up all the pleasures of life and only survived on fruits and root vegetables, as did both Kunti and Madri. The king-turned-hermit spent much time in meditation. The trio did not stay in one place for too long, as Pandu didn't want to be attached to a materialistic lifestyle. Madri was experiencing a new side of love and devotion, devoid of luxury but rich in companionship and friendship.

They slowly moved towards the higher mountainous regions. Spotting a peaceful place on the upper hills near Rudra Prayag, where the river Alaknanda met with Bhagirathi, they decided to settle down for a few months. In the mornings, Pandu would light a sacrificial fire and perform homa while Madri would sit next to him, listening to the chanting of mantras. Sometimes, the session would end with all three of them discussing the Vedic shlokas, the auspicious verses.

One day, Pandu saw a group of ascetics going in the direction of Badri Vishal up a rough and bleak mountain.

Upon asking, he came to know that they were heading towards Brahmalok, the divine abode. Keen to follow them, Pandu asked their permission to join the group. He was told by the saints that it was very difficult terrain, and they didn't think it was practical for him to follow their group with two delicate ladies in tow. They also indicated that as he was a grihastha—a married person—he was liable to have progeny to qualify for venturing further into his spiritual life. He had not yet performed his duties in life and could not advance in the direction of salvation.

Pandu looked dismayed. Madri watched as he requested the saints to guide him towards his religious duties and help him find a way to procreate his successor. They reminded Pandu of the story of his own birth by niyoga and said that they could visualize that Pandu would be the father of handsome, valiant boys. Madri tried to ask him about it, but he wouldn't say a word, and the next day she saw Pandu taking Kunti aside, wishing to speak with her in private.

Later, upon endless requests to Kunti, Madri found out that Pandu had come to her, lamenting how his inability to produce a son was hampering his spiritual growth. He had asked Kunti, his first queen, to get pregnant by some wise man, just as his mother had done, and bear children for Pandu.

Aghast at his suggestion, Kunti made it clear that she couldn't mate with another man as the wife of Pandu. But Pandu insisted that the sages themselves had told him that there were many ways of getting an heir if a man himself was unable to do so, one of those being niyoga, the son conceived by his wife from the seed of a good and selfless man.

Kunti then revealed to Madri what she had disclosed to Pandu at that moment: When she was young, upon pleasing Rishi Durvasa with her service, he had given her a boon and a mantra to invoke any god of her choice and beget a son who would bear qualities of that celestial god. She also hesitantly mentioned that, as a young girl, she had tried the mantra and invoked Surya. He had immediately materialized, and she had given birth to a beautiful boy with a golden halo. She had had to give him away because she was unmarried.

Kunti had offered to look for her uniquely born son for Pandu, but Pandu had declined, saying that she was not his wife at that time and that, if she possessed knowledge of such a mantra, she could use it now, in his time of need. At Pandu's request, Kunti decided to invoke Dharmaraj to conceive a son with dharmic qualities. In due time, their first son, Yudhishthir, was born to Kunti, but this left Madri feeling upset and excluded. As she coped with her sorrow, Kunti, following Pandu's wishes, invoked the mighty Pavan Dev and bore Bhim, and later, Indra Dev to bear Arjun.

As the babies grew, so did Madri's anguish. Madri loved Yudhishthir and took any chance to help Kunti with the children. But she was undeniably hurt. Pandu had enjoyed her company as his consort, but when it came to getting sons, he had explicitly chosen Kunti, and not her. As the boys got bigger, Madri started to sense the futility of her existence.

Had Pandu's love for her diminished?

Kunti was blessed with the mantra, but what about her?

Madri's love for the boys had given her a taste of motherhood. She craved the experience herself. A low flame of envy burnt in the depths of her heart. She had given up all the comforts of life to be with Pandu, even her precious veena, which she missed so much. But it seemed her presence now was undesirable. She decided to confront Pandu.

The morning sun saw Madri sitting under a banyan tree, her eyes closed with resolve. The daily activity around her had started. The boys were running around—Kunti was calling them in a hushed voice, trying not to disturb Madri's meditation. Pandu noticed Madri as he was getting ready for his morning rituals. He went and sat next to her and softly called out her name.

'Madri, is something bothering you?'

Madri opened her eyes devoid of any emotion, cleared her dry throat, and said, 'My Lord, my life is as dry as these falling leaves. I am happy to see you and Kunti didi enjoy raising your sons. But I have lost everything—without your love and companionship, my life is futile. I beg you to request Kunti didi to help me in begetting a son. I long for motherhood.'

Pandu pressed her hand and promised to ask Kunti if she would share her mantra with Madri. Kunti willingly agreed and asked Madri to invoke a deity of her choice. Madri could not believe her ears.

Madri asked to be given a day to think about which deity to invoke. She spent a sleepless night trying to decide which deity could fulfil her wish. Kunti already had three sons from three powerful deities. Who could she choose to compete with that? Her first thought was Vishnu—Narayan himself. But she forced herself to shrug the thought away, as she did not think it would be possible and she might lose her chance. She tossed and turned for a while before coming out of the cottage. She started walking around, but after a while, she sat on a rock, exhausted. Lost in her thoughts, she slowly saw the sky turning pink, and a glimpse of the sun resolved her dilemma. She thought for a few moments, and a decision was made.

On the chosen day, Madri woke up before sunrise, took a dip in the freezing Alakananda River, and prayed to Lord Rudra, asking for his blessing. She walked up to Kunti, who was already waiting to recite her mantra, folded her hands, and invoked the celestial demigods, the Ashwini Kumars, the twin sons of the all-powerful Surya. Her happiness knew no bounds when, in due course, she begot beautiful twin sons, whom she named Nakul and Sahadev. She felt a sense of satisfaction as she realized how smart she had been to get two sons in one chance.

A few months later, at Madri's insistence, Pandu requested Kunti to give her mantra to Madri once again. But this time, Kunti flatly refused. Madri suspected that Kunti was shocked at her cunning—in invoking the twin gods and getting two sons—and now did not wish to give her another chance. Madri moved on with ease.

The princes and their baby brothers changed the lives of their parents. Pandu was now less rigid in his strict regime and could often be found delightedly playing with his sons. His loss of interest in family life took a back seat as he watched his sons grow up.

Spring was in the air. The chill of the Himalayan winds had reduced considerably. The forest was blooming with Krishnachuda, the flame of the forest. The bright red and yellow flowers overcame the gloominess of winter and turned the forest vibrant with the colours of imminent spring. The winds were loaded with the fragrance of various kinds of vegetation.

Madri had, over time, planted some medicinal plants around their cottage that helped with minor ailments as well as purified the air around their beautiful abode. She had also planted various flower-laden creepers and adorned the walls with tribal art that she had learnt from the nearby ashram women. In the forest behind the cottage was a stream with crystal clear water flowing down from the hills of the Himalayas.

The princes were being raised in natural surroundings with much love and care. Pandu focused on their physical fitness and started to teach them archery and wrestling at a very young age. Kunti oversaw teaching them scriptures and shastras. She also used to tell them stories of their brave ancestors and other famous kings. Similarly, their finer faculties were being developed by Madri's deep aesthetic sense. The boys loved to do little chores for the mothers.

Every day, the boys, led by Yudhishthir, sat down under the banyan tree a little away from the cottage to learn their lessons of shastras. This was the time of the day when the elder ones recited shlokas—the Vedic verses—while the younger two, who were just toddlers, played with pebbles.

The kitchen garden behind the cottage, planted by Madri, offered many vegetables and fruits. Kunti picked some kandamools—root vegetables—and some fruits and sat down to chop them, keeping an eye on the boys as she cooked meals for the family.

Madri, lost in reverie amidst the music of chirping birds, suddenly noticed a deer rush through the front yard of the cottage towards the forest behind. Unmindfully, she followed the deer into the dense forest.

It had been such a peaceful, harmonious time for Madri and her family. Along with that peace came a lowering of guard, a desire to follow one's heart, and even a deceitful sense of invincibility.

Hadn't she seen Pandu stroll towards the forest a little while ago? Was he still around? Should she look for him besides the stream?

It was in this daydreamy frame of mind that she and Pandu found each other in a state of bliss in the forest.

Suddenly Madri's bone-chilling scream rode the wave of the heavy wind, piercing the stillness of the dense forest. The bowl full of chopped vegetables slipped from Kunti's hands.

'Kunti didi, please come,' pleaded Madri's shrill voice from a distance. Kunti left the kitchen fire burning and ran towards the sound which seemed to be coming from the stream side.

Madri saw Kunti running towards her with all the princes in tow. They had also come running, hearing the sound, to see what had happened. Bhim was carrying his little brothers on his two shoulders.

Madri beseeched her to leave the boys at a distance and come nearer. The trembling in her voice was evident. As Kunti reached nearer, she could now see two bodies entangled intimately at a distance. In an instant, as Kunti understood what had transpired, Madri's face turned a shade of beetroot red with shame and agony. Kunti gestured to Yudhishthir, the eldest of them all, to stay back with his brothers.

It required their combined strength to pick up the muscular, now still, body of Pandu from atop Madri. Slowly, they both laid him down on one side. Their worst fears came true as they realized that he was not breathing.

Madri could not stop wailing and cursing herself until her voice ran hoarse.

Even as the distraught Madri was inconsolable, she turned to look at Kunti, who was quiet—very, very quiet—her jaws tightly clenched. Madri knew that Kunti had spent years taking care of Pandu, helping him curb his bodily desires, motivating him towards the life of a hermit. She could not look up and meet Kunti's eyes. She had cheated and wronged her Didi, her mentor, her only friend. She pulled her shawl over her bosom, evened her clothes and dishevelled hair, and sobbed uncontrollably.

Hearing all the commotion, sages from the nearby hermitage quickly arrived. It did not take much for the wise ones to understand what had happened. Pandu's curse and the reason for his being in the forest were common knowledge. They started to prepare a pyre for the lifeless body of Pandu, whose prana, the life force, had left him the instant he had tried to mate with his beloved wife.

Madri's cheeks burnt with shame and guilt at the very thought of it. She was finding it difficult to breathe, as if something inside her was choking her.

By now, the princes also understood that their father was no longer alive. The three elder princes were sobbing, standing huddled together. Nakul and Sahdev started wailing as soon as they saw their mother. They raised their arms to leap towards her. Their combined cries of anguish rang through the quiet of the forest.

Madri suddenly pushed her boys aside, held them each firmly by one arm, and left them near the stone-like figure of the grieving Kunti. Avoiding the question mark in Kunti's gaze, who had looked up at Madri's sudden action, her voice boomed over the gloom in a strong declaration, 'I will accompany my beloved husband on his final journey.'

Tormented by her words Kunti argued that it was the right of the first wife, and, if anyone had to go, it would be her. The hermit women from the ashrams nearby came forward and tried to console them. The sages advised both not to entertain such horrifying thoughts. Their sons were still young; they needed their mothers. It was now the mothers' duty to raise them well.

But Madri was not at all willing to change her mind. She turned to Kunti with folded hands and said, 'Didi, you have been like my elder sister, my guru, guiding me in my weaker moments. Please try to understand me. All my life I have loved my husband with absolute devotion, totally dedicated myself to his wishes. My life is meaningless without him. This is my moment of Purushartha, the only way I can walk on the path of moksha after sharing a great life of dharma with my lord. I do not consider myself capable and strong enough to raise my boys, as well as yours, as my own. My heart is deeply anguished. You are strong-willed. You must stand by our sons as their pillar of strength. Please take them to Hastinapur, their rightful place, where they will be raised as princes and bring glory to the Kuru clan and their departed father. I have full faith in you that you will raise my sons as your own.

Please forgive me for leaving you alone in this moment of grief with such a responsibility. But it is practically impossible for me to take a single breath in this ill-fated place.'

Kunti was speechless and looked at Madri blankly. Madri knew that Kunti's loss was irreparable too. Yet, she was the only one with the strength to survive this calamity—not for herself but for their sons. Kunti glanced at Nakul and Sahadev, stepped forward, and bent down to hold the two little princes close to her heart, wiping tears from their cheeks as her own eyes started to burn.

The sages helped Yudhishthir, now almost sixteen, perform the last rites of their father while holding little Nakul, the elder of Madri's sons, in his arms. Madri sat on the pyre with Pandu's head in her lap, looking at Kunti and their sons with glazed eyes that envisaged the great Pandavas, the sons of valiant Pandu, raised ably by Kunti. With such visions of their bright future, she closed her eyes as the pyre was lit.

Kunti stood there, tears finally rolling down her swollen eyes. As the Pandava princes sobbed uncontrollably, she stood with her arms around them, an embodiment of strength.

A few weeks later, Kunti arrived in Hastinapur with her five sons, the Pandavas, carrying the resolve of not just one mother, but two. Madri's spirit lived on in her Didi's heart, driving Kunti to ensure that her sons were given a good life and their rightful place as the heirs of Pandu.

6

Vikarna: The Price of Blood

Raghu Ram Sola

Part 1: The Conflicted Warrior

The sun had not yet risen. Thirteen days of war had taken their toll on Vikarna. The wounds were still coarse, and the chilly breeze was making them ache. Still, Vikarna stood in his chariot, unflinching. Dushasana, his elder brother, accompanied him along with thousands of Gandhara soldiers. None of them had slept the previous night. Most of the soldiers were yawning.

'These were the days of valour. Every day, for the past thirteen days, men faced hopeless odds. Some survived, and many lucky ones died. It was strange how war makes people conscious of their own mortality, and yet people sacrifice their lives for something ... someone they believe in,' Vikarna thought. Yesterday, Vikarna saw one such sacrifice. Brave Abhimanyu, the beloved son of the mighty warrior Arjun, had pierced the Padmavyuha formation to save the Pandava side from imminent defeat and died. Vikarna regretted the role he had played in it.

Jayadrath, Vikarna's brother-in-law, checked the progress of other warriors, preventing them from aiding Abhimanyu. Now Jayadrath was hiding from Arjun, quivering with dread.

Vikarna didn't know what he was fighting for. He didn't believe in his side, and he had no love for Jayadratha.

Vikarna at least knew why he was fighting the war. It was his dharma. Even if it meant he would aid adharma, it was his dharma. He didn't leave to join Yudhishthir like Yuyutsu did because it was his dharma. He remembered the wise words of his cousin when everything between them had been alright. It was his dharma. It was his dharma to die a meaningless death fighting for a losing side. It was his dharma.

'We will win the war by the end of today, brother,' Dushasana interrupted Vikarna's thoughts. He was a very tall, well-built person. 'It's not possible for Arjun to find our useless brother-in-law in time. Even if, by some miracle, he finds him, our greatest warriors will protect him. He will definitely fail, and when he fails, Arjun will enter the pyre. Without him, the Pandavas stand no chance.'

'That's true,' Vikarna agreed, 'but we cannot underestimate Arjun. There are tales that he even fought Mahadev and came out unscathed.'

Dushasana's lips turned into a smile, and then he shook with mirth. 'Your large ears will believe everything! Stories propagated by jungle folk—yes, that's what they are. There they were born, there they lived, and there they ruled. Even, if by some miracle, Arjun kills him, he will still die because of the curse Jayadrath's father has set about his son's killer. Haha, that useless brother-in-law turned out to be the most valuable pawn we poss…'

The loud sounds of Devadatt and Panchajanya, the famed conches of Arjun and his charioteer Krishna, cut him off. They were boldly advertising their location and daring anyone to attack. The sky was now crimson red, perhaps the colour of Arjun's eyes. Before they could even realize what was happening, an arrow flew way over their heads and towards Jayadrath. It would have beheaded him if Ashwatthama, the son of Dronacharya, hadn't cut it off.

'Be careful,' the son of their preceptor shouted, 'it's Arjun! He can fire arrows a very long distance. He may not see Jayadrath. He may not be near him, but he can still kill him.'

Vikarna cursed himself for being careless and looked in the direction from which the arrow had come with his large eyes. His tall, dark body, now pumped with adrenaline, no longer felt pain. 'It's my dharma,' he remembered once again.

'Aim your bows, and cut off any incoming arrows,' Vikarna ordered the soldiers.

The day ahead was filled with darkness and sorrow, the same as the past thirteen days. But all that misery was nothing compared to the incident that happened long ago…

Part 2: Homecoming

Vikarna observed the crowds from his seat on top of the elephant. They were everywhere. Some were standing on the tops of towers constructed eons ago by their forefathers. Most of the people were outside. At least the clouds were dark, and the winds were pleasant.

Vikarna's lips turned into a smile. 'I will meet my cousins today,' he thought. He noticed the excitement in the crowd and instructed the soldiers to prevent any stampede.

The last time he had seen them was when they had come back after spending around six years in exile—after escaping from a botched attempt to burn them alive. Vikarna distinctly remembered that day. His father, Dhritarashtra, convinced by Vikarna's uncle Vidura to bridge the familial gap and award the Pandavas their fair share of the land, sent him to receive them. He remembered their cheerful faces and sad smiles that followed. Dhritarashtra had given them infertile land filled with rocks and wild serpents, basically a desert, for their share. Somehow, they turned it around and established Bharatavarsha's greatest empire. They were now coming to play a game of dice with Vikarna's brother, Duryodhana.

Vikarna's smile faded at the thought of his brother. As a child, Vikarna had followed him everywhere and clung to him like a cloth. He loved and admired Duryodhana. He had picked up fights for him and tried to humiliate his cousins. But as he grew and learnt right from wrong, he regretted those actions. The admiration he once held for his brother turned into concern. He wanted to apologize to the Pandavas for his behaviour, but he could not bring himself to say those words. Instead, he asked Arjun to teach him archery. The third Pandava, understanding he was trying to make amends, gladly accepted him as an apprentice. Ever since then, the Pandavas treated him as their own brother, but his relationship with his own brothers diminished. They began putting a distance between themselves and him and stopped sharing their secrets. They loved him still, and neither did Vikarna stop loving them, but he became a spectator, not a participant.

The pretext of a friendly game might have fooled everyone, perhaps even the Pandavas, but Vikarna knew his brothers too well. His heart felt heavy. He was not worried about the Pandavas—no, they could handle anything that was thrown at them. He was worried about his own brothers. If they were to botch whatever they were planning one more time, they would surely face the wrath of the Pandavas. How many times could they forgive? He had to decide between the adharma that his brothers were hosting and the dharma that was with the Pandavas.

All his worries disappeared at the sight of the approaching chariots.

They arrived at the exact auspicious moment they had said they would. They carried heaps of gold and gemstones, the best of clothes and perfumes, and had weapons decked with gold and horses clad in beautiful white armour. They brought the stoneware made by the Pandavas themselves, thanks to their time at a potter's house during exile. Guarding either side of Yudhishthir were two tall men, one almost eight feet tall and exceptionally well built. His armour was unduly small for him—it looked as if he were popping out of it. He bore a large mace and had a shaved face. His presence inspired both security and terror. The other was dark, and his hands reached beyond his knees. Unlike his brother, he had grown a moustache. He carried a heavy bow and two quivers. Bhim and Arjun. They were protecting their king, Yudhishthir, on either side.

'How are you, brother?' Bhim shouted, jumped out of his chariot, and rushed towards Vikarna as soon as he saw him. He would have knocked him down if not for the timely intervention of Arjun.

'Be careful, brother. He has to be alive to feel your love,' Arjun teased Bhim and bent down to touch Vikarna's feet, seeking his blessings.

'Be noble and bring great renown to our clan,' Vikarna blessed him and brought him to his feet.

'Don't even think about it, I am only eighteen days older than you.' Bhim was about to protest, but he was late.

'Ayushman bhava,' Bhim blessed, brought Vikarna to his feet, and hugged him.

'Save some blessings for us too!' Nakul and Sahadev, who were guarding the rear wheels of Yudhishthir, exclaimed as they rushed towards Vikarna and fell at his feet. Vikarna blessed them and then sought blessings from Yudhishthir.

'It feels nice to be here. Even after all these years, it feels like…' Yudhishthir hesitated.

'Welcome home, Samrat Yudhishthir,' Vikarna said cheerfully.

All their lips turned into smiles at his welcome.

Yudhishthir greeted the people of Hastinapur, while his brothers distributed the gifts. After meeting every person who had arrived there and after learning of their well-being,

Yudhishthir slowly turned to Vikarna and said, 'Shall we seek the blessings of the king and our aunt, Gandhari?'

Once they were in relative privacy and after making sure no one was within earshot, Vikarna voiced his concerns to Yudhishthir and his brothers.

'I am aware of Duryodhana's treachery, Vikarna. He poisoned Bhim the last time we trusted him,' Yudhishthir said.

'Then why did you come?' Vikarna asked and instantly regretted the phrasing. It sounded as if he didn't want them there.

Yudhishthir's lips turned into a benevolent smile. He said, 'I didn't want to come. Even our uncle Vidura advised us not to. Even so, it's my dharma to come.'

'Does dharma dictate you play a game of dice?' Vikarna, now confused, wanted to understand the nuances of dharma and asked this question as an eager disciple, but once again regretted the phrasing, as it had come out sounding like a taunt.

'You shouldn't speak to our brother like that. Where are your manners?' Bhim mockingly chided him and pulled his large ears.

Vikarna panicked and apologetically looked at the brothers. He wanted to explain but couldn't form the words properly. He said, 'No, I didn't … I am…'

'He is just playing with you,' Arjun's lips turned into a smile.

They laughed for a while.

'Vikarna,' Yudhishthir addressed him like a teacher addresses a pupil. 'We all have listened to the story of King Ram, who went to the forests on the command of his father. In a way, Dhritarashtra is our father, and we must follow his wishes as commands.'

'Ram followed the orders of a loving father who was forced to do so out of a word,' Vikarna observed.

'We can't choose our fathers, Vikarna, but we can choose our dharma,' Yudhishthir replied, his lips creasing into a knowing smile. He knew why Vikarna had asked that question. One cannot choose brothers just as one cannot choose fathers.

'Will you follow his commands even if he asks you to lay down your life or give your kingdom to Duryodhana?'

'Unless it is in protecting others, it is against dharma to give up one's own life. As a responsible king, my duty to my subjects comes first,' he answered.

Vikarna looked around to check for eavesdroppers. He hesitated for a couple of seconds and then said slowly, in a whisper, 'So I have to follow Duryodhana?'

'Follow him unless he asks you to commit adharma. Advise him until he doesn't want it. Be there for him,' Yudhishthir said.

Vikarna stayed with them, and the Pandavas spent the rest of their evening visiting various temples and well-wishers. They met the Kuru elders: Bhishma; their preceptor, Drona; and his son Ashwatthama, who were also visiting Hastinapur from their kingdom in northern Panchala. Then they took the blessings of Dhritarashtra and Gandhari and were on their way to Vidura's home.

They spent the evening at Vidura's home. Even though he managed the treasury, his home was not extravagant. He served them home-cooked meals—nothing too fancy but very good.

'We have visited so many places after coming here, Uncle Vidura, but this is the place that truly felt like home.' Bhim voiced everyone's feelings while parting.

He smiled and addressed Yudhishthir. 'Be careful, Yudhishthir. I warned you against coming here. Here you have no allies, and they are planning to use your dharma against you.'

'I will be careful, Uncle. Besides, we have you, Pitamah Bhishma, and our preceptor, Drona, to come to our aid if something goes wrong.'

Vidura smiled weakly and excused them after asking Vikarna to stay behind.

'We will be the only allies he will have if things go south. I hope I can count on your help,' he said. His eyes became moist and deprived of light. 'I tried my best to stop the king from making this mistake, and I tried my best to stop Yudhishthir from coming, but my efforts have been in vain. Drona is practically a slave to the throne. Bhishma has turned a blind eye so far against the atrocities committed against the Pandavas, so I doubt he will do anything different now.' His eyes began to tear up. He forgot his surroundings and spoke to himself, 'We are the only help.'

'I will always be on your side, Uncle,' Vikarna said. He placed his arms around his uncle and wiped his tears. 'Together, we will protect them.'

Arjuna joined them, hearing the last words from Vikarna. He questioned what it was about.

'Nothing. He just wants my help with something,' Vikarna replied.

Vikarna accompanied them to their guest houses and left. The next day, the Pandava wives arrived. Vikarna greeted his sister-in-law, Draupadi. He had not seen her since she was crowned Empress of Bharatavarsha at Rajasuya yajna, almost a year ago. Vikarna's admiration for Draupadi was something words couldn't express. She brought prosperity to beggars and helped them establish a great empire. Draupadi also managed the treasury of Indraprastha, a job impossible to do because one had to manage between helping the weak, developing the kingdom, and keeping the treasury afloat. She also managed the household by waking up before everyone else and going to bed only after everyone was asleep. She cooked and served the meals daily for whoever was in need. Vikarna was in awe of her industriousness and attention to detail, remembering the names of thousands of dasis and workers at the Pandava Palace, the Sabha built by Maya Danava.

Part 3: The Day of the Dice

The fateful day to play the game of dice arrived. It was going to take place in the newly constructed palace for Duryodhana in Jayantha.

The hall was oval in shape. Along the circumference, there were seats for Kuru elders and guests. At one end of the major axis, a throne was present on which King Dhritarashtra sat, and, at the centre of the oval, there was a carpet on which Samrat Yudhishthir sat facing north and Duryodhana south. To Vikarna's surprise, there were no windows. Slowly, all the guests and Kuru elders sat down in their respective seats to enjoy the match.

'Shall we begin the game, Maharaj?' Duryodhana bowed to the king and asked his permission.

'You may begin.' Dhritarashtra waved his hand and relaxed on the throne.

At Duryodhana's signal, a priest stood up and said, 'On behalf of King Dhritarashtra and Prince Duryodhana, I welcome you all with a humble heart to the game of dice. It is going to take place between our own prince, Duryodhana, and Yudhishthir from Indraprastha. I will explain the rules of the dice game to people who are not familiar with them. In my hands are the dice that will be used for the game.' He lifted his hand and showed a couple of cuboids to the crowd. 'The first dice has numbers from one to four, and the second one has numbers from five to eight.' He dramatically paused and continued. 'Both sides have to guess a number, and whichever is closest to the actual outcome wins. Since the numbers are very limited, the contenders cannot choose the same set of numbers consecutively. Whoever wins gets the chance to roll the dice. Since Kshatriyas are going to play the game, they are going to stake something for each game, and whoever wins gets them all. In case of a tie, the game will be voided,'

They started the game, and Duryodhana, who had been trained by Shakuni, initially had the upper hand, but Yudhishthir speedily caught up to him with his understanding of probabilities and kept on winning. The game went on for hours. There was no way for Vikarna to tell what part of the day it was because of the absence of windows. Both of them started getting tired but kept on playing, with Yudhishthir leading. The audience lost interest in them but were too polite to leave. They did not want to anger the kings of Hastinapur and Indraprastha.

'Brother Yudhishthir, I know you are an excellent player, and I don't even know the basics of it. To keep the game challenging, I would like to nominate Uncle Shakuni to play on my behalf. You are not afraid of any fair competition, are you?'

To Vikarna's knowledge, Yudhishthir was also a novice, and it would have been a fair game between him and Duryodana, meanwhile Shakuni was an expert dice player.

'I accept,' Yudhishthir agreed, to Vikarna's surprise.

'Brother...' Bhim protested.

'Very well then,' Duryodhana called Shakuni to take his seat, and he sat beside him.

'There is no valour in playing a dishonest game, Uncle. Bound by my Kshatriya dharma, I am continuing the game. Do not defeat us through crooked means.'

'What are your numbers, Yudhishthir?' Shakuni asked with dice in his palms.

Yudhishthir said, 'One and eight.'

'My numbers are three and seven,' Shakuni replied.

Shakuni carefully rolled the dice with his palms and won the game.

'What are the odds of that?' Vikarna thought 'One in sixteen?'

Again, Shakuni asked for a fresh set of numbers, and this time too, he won.

Vikarna now calculated the odds to be one in two hundred and fifty-six.

'This is crazy,' Vikarna thought, and kept on watching the game.

Yudhishthir kept on losing, Shakuni kept on winning, and Vikarna lost track of probabilities when Shakuni crossed the one-in-a-million mark.

'He is good, but not that good. Surely there must be some kind of cheating going on,' Vikarna thought, but his brothers started enjoying the game, oblivious to the deception.

To Vikarna's surprise, Yudhishthir kept on playing and kept on losing.

Slowly, Yudhishthir lost his kingdom, his brothers, and himself. The brothers still stood by Yudhishthir's side, willing to follow him even to death.

The entire sabha had gone silent by now. The reality of the situation sank into everyone's hearts. Their eyes eagerly waited to see what would happen next. Some people couldn't concentrate because of exhaustion.

Shakuni's lips turned into a sly smile. He looked at the glowing Duryodhana. They eagerly waited for one of the brothers to protest and disown Yudhishthir, but it didn't happen. Realizing they had to do something more, Shakuni, with a mocking smile, said, 'Fear not, Sevak Yudhishthir, there is still hope for you. Gamble your wife, Draupadi, and you may win everything back. It's an ideal deal for you, isn't it? With just one roll, you will gain everything you have lost—all your brothers, your wealth and kingdom, everything,'

'And the possibility of losing everything,' Vikarna muttered under his breath. 'Surely Yudhishthir cannot stake Draupadi!' he thought.

But Vikarna was wrong.

Yudhishthir described the physical beauty of Draupadi down to little details like hair on her body and staked her.

'Why is he doing that?' Vikarna was confused.

And Yudhishthir lost.

Vikarna's heart was filled with fear. His body felt weightless. And his body temperature rose. The entire sabha became silent. *What worse could happen next?*

As if answering their questions, Duryodhana broke the silence, 'Vidura, bring Draupadi here. It would please me to see her clean the floors and serve me along with the other maids. Later, we can send her to the whorehouse.'

Vikarna wanted to protest but could not form the words. He looked at the Pandavas. Tears were flowing from their eyes. Yudhishthir turned his face down, away from all the eyes.

Bhim started shaking violently and tried to get up and bash everyone there with his mace, but Arjun restrained his brother. Then his eyes darted to Karna, Duryodhana's so-called friend, who was smiling shamelessly at the turn of events. Duryodhana was glowing with pride, and Dushasana was by his side to do whatever his brother required.

Vikarna's eyes then shifted to Bhishma. *Surely he must object to this.* However, he did nothing. Then Vikarna looked at his father. *Surely he can't do this to his brother's children.* Dhritarashtra was smiling when he thought no one was looking. Vikarna then searched for his mother, but she was not there. Then, his large eyes finally turned to Vidura. His head was in the palms of his hands. After hearing Duryodhana's command, he rubbed his eyes and slowly stood up.

'Now everything depends on you, Uncle,' Vikarna thought.

Vidura adjusted his throat and, in a serene voice, said, 'Duryodhana, you are angering people superior to you. You have bound them for now, like a lion in a cage. But once they break free, you will have no place to run and no place to seek refuge. They will even go to the base of the ocean to kill you. Bhim will consume you and your brothers like fire. Arjun will resemble Pasupati and will destroy your forces. Yudhishthir will win. Dharma will win. Don't bring disaster to our clan. You have everything. Ninety-nine brothers will do anything for you. You have a healthy body, a kingdom to rule. You can have anything you wish for. Why are you jealous of your cousins? It is not too late. You can still turn it around. O Duryodhana! Do not lose everything on account of your greed and jealousy,'

'Oh Ksatta! Do not lecture us on morals. You should obey my order and bring Draupadi here,' Duryodhana mocked him.

Vikarna's eyes turned red, and he was about to come to Vidura's aid but, before he could respond, Vidura replied, 'The wise seek the advice of learned people. O Duryodhana! You have no desire to do what is right. You will only do what pleases you. So, whatever I say is like the rain on the ocean, but I will not take part in your adharma. Having lost himself first, Yudhishthir had no right to stake Draupadi. He, however, staked her under the dharma of a slave, to follow the commands of his master. So, the stake is not valid.'

Vikarna's heart filled with a flickering hope. He had always admired Vidura for his knowledge of dharma, but at this moment his admiration changed into something more, something words could not express. Even in this dire situation, he clung to dharma and found a way out. It is true that dharma will always protect those who seek refuge in it. *Dharmo rakshati rakshitah.* His hope, however, was short-lived.

Duryodhana called a servant. 'Pratikamin, do not fear those servants. Bring me Draupadi. Vidura has always been on their side and still fears them.'

Vikarna's heart sank with sorrow and horror. He frantically searched everywhere for a person who would object but found no one apart from Vidura. In the absence of windows, he could not make out what time it was. It could be night or it could even be the next day. After what felt like an eternity, the servant finally returned without Draupadi.

'Why are you here alone? Where is she?' Duryodhana asked him in an angry voice. From the years growing up with his brother, Vikarna knew it was not anger—he was merely enjoying the sport of hunting. The longer the delay, the tougher the prey, and the more satisfaction he would feel.

'Draupadi has asked me to ask Yudhishthir whether he lost himself first or her.' Everyone in the sabha looked at Yudhishthir, expecting a reply. Most of them were tired and were not paying attention to the game and could not remember who lost first. Vikarna and a handful of people knew the exact order but were too afraid to speak. But Yudhishthir did not reply.

'Why is he silent?' Vikarna wondered.

Duryodhana broke the silence once again. 'Bring her here, and let her pose the question.'

The servant looked ashamed, admitted being afraid of Draupadi, and refused to go.

Duryodhana was amused and said, 'Brother Dushasana, bring her here. We have nothing to fear. Don't be afraid of Bhim. He can't do anything.,'

Dushasana dutifully left, and the entire Sabha felt the tension. After what seemed like an eternity, Dushasana returned with Draupadi. She was clad only in a single garment.

'I am in the assembly of…' Draupadi was about to speak, but Dushasana didn't let her. He caught her by the hair and started pulling her along with him. Draupadi instinctively put one arm on her cloth to not let it loose, and with another hand, she tried to pull Dushasana's hand away from her hair. Dushasana's lips turned into a crooked smile.

He shouted, 'My dear brother, I have brought a beautiful whore for you. This one is feisty, just like you love them. Oh, maybe I should show her to the court and let them take their turns with her. After all, you are a generous prince.'

'You are right, brother! You are right indeed. What will people say about me if I don't share such a beautiful vessel?'

Vikarna's eyes turned bright red, and tears started pouring out. He couldn't see anything. He didn't want to. But he had to do something, anything.

Then he saw Draupadi bending over and whispering something to his brother. He wondered what it could be, but his question was immediately answered.

'Your husband has staked you and lost. We won you in accordance with dharma. Plead if you want to, but you have no protectors. Masters do whatever they want with their slaves. This may be the time of your menses, but whether you are clad in a single garment or no garment at all, you have to please your masters,' he loudly mocked and laughed.

Dushasana then dragged her around the sabha, and during their hustle, her garment started loosening to Vikarna's horror. He closed his eyes out of mortification and heard Draupadi's voice, pleading with Dushasana to stop. She begged the Kuru elders for justice. Dushasana ignored her pleas and, calling her a slave, marched her across the courtroom, dragging her by the hair.

It was Bhishma's voice that prompted Vikarna to open his eyes. Filled with tears, he couldn't see anything. He rubbed them and looked at the Pitamah.

'Oh, fortunate one! Dharma is subtle, and I do not understand the depths of it. As a slave, Yudhishthir does not possess property and thus cannot stake you. However, women are also said to be the property of their husbands. O sinless one! Yudhishthir will not abandon truth. He himself is silent. He has voluntarily played with Shakuni and lost. How can I say anything for certain? Dharma is nothing but what the powerful ones say it is. Even Yudhishthir is not thinking that Shakuni deceived him.'

'O Pitamah! Yudhishthir was unskilled, and skilled ones challenged him. Bound by his Kshatriya dharma, he was forced to play. Being unskilled, he understood the game only after everything was lost,' Draupadi replied.

Draupadi had done nothing to deserve this kind of humiliation. Even in this situation, she did not blame Yudhishthir and stood by his side. She was being targeted by his wretched brothers to cause disunion among the Pandavas, and it was working. Vikarna saw Bhim and Arjun arguing between themselves. Bhim openly expressed his anger towards Yudhishthir, while Arjun supported Yudhishthir.

The entire sabha was watching them silently. No one dared utter a word for fear of Duryodhana. The person who was daring enough to oppose him was termed a blind supporter of the Pandavas. If anyone had to do something, it had to be him—a brother of Duryodhana. No one could call him biased towards the Pandavas. He had to speak now. He remembered Yudhishthir's words. 'Follow him unless he asks you to commit adharma. Advise him until he doesn't want it. Be there for him.' He had to advise his brother. Vikarna made up his mind and stood up to address the court.

'O kings and elders! Answer the question posed by my sister-in-law. If we do not answer it, we will certainly go to hell. O Bhishma! You have vowed to remain celibate for your father and thus robbed this kingdom of an effective ruler. You are a fearless warrior and a valued member of the Kauravas. Speak your mind; don't be afraid. O Drona and Kripa! You have taught us everything we know. You have taught us about dharma, the merits it grants, and how it will destroy those who ignore it. Still, you are silent. O Father! These are the children of your brother. Draupadi is your daughter-in-law. Why are you silent against such an atrocity committed against your own? O kings and elders! Please address the question posed by the intelligent Yagnaseni.' He paused and looked at everyone in the sabha. They continued to remain silent, afraid of Duryodhana.

Vikarna almost lost the will to go on after their inaction, but then he looked at the pitiful state of Draupadi and was persuaded to continue. 'O Kauravas, kings, and elders! Even if you say nothing, I will speak my mind. King Yudhishthir, having lost himself first, staked Draupadi, the common wife of all the Pandavas. Shakuni deceived the king and won. How else can he win consecutive games? Knowing fully well that Yudhishthir does not have the right to stake Draupadi, he forced him to do so. Fie on that wretch! Where is your valour if you cannot protect a helpless woman? What is the use of learning to use various weapons if you can't even protect a single person? Speak your mind and pick up your side, wise ones! Otherwise, we will all burn in hell.'

Vikarna didn't know what had come over him. He wanted to sound neutral, but he had picked his side and dared everyone else to do the same. Vikarna could no longer have a proper relationship with his siblings and would be forced to live like Yuyutsu, their half-brother. He would be called a traitor, and his royal status would be just in name. But all of this would have been worth it to save his sister-in-law.

His effort had not gone in vain. The sabha was soon filled with whispers.

'Yes, what Prince Vikarna has said is right. Shame on Shakuni for cheating the Pandavas through a deceitful game,' someone said.

'Shame on Dushasana for dragging his own sister-in-law to the sabha in such a state,' someone else echoed.

'Is it not enough to rob Yudhishthir from us? What sin must we have done to see him in such a state? Fie on Duryodhana for such greed.'

'Yagnaseni Draupadi is such a virtuous woman. She served us like her own family. She does not deserve this treatment from these insolent wretches.'

Vidura threw Vikarna an approving look, but Vikarna was too excited to notice. He could not feel his legs and hands. His breathing quickened, and his entire body started sweating. A chill ran through his heart, immediately filling it with warmth. He could not hear anything, but somehow he knew they were approving his argument. He looked at the Pandavas and Draupadi and perceived their gratitude. Then he looked at his brother, Duryodhana. He had lost his cool, assured composure, and his eyes were bright red with rage. Dushasana was unsure of what to do next. Then his gaze turned to Karna. Once again, a chill ran through his heart. He did not know why.

Duryodhana had ninety-nine brothers, but none of them were as close to him as Karna. Whenever Vikarna or Yuyutsu tried to advise something good to Duryodhana, he foiled their attempts. Karna slowly arose from his seat to address the sabha, ready to shatter Vikarna's attempt.

'O child! You are but a juvenile, and you are trying to speak like an elder. O foolish one! You do not know what dharma is or what adharma is, and yet you are speaking as if you know everything. You think Dushasana is wrong for dragging Draupadi to the sabha like this. By the decree of gods, a woman should not have more than one husband, but this whore married five of them. In accordance with dharma, we should parade her around the kingdom bereft of clothes. What is wrong with a woman having five husbands to have some more? O Dushasana! Vikarna is a child. Don't listen to him. Strip away her clothes, and teach her a lesson on dharma.'

Without wasting a single moment, Dushasana tried to pull away Draupadi's garment. Draupadi desperately clung to it, but her strength was no match for Vikarna's brother.

Vikarna tried to protest, but what happened next shocked everyone assembled at the sabha.

Garment after garment appeared out of nowhere and clung to Draupadi's body. It appeared as if an invisible force had come to her aid. The force of dharma, the force of Lord Krishna. Dushasana continued pulling. There was no end to those garments, but still, he continued with all his might.

Vikarna could not believe what was happening before his eyes. He was exhausted and thought his eyes were playing tricks on him. Then he saw the sabha as people rose to break into applause. They started praising Draupadi after witnessing this miracle. Then the admiration for Draupadi turned into anger towards Dushasana and Duryodhana for committing such shameless transgression against their own sister-in-law—one who was protected by gods, no less.

Dushasana collapsed from exhaustion.

Vikarna's eyes were once again filled with tears. This time, they were tears of joy. His entire body felt numb, and a wave of relief washed over him.

Vidura once again rose and spoke. 'Draupadi is weeping for justice. We, the learned ones, have failed to give it to her so far. O kings! O learned ones! O warriors! Speak your mind like young Vikarna. Those who know about dharma and still sit idle will surely be guilty of the sin of lying by half. Those who, out of fear, answer falsely will surely be guilty of lying. So, virtuous ones! Speak your mind. Do what is right.'

Draupadi, now having regained some control, once again addressed the assembly. 'O Kuru elders! In my distress, I have failed to offer salutations.' She held her hands up in salutation and sought the elders's blessings.

Vikarna was surprised. Was she offering homage to the people who had failed to protect her? He knew he would never do such a thing if he had been in such a position and, with that realization, his admiration grew.

Duryodhana then once again tried to cause a rift between the brothers by promising to free them if they relinquished Yudhishthir as their lord. But the Pandavas and Draupadi stood by his side. Angered at Duryodhana and Dushasana, Bhim vowed to kill them. Arjun vowed to kill Karna and Sahadev to kill Shakuni. Bad omens arose, and, upon hearing them, Gandhari came to the court and persuaded the king to set the Pandavas free. Yudhishthir once again played the game and lost. According to the conditions of the game, they were to spend twelve years in the forest and one year in hiding. After thirteen years had elapsed, Pandavas having foiled all strategems applied by Duryodhana, asked for their kingdom, Duryodhana refused, and that had led to the War.

Part 4: The Eclipse

The sun had reached its peak. Like the morning cold, the temperature was unpleasant. It was a wonder how two extremes could cause the same effect. Vikarna could smell death. The stench was bearable at dawn, but now the assault on the nose was too much. He fought the urge to puke. He desperately wanted to tie a cloth around his nose but thought better of it. He knew how the war was unfolding from scouts. He knew Arjun had pierced their formation, and even Bhim and Satyaki had broken through.

'One more day of loss. When will my brother learn it is futile to fight this war?' Vikarna wondered.

'O brother! You are again thinking too much,' Dushasana spoke.

'What's there to think? We are losing once again. We can't let Arjun kill our brother-in-law, but I am in serious mind to cut our losses.'

'What do you mean?' Dushasana asked.

'We kept an army between him and Jayadrath, but by the end of today, I think we will lose both the army and our brother-in-law.'

'Don't be a cynic, Vikarna. What can Arjun do all alone? If push comes to shove, our Karna will stop Arjun in his tracks.'

Vikarna broke into a dry smile. 'Do you trust him that much?'

'Yes, I trust him with my life,' Dushasana replied.

'There is no arguing with you,' Vikarna said. 'But Arjun is not alone. Bhim and Satyaki also broke into our formation and are trying to catch up with him.'

'Yes, Bhim will be a problem. Out of all the Pandavas, he is the one I fear.'

'You and me both, brother,' Vikarna said with a smile.

'Then why did you help him? Why? I was trying to humiliate him by humiliating his wife, but you spoke for her.'

'I didn't do it for them. I did it for us. It's against dharma. Don't you think it would have been better if we gave the Pandavas their own kingdom? We could have easily coexisted, and together we would have been unstoppable.'

Dushasana was about to say something

'I know what you are going to say, brother. I know you hate them, but why must we hate them? What have they done to us? Instead, they helped us in our time of need. Anyway, there is no use in debating the what ifs.'

An uncomfortable silence settled between them.

Then Vikarna received orders to protect Karna from Bhim, so he instructed his charioteer, Agnidhra, to take his chariot towards Karna. Some of Vikarna's brothers also joined him on the way.

All seven of them turned their chariots towards Bhim and reached him with the speed of wind. Then Vikarna saw how Karna was paralyzed with fear. Petrified, Karna was unable to even knock an arrow on to his bow and was chased by

Bhima on his chariot. Bhim was wrath personified. He killed anyone who dared come between him and his prey. He was firing arrows at Karna. Karna's flag was cut off, his armour was broken, and the chariot was barely holding together. Karna's charioteer drove the car towards Vikarna and his brothers. Agnidhra, Vikarna's charioteer, without requiring instructions, inserted the chariot between Bhim and Karna.

'Move away!' Bhim shouted, his eyes red with anger. A chill ran down Vikarna's spine.

'I can't,' Vikarna shouted back.

Vikarna's brothers, meanwhile, surrounded Bhim from all directions. They formed a circle around him. The burly second Pandava tried to break free, but they moved with him to make sure that their target remained at the centre. They also moved along the circumference.

'Don't give him a chance to attack. Fire at him at once,' Vikarna shouted to his brothers. He drew a large bow, yoked an arrow to it, pulled the string back to his ear, and released it, not taking the time to aim. Vikarna's brothers followed his lead. Aim didn't matter now, not with Bhim surrounded.

Bhim tossed away his bow and picked up a couple of blunt swords with both of his hands. He bent over with his giant body and started cutting off the arrows coming towards his charioteer, Vishoka. Vishoka focused his efforts on steering the horses away from danger. He was calm and showed exceptional ability. He changed directions and tried to close the distance, but arrows from the Kaurava brothers blocked the way. Then he turned the chariot in circles to make it difficult for the Kauravas to aim. The white horses, clad in light golden armour, instinctively dodged the arrows. The horses neighed and pranced. They kicked any of the soldiers who were stupid enough to come towards them, and Bhim finished them off.

Vikarna continued firing the arrows at the horses, at Vishoka, and at Bhim, not giving them any chance to recover.

A few of Vikarna's brothers grew tired. They began targeting only Bhim.

'Aim for all,' Vikarna shouted, but his brothers ignored him.

Vishoka closed the distance to the nearest Kaurava when the horses were out of danger. Bhim seized the opportunity. He tossed away the blunt sword, picked up a sharp one, and slashed at Vikarna's brother, breaking his bow in two. Before Vikarna could react, Bhim beheaded the Kaurava. His blood splashed on Bhim's face.

Vikarna's heart skipped a beat. Before he could absorb what had happened, Vishoka moved the chariot towards another of Vikarna's brothers. The chariot's left side was now facing Vikarna. Bhim raised his sword once again, and Vikarna's brother lifted his bow with both of his hands, covering his face and upper body.

Vikarna knew what Bhim's next two moves would be, and he instinctively picked up a javelin and hurled it towards Bhim. The second Pandava, with a speed that belied his size, leapt back into the chariot and away from Vikarna's brother. Vikarna picked up another javelin and threw it at Bhim's left chariot wheel. Vishoka hurtled the chariot forward, and the javelin barely missed the chariot's rear end.

Vikarna signalled his charioteer, Agnidhra, to follow Bhim. Vishoka kept the chariot moving towards the next brother in a linear path, and Bhim turned back on his chariot to face Vikarna. Vikarna picked up another javelin and hurled it at Bhim's chest. Bhim threw away his swords and picked up a mace with both his hands, turned a little to his right, and dodged the javelin's sharp end. Before the javelin could reach Vishoka, he flung it towards the ground. The spear clanged against the floor and flew away from the chariot as if it were made of cloth. Bhim tossed away his mace and picked up a lasso, and Vikarna simultaneously bent down to pick up another javelin and hurled it.

Bhim guided the lasso to catch the javelin in mid-air and form a knot around it. He then jumped from the rear end of his chariot, and Vishoka moved away just as Bhim turned the javelin in a full circle and hurtled it back towards Vikarna. Then he ran towards Vikarna, ready to tie him up with the lasso.

The javelin pierced Agnidhra's heart, and blood sprayed on Vikarna's face. With his right hand, Vikarna wiped it off. Agnidhra coughed up more blood and fell on the horses. That threw them off the rhythm. They neighed and tried to run in opposite directions, causing the car to halt suddenly. This threw Vikarna off his balance, and he fell face-first on the chariot. Vikarna could feel his own warm breath on his face. He tried to move his hands, but they were tied to his body with the noose. Vikarna did not see when Bhim did that. Normally, he would have been able to stand up without the help of his hands but was unable to do so now because of the weight of the armour. Vikarna could see nothing. But he could hear the panicked cries of his brothers.

'Don't touch my brothers,' Vikarna shouted. 'Don't you dare! You couldn't even help your wife back then, and now you are ready to kill my brothers to prove your worth. Come back to me, you coward, come back to me.'

He could hear Bhim's violent roar that sounded like a boar, the Varaha.

Sweat trickled down Vikarna's forehead. His mouth felt dry. He struggled to get back on his feet and break free of his bond. Vikarna was making progress, but not at the pace he was hoping for. He continued shouting insults at his cousin, but the panicked cries of his brothers were reduced to nothing. By the time he broke free, none of the brothers who were accompanying him were alive.

Bhim stood on the ground, bathed in the blood of his brothers. Vikarna could see blood dripping from Bhim's chin.

Bhim held the large mace in his hands. Vishoka and chariot were at a distance from Bhim's fatal slashings as if Bhim didn't want his chariot stained accidentally by Kaurava blood.

Vikarna's body felt numb. His charioteer was dead, his horses unresponsive. He picked up his bow mechanically. 'You know, I am hiding behind dharma just like you did,' he muttered, as he fired an arrow aimlessly. It didn't hit Bhim. 'I didn't want to fight my brothers by joining you, and now you killed most of them.'

Vikarna then ran towards Bhim, firing arrows rapidly. Bhim dodged them and hit Vikarna with his mace. Vikarna's armour shattered. The second Pandava then picked up an arrow from the ground and, with his left hand, stabbed Vikarna just above the ankle. Vikarna didn't feel the pain. He hit Bhim with his bow, stepped back, and released an arrow. It dug into Bhim's right shoulder. Vikarna then collapsed on his right foot. He cursed Bhim and pulled the arrow out. The burly second Pandava also removed the arrow with his right hand.

'Don't,' Bhim begged, 'please don't. I don't want to kill you.'

Vikarna ignored him. He could feel the tears on his cheeks as he released another arrow. Bhim dodged it. In the next moment, he hit Vikarna on his right shoulder with the mace, shattering the bone. Vikarna lost his grip on the bow, and it fell from his hands. Vikarna then picked up a sword from the scabbard tied around his waist. Bhim did not waste another second. The second Pandava pulled out his own sword and stabbed Vikarna in the chest. Vikarna coughed up some blood onto Bhim's chest and collapsed on the ground.

'Why was it like this?' Vikarna's heart screamed. He could see his mother and remembered her words.

'What happened? How did you get these wounds?' Gandhari asked Vikarna, feeling his wounds with her hands.

'From that Bhim,' Vikarna replied, his eyes filled with helpless anger.

'What did you do?' Gandhari smiled.

'I did nothing,' Vikarna replied instinctively.

Vikarna felt her gaze despite her blindfold.

Then he mumbled, 'I said, "You are not worthy to stay in this palace. Go to the jungle and stay there. Maybe my brother will let you live." Bhim beat me up for that.'

'Don't you think you are in the wrong?' Gandhari smiled.

'How am I wrong? They came out of nowhere, and suddenly they want the throne that is our brother's.'

'They are not strangers. They are your cousins. One day, you might need to choose sides. But until then, don't treat them any different from your own brothers.'

The ten-year-old Vikarna didn't understand what his mother had said then, but he followed her words anyway.

He looked at Bhim. His face was covered in blood. The blood of Vikarna's brothers. But, behind that, he saw the face of the cousin he once loved ... still loved.

'I am sorry,' Vikarna tried to say, but nothing came out.

Vikarna saw Bhim rush to his side. Vikarna could feel the warm tears falling on his cheeks. He could hear Bhim say something but couldn't understand what it was. It didn't matter now. His heart was filled with warmth before turning eternally cold.

7

Duhshala: Dead Man Walking

Ananya Ganesh

The sun was beating down on the camp at the fringe of the battlefield. Servants were weaving in and out of the areas between tents, occasionally ducking in, then leaving discreetly, a pile of clothes or dishes in hand.

Duhshala was resting inside her tent. A maid was moving a wide, bamboo fan at her side, pushing currents of air onto her face. The maid, meanwhile, was plastered with sweat.

Another maid entered through the half-open tent flap and bowed. She carried in her hand a tray of coconut sweets. Duhshala frowned. She didn't like coconut.

'Dushasana!' Duryodhana, her brother, shouted. 'Come on outside! We're going to play!'

'Can I come?' Duhshala wanted to ask. But the words didn't come. They remained lodged in her throat, creating a lump, an impassable barrier.

Duryodhana passed her on his way out, younger brother Dushasana in tow. Duryodhana saw her and flashed a tentative half-smile. Dushasana did not spare her even a glance.

Duhshala looked behind them and sighed. Her mother appeared from one of the multiple doorways.

'Duryodhana?'

'He just left. Should I call him back?' Duhshala replied.

'No, no need. I made some sweets for him.'

'Oh.'

'Do you want some?'

'Which ones?'

'Coconut. Come, they are in the antechamber.'

Duhshala didn't like coconut. She stood up anyway.

The servant was gone. Another had replaced the one standing by her side. Duhshala opened her eyes and stared at the small section of the common area she could see through the tent flap. She spied an ochre leaf, hanging from a tree. A short gust of wind blew, and the leaf gently fell to the ground. Duhshala felt a sudden urge to pick it up, to hang it back on the tree, as if by doing so she can stop the war, but she could not bring herself to get up or, indeed, to do anything.

A maidservant rushed into Duhshala's chamber. Her eyebrows were creased, and she looked horrified, as if she had seen something she could not forget. She bowed but immediately straightened and began talking hurriedly, the words tumbling out of her mouth.

'Draupadi … Dushasana … Yudhishthir gambled … taking her…'

Duhshala didn't catch everything, but she heard enough to get the main idea, and immediately a cold terror gripped her stomach. It felt like a cold abyss had opened inside her, and it drew everything down. She couldn't open her mouth to form the words as a wave of horror crashed over her.

She knew what she wanted to do. She wanted to get up, march to the court, and stand right in front of Yudhishthir. She wanted to scream at him—that a woman is not property, she is not yours to trade away. She knew that all the revered elders would not have said anything against the gamble or the stakes. Scorn rose within her.

More than anything, she wanted to stride up to Dushasana, grab him by the ear, and slap him for his blatant disrespect of Draupadi's dignity.

Just as fast as it rose within her, the anger subsided. She deflated visibly, like a balloon, and felt her shoulders droop. She thought about her scorn for the elders, who didn't say anything, and felt bitter self-loathing for staying silent.

She heard footsteps and looked up. Her mother stood in the doorway, the blindfold tied securely around her eyes as always. Duhshala didn't know how she could tell, but somehow she knew Gandhari had heard the news.

Gandhari made her way to the couch where Duhshala was sitting. She took a seat and leaned back, and Duhshala collapsed against her shoulder. Gandhari placed an arm around her.

Gandhari had never been particularly affectionate towards Duhshala. Their relationship had always been the bare minimum. When she was young, Duhshala loved hearing the story of her conception—how Gandhari had desperately wanted a daughter, and so Ved Vyas divided the lump into 101 pieces. Listening to the story gave Duhshala hope—that if she was the daughter Gandhari wanted so desperately, surely Gandhari would love her more. But it had never been so. Gandhari had always lavished her attention on Duryodhana and Dushasana. Duhshala and Yuyutsu had often been the black sheep, the odd ones out.

Gandhari pulled Duhshala closer. In that moment, Duhshala felt a rare moment of connection with her mother, possibly the first one ever. Gandhari, the woman who had eyes but could not see, and Duhshala who had a voice but could not speak.

'I know.'

Duhshala's mind shifted to Abhimanyu. She'd never met him. By the time he was born, the Kauravas and Pandavas were already feuding fiercely. But she'd heard the stories. They said he was like Arjun on the battlefield.

And she had also heard her brothers and husband talking. Plotting. About Abhimanyu. And how to take him down. She couldn't help but feel sorry for him. Such a young age, and not only was he participating in a war, but his blood uncles were scheming against him. Once more, she wanted to do something but couldn't. At this very moment, he must be out there, fighting for his life.

She thought of her son, Suratha, out on the battlefield, and sent out a quick prayer that he should remain safe. Just like she had done that morning.

It was evening now. The sun had set, and remnants of light still shone over the horizon, casting faint streaks of orange-purple clouds into the sky. But the warriors had all returned. In the other camp, Duhshala thought, it must be the same.

Her husband had returned too. He was removing his armour and bathing, but Duhshala knew that in the fifteen minutes between now and his entering the tent they shared, she was expected to have changed her clothes and be ready for him.

She got up and disappeared into a smaller tent on the side, where her ladies-in-waiting were ready for her. They had laid out a magenta and yellow sari for her. She wrinkled her nose and cast it aside in favour of a green and red one. They helped her drape it, and within ten minutes, Duhshala was in the main chamber again. Jayadrath entered, looking arrogant as always.

Ever since his humiliation in the forest at the hands of the Pandavas, he had spent his evenings plotting revenge. Today, it appeared he had finally got it because a gloating smirk covered his face. It was not a good look on him. He took a seat on the bench and beckoned for Duhshala to join him. She moved over, but at that moment, a still-armoured messenger entered the tent unbidden. He was flushed and panting but managed to call Jayadrath to the main tent before exiting.

'Stay here,' Jayadrath stated before striding out of the tent. Duhshala wanted to follow but was left in her seat by the same impulse that restricted her all those times before. This time, she made a conscious effort, got up, and walked behind her husband. One of her maids scurried behind her.

She reached the main tent in time to hear Duryodhana's last words.

'…Arjun's pledge.'

She entered and saw Jayadrath collapsed on the couch at the far end of the tent. He looked pale, the colour of flour, and Duhshala was immediately concerned.

'Pledged what?'

'Duhshala? Why are you here?' Duryodhana asked. Jayadrath looked as if he wanted to say something, but when he opened his mouth no words materialized.

'Pledged *what?*' she asked again, this time with more force. 'Tell me. I have the right to know. I've watched you fight this meaningless war for weeks and said nothing. I've watched you dismiss me for years and put up with it. I've watched you practically sell me off to the bidder who offers the best alliance for you, and even then, I said nothing. Tell me!'

Duryodhana was taken aback, but he didn't protest. Then he put his hand up to his forehead and sat down on a plush couch. At the back of her mind, Duhshala found herself wondering about the luxury of the couch, especially in the middle of a devastating war.

'Alright. I suppose you have to know, and it is probably better that you hear it from us first, lest anything…' —here he looked at Jayadrath out of the corner of his eye—'... untoward happens.'

'Abhimanyu died today. It wasn't a fair fight.'

Duhshala opened her mouth, ready to spill some more of the hot lava that has been slowly bubbling to a boil her whole life, but Duryodhana held up his hand.

'I know what you're going to say. It wasn't a fair fight. But, Duhshala, you have to understand that all's fair in love and war. Really, if you think about it, it's the Pandavas who are to blame for sending him in the first place. Once he was in the field...'

Duryodhana's eyes passed over Duhshala, as if he expected an outburst. He took a glass of water from the corner of the chamber, where a servant stood with a tray.

'All the same, I cannot believe what happened today. It will haunt me for the rest of my life and beyond, but it must be said that your husband displayed immense bravery in holding off the four Pandavas who made it to the Chakravyuh. We succeeded in diverting Arjun today. It's a sign, Duhshala. Don't you see? The battle is taking a turn, and it is in our favour. We can *do this*. Everything is on our side. And the sooner this is over, the sooner we can go home. The troops saw what happened today. They saw Jayadrath holding off the four Pandavas. They have hope again, Duhshala. And it's because of your husband. You should be proud today.'

Proud? Duhshala thought scornfully. Unlike everyone else here, she knew the less-than-noble origin of the boon that Shiv gave Jayadrath. A boon that was the direct result of Jayadrath's humiliation at the hands of the Pandavas after he kidnapped Draupadi. She imagined that if Duryodhana knew, he too would not hesitate in scorning Jayadrath. Say what you will about him, Duryodhana was, at the very least, a dharmic man. Then she remembered Draupadi being dragged out of the women's chambers by the hair and hesitated.

Why had Duryodhana not said anything then? That was not the brother she knew while growing up.

'But he found out, and our spy has just returned from the Pandava camp. He says, and I find it hard to disbelieve, that Arjun has vowed to … to *kill* Jayadrath before dusk tomorrow.'

Everything spun in Duhshala's head. Duryodhana kept talking, saying something about how they would do everything to keep Jayadrath safe, but it all sailed over her head. Because she knew, and she knew it as soon as she heard about Arjun's pledge. She knew it was over. Jayadrath was a dead man as soon as Arjun stepped onto the battlefield tomorrow.

And inside, Duhshala could not help but feel slightly relieved. She remembered all those years ago, in Dhritarahstra's court, at the game of dice, how she had wanted to say something as Dushasana dragged Draupadi out.

She remembered, more recently, the moment in the forest when, once again, Draupadi had been targeted, this time by Jayadrath. And how her cousins had caught him—of course, they would catch him—but let him go because of her and how she had begged. Not for her benefit, but so that their son would still have a father.

She remembered Draupadi's indignation when Bhim cut off Jayadrath's hair but let him go, and felt a surprisingly strong pang of sisterhood. In a way, Jayadrath got his just desserts.

She thought about waking up in two days, without Jayadrath around. Surprisingly, she felt relief. Throughout her life, she'd never really been able to come into her own. Partly because of her own tendency to be timid but also because of the others around her who outshone her. Jayadrath was the least deserving of them; just the accident of his birth in a powerful kingdom elevated him to their level. Maybe it was now time for Duhshala to come to the fore.

'Rest assured, we'll do our best to keep him safe.'

She blinked. She hadn't realized Duryodhana was still talking. Jayadrath had by now regained most of the colour on his face. If it were possible, he now looked almost as arrogant as before, although there was something in his eyes.

Fool, she wanted to sneer. *If Arjun has pledged it, you are a dead man walking.* She took a deep breath and looked Duryodhana in the eye. A cold smile appeared at the corner of her mouth.

'I'm sure you'll try.'

8

Pandu

Sumathi Sridhar

Kama: The Desire That Burns

Pandu impatiently pushed aside the thick forest bushes as he moved forward to gain a good view of his game. It was autumn. The leaves shed by the trees littered the forest floor. He trod carefully as he didn't want the dried foliage crackling loudly under his feet. His heart was beating wildly against his chest, partly from excitement and anticipation, and partly from the long and swift paces he had taken to reach the spot.

There was his kill!

Straight ahead, on the forest floor, lay a deer, in an ever-growing pool of blood, its body writhing in pain. Pandu observed that his arrows had torn through the deer's flesh, cutting into it deeply. That explained the copious blood.

For a moment, he felt a soaring sense of elation, the insane high that came with conquering, with killing.

And then, he saw the doe … and froze.

She stood beside the deer, staring at Pandu with her large, melancholic eyes. Her perked-up ears signalled her alertness, her keen assessment of the clear and present danger. Yet, she had not bolted on seeing him.

Frowning involuntarily, Pandu tried to recollect if he had noticed the doe when he had taken aim.

Or had he turned blind momentarily in his desperate desire for a hunt?

Trying to ignore a knot that was forming in his stomach, Pandu returned his attention to the dying deer. It had its eyes closed, and its breathing appeared to be slowing down. A sign of life in its final rhythm.

The doe had probably realized it too. She now crouched down and moved closer to her dying mate but kept her large, mournful eyes fixed on Pandu.

Was it the agony of unfulfilled love that he saw in her eyes? The ache from a glorious moment of union that was brutally cut short? Or was he imagining it? He couldn't tell.

The knot in his stomach had now spread to his chest and was making him breathless. He wanted to simply go! Leave the place! And, let the doe grieve in peace…

He turned on his heels and started to walk back swiftly, the harsh rays of the midday sun beating upon his back.

As he staggered back to his chariot, his mind pitilessly recalled the sacred code of the warriors. 'It is a sin to kill a being engaged in the act of love. For, love begets life!'

He, Pandu, of the great Bharata lineage, the illustrious Kuru clan that was known for unfailingly upholding dharma, had committed the sin. Of cruelly extinguishing the possibility of life!

Thanks to his excessive lust for hunting!

Dharma: The Right Thing to Do

Back in his forest camp, Pandu paced his chamber restlessly, as the day's events and its myriad implications played out in an unending loop inside his head.

Excessive lust for hunting? Indeed! Undue fondness for the game had always been his weakness. His close aides, who joined him frequently on his grand hunting expeditions, had always warned him about his overindulgence in the sport. He had always argued back. 'Hunting was an important pursuit for kings. That's how they honed their archery skills. Weren't the bow and arrow a warrior's best friends?' But what he never shared with them was the secret sense of triumph and power that a good hunt always gave him. In no other aspect of his life did he feel like a real man—not even when he sat on the Kuru throne as the undisputed sovereign of the great Hastinapur.

'Undisputed? Really! Whom am I deceiving?' he thought to himself, bitterly.

He knew that his subjects thought of him only as a proxy king. Proxy to his uncle Bhishma, who had abdicated in favour of his stepmother Satyavati's sons and grandsons before they were even conceived.

Bhishma had forsaken not just his crown but also his sex life and the opportunity of raising a family so that his stepbrothers' descendants could enjoy the sole, uncontested right to kingship. As Satyavati's grandson, Pandu's sovereignty had thus been built on his uncle's supreme sacrifice. What made Pandu's kingship more complicated was that he had bypassed not just Bhishma but also his own elder stepbrother, Dhritarashtra, whose visual impairment had disqualified his claim to the throne.

Pandu often felt fake, living off such borrowed kingship, when he was neither the eldest nor, in his own opinion, the ablest.

Hunting had been his only solace, a sport where, unlike in palace politics, he was his own master. A game that gave him enormous power over beings. Not borrowed, not bequeathed, but earned. With tools and skills.

That was why, when Bhishma and Satyavati had suggested to him the idea of a forest retreat, he had been thrilled.

Of course, the elders had had a different agenda. Well, he had had his.

Unfortunately, things had not panned out as he had expected. Not in the least. Worse, in an ironic turn of fate, he had ended up defeating the very purpose of his sojourn.

It had been his grandmother Satyavati's idea to give him a temporary break from his burdensome royal duties and send him to the forests where he could spend more time in the pleasurable company of his wives. Of course, Pandu knew there was nothing altruistic about Satyavati's idea. She was obviously anxious about the future of the Kuru line, given its troubled past.

His past.

Now, maybe, his future…

Pandu knew that, after the retreat, he would be expected to pay back and show results. With sons. Sons, who would continue the Kuru line after him.

'What a cruel joke! For all of Satyavati's efforts, I am probably going the same way as Bhishma. Kingdom, women, everything at hand, but nowhere to go!'

'Strange, how history repeats itself,' thought Pandu to himself and broke into a hollow laugh. His laughter was caught by the chamber walls that echoed loudly and snapped him out of his musings.

Thrown back into the real world, he was shocked to find the world outside had turned dark and cold. Chilly winds were blowing in from the north. The light in the sky was fading. The setting sun had tucked in its resplendent rays and retired early for the night, signalling the approaching winter.

With effort, Pandu withdrew his gaze back into his chamber and sighed. The surrounding darkness suffocated him.

Returning to his camp straight from the forest at noon, he had confined himself to his chamber, leaving explicit instructions not to be disturbed. He had no idea how long he had remained confined to his chamber or to his thoughts. As he had demanded complete privacy, no one had come to his chamber to light the oil lamps or kindle the fire in the hearth. 'Maybe,' he thought, 'it was time for some light and warmth.'

Squaring up his sagging shoulders, he called for his camp guards.

Within minutes, his chamber was transformed. Brightened by the glow of the scented oil lamps and warmed by the crackling fire in the hearth, Pandu's mood lifted, slightly.

Looking around, his eyes fell on a table. On it was a large silver plate, laden with once-fresh fruits and berries, a curd and barley preparation, and his favourite dish, roasted venison. A feast fit for a king. He remembered it being served hours back. He had not asked for it but knew who had sent it.

'It's time to meet my wives...' he told himself and sighed.

Pandu's chief queen Kunti walked into his chamber. Quite unlike her usual self, she appeared anxious and a bit flustered. Looking at her, Pandu felt a pang of guilt. He had always admired her regal bearing, her quiet poise. Now was clearly not the best of times in her life. And he was to blame for that.

Madri, his younger queen, followed Kunti, looking calm and gloriously desirable, as always. The light from the lamps in the room only served to heighten her flawless, wheatish-yellow complexion that glowed like the gold she wore.

He fought the urge to reach out and embrace them both. His mind and body ached for some comforting touch. But he restrained himself.

For, he had made up his mind.

Madri walked up to him and pointing to the untouched food on the silver plate, said, 'My Lord, I see you have not eaten at all.' She sounded worried.

Pandu rewarded her concern with a wry smile. 'Dearest Madri, I can hardly afford to dine like a king anymore.'

He saw Kunti and Madri exchange looks. Anxious looks.

Looking into their worried faces, Pandu started, 'My dear queens, I'm sorry I shut myself in, and you out, for so long. But I needed the time to sort things out for myself first before meeting you both.'

Madri opened her mouth to speak, but Pandu stopped her, signalling her to wait. 'Please allow me to finish,' he pleaded.

He then paused, took a deep breath, and trudged on. 'The Kuru elders sent us here so we may produce an heir for the Kuru throne. Unfortunately, what has happened today has changed everything.' He paused and cast a sideways glance at Kunti and Madri.

Their unsurprised faces surprised him a bit.

'Do they know, already?' he wondered. 'Maybe my charioteer has talked…'

Picking up his next words carefully, Pandu continued, 'As a king, my primary duty is to protect my subjects and ensure that life flourishes and prospers in my kingdom. Sadly, by a cruel twist of destiny, I've failed in that duty.'

He knew he sounded vain uttering these words. As if he were pronouncing a royal diktat, rather than having an intimate conversation with his wives. But he didn't know how else to deal the blow.

Before he could continue further, Madri interrupted him. 'My Lord, forgive me for speaking out of turn, but since when has hunting animals become adharma in the Kuru kingdom?' Her voice had taken on an edge.

'They do know!' he thought, his suspicions now confirmed.

Meeting Madri's eyes squarely, he answered, 'My dear queen, it is not about the killing, but about the timing. I've committed a heinous, inhuman act, by killing a deer when it was pleasuring its mate….' His voice trailed off as he remembered the look in the doe's eyes once again.

'I have behaved like an animal, without empathy, and I deserve to be punished. Worse, I have brought shame to my warrior clan by breaking our most sacred canon,' he added, sounding miserable.

He paused and stared out of the chamber window into the dark, chilly night for several seconds, before continuing. 'Through my unthinking act, I have lost the moral authority to lead our clan or … to fulfil my duties as a husband,' he finished, softly.

Gathering his courage, he now turned around to look at his wives, his eyes begging for support. He desperately hoped they understood what it all meant. Looking into the two pairs of eyes that stared back in shock, he knew! His words had hit home.

There was a brief silence, before Kunti reacted. 'My Lord, you disappoint me! In your present state of agitation, you are only thinking of yourself. Have you thought of what your decision means to others? What about our family? Our elders? Our ancestors? Don't you think you owe it to your ancestors to produce sons and identify a successor before giving up Hastinapur?'

Her voice was shrill and her tone sharp. Pandu looked up at her. He could see the leaping yellow flames from the hearth reflected in her dark, beautiful eyes. The fire in them seemed to sear his soul. With great effort, he looked away.

Kunti had always been his conscience-keeper. She asked the hardest questions.

Unfortunately, he had no answers for her. What had to happen had happened. Was there any point in fretting over it now?

But Kunti was relentless. She responded to his silence with more questions. 'Forget our ancestors. Tell me, O king, isn't it great adharma to forsake your own kin, your wives, who are dependent on you?' she asked pointedly.

Pandu could sense the bitterness in her voice. Kunti had dreamed of having many sons, and the first among them succeeding Pandu. He had let her down too. Again, there was very little he could do about it now.

Unable to meet Kunti's accusing eyes, he turned to Madri for support. 'My dear queen, don't you understand? How can I, a descendant of the great Kurus, who hold equity and justice above everything, continue to indulge in carnal pleasures and dream of progeny, when I have brutally stopped another creature from doing so?' he wailed. 'To me, that would be adharma. My elder brother Dhritarashtra was not allowed to be the monarch because he can't see. I will prove myself to be no better when I, blessed with the gift of vision, refuse to see and acknowledge my own acts of adharma. I can never forgive myself nor will my forefathers,' he added emphatically. There was a certain finality to his tone now.

'Being the king of the Kurus, there is no one who wields the authority to punish me. So, it's only fair I award punishment to myself, appropriate to the horrendous deed I've committed.'

He paused before continuing, 'As an act of atonement, I vow to give up the Kuru throne in favour of my brother, Dhritarashtra. I also vow to renounce the pleasures of the flesh forever. Henceforth, I shall not touch a woman with desire in my heart. I shall give up Hastinapur, retire to the forests permanently, and live the life of a recluse. That, I think, would be dharma, the right thing to do. If by chance or by choice, I ever fail to keep my vows or violate them in any manner to fulfill my lust, may my body perish that very instant!' He finished, almost choking on his last words.

There was stunned silence in the room for several minutes. Somewhere, far away in the forest, Pandu heard a bird cooing, calling out to its mate. It seemed to be in great pain.

Artha: Wealth to Be Earned

Along with the first flush of snow came the news. Dhritarashtra's wife, Gandhari, was pregnant. The royal messenger was also pleased to inform them that Sage Krishna Dwaipayan had blessed Gandhari with a hundred sons.

Pandu received the news with mixed feelings. He was happy for his brother, of course. But not wholeheartedly. A part of him felt a mixture of emotions ranging from depression to jealousy, which was only natural in his case, as he reasoned to himself.

Pandu had always had a soft spot for his stepbrother, who had been born blind. Too much had been taken away from him unjustly. It was cruel how people like Dhritarashtra were punished twice—once by God and once again by man.

But now the tide seemed to be turning in his brother's favour. Not only had he got the reins of Hastinapur back from Pandu, but he was going to become a father too, which he, Pandu, could never be. And it broke his heart to think that.

As king of the Kurus, he often consoled himself saying that he had done the right thing by opting for the life of a recluse. But, as man and husband, the choices he had made had not been easy on him or his wives. Often, he lamented to himself wondering why he had been singled out for such ill-fate. Why did he have to bear the wrath of his ancestors? Why did he have to suffer the spartan life of a recluse in this harsh terrain? These questions continued to haunt Pandu even as he tried to settle into his new life in the deep forests, far away from Hastinapur.

'Well, at least, I am not alone,' Pandu consoled himself. His wonderful wives were by his side, and he was grateful for that. They made his life tolerable. He shuddered as he remembered how close he had come to losing them.

When he had announced his decision to give up his kingdom and his family and embrace a solitary life in the forests, Kunti had put her foot down. 'My Lord, you are not going alone. We are also going with you. Haven't you always said, how a man's wives are his best friends? My lord, I assure you, we will not come in the way of your vows. In fact, both Madri and I can help you with your expiatory rituals.' Kunti had been persuasive. And he had buckled. Today, he was happy he had bowed to his wife's greater wisdom.

'In any case, without you, Hastinapur has no use for us,' she had added, wistfully, in her final winning argument. Sadly, Kunti had been right. With Pandu alive and as a recluse, the palace had no place for his queens. Not until they had children. More specifically, sons.

Well, he wanted them too. Now more so, after hearing about Dhritarashtra, Gandhari, and their prophesied hundred sons. Sons, who would ensure that the gates of the heavens opened up for him after his death. Sons who would enable his own ancestors to come back to earth, taking on new lives. He would have children who would guarantee his immortality, as he would continue to exist through them, their offspring, and so on, indefinitely.

He had talked to many sages, many wise men who lived in the forests, about his situation. They had heard him out patiently and were unanimous in their message for him. He was destined to have sons of his own—wise, powerful sons, gifts from the gods themselves. That day was not far away.

Although their words did soothe his troubled mind temporarily, his worries came flooding back till he was left with no choice but to accept the only way out. Not an easy way, but a time-tested way. The way he had been conceived.

Niyoga!

He had been mulling over the idea for a while. After much deliberation, one day, he gently proposed it to Kunti. He had not expected to push his idea through without a skirmish, but he had certainly not expected a full-blown battle.

Kunti was shocked and disgusted.

'My Lord, how can you even come up with this suggestion? How can I offer myself to a complete stranger, an ordinary man, when I have accepted you, the king of the Kurus, as my soulmate? I find the idea foul and insensitive,' she shot back with fury.

Unmoved, Pandu persisted. 'But the men I have in mind are not ordinary people. They are virtuous Brahmins, who have gained superiority over their minds through severe austerities. Their seed is potent and can bear us really powerful progeny. Don't forget, Dhritarashtra and I were conceived this way.'

He hoped that would clinch his argument. But Kunti was a tough opponent. She fought back, tooth and nail.

'My Lord, in your overwhelming desire to have children, you are not thinking through all the implications. Don't you know what your own mother and aunt went through? How can you, of all people, forget how your mother's experience has affected you? How can you forget your elder brother, who continues to suffer as a victim of this barbaric arrangement? The haste shown by Queen Mother Satyavati in this regard has proven to be a curse for the family. Surely, you realize that?' finished Kunti, ending her bitter tirade.

Pandu was totally taken aback by Kunti's rancour. But, to his annoyance, he realized that she was right. Once again.

Niyoga had not been easy on his mother and aunt. Satyavati had given them no choice. They had been forced to bear children for the family through her son, Sage Dwaipayan, who had approached them in his most uncouth, undesirable self. No woman could have willingly received the sage in the form he was then.

And it was true that the healthiest children were conceived only when the union was a happy one. 'My mother's experience was definitely not a happy one,' thought Pandu, as he recollected his own unhappy childhood spent struggling with a jaundiced liver, a condition that had given his skin a yellow tone and his name that meant 'pale'.

Kunti's logic was unbeatable. Unarguable. He had now reached a dead end in his quest.

'I'm certainly destined for the sonless hell,' he thought, dejectedly. 'When my body perishes, so will my ancestors…'

These reflections kept him awake through the night, till eventually, the night goddess Ratri made her unwilling way to Ushas, the damsel of dawn.

With dawn, came hope.

Kunti appeared to have calmed down after her heated outburst of the previous night.

At the first opportunity of finding themselves alone, she resumed the conversation. 'My Lord, your worry is not yours alone. It is mine too. I gave it a lot of thought last night. We'll find another way out of our problem.'

Pandu listened to Kunti with disinterest. He was not sure what 'other way' they could possibly find. To him, the situation looked hopeless.

Undeterred by his indifference, she continued, 'I have a plan, a means through which we can have children. Your children, my children, our children,' sounding excited.

Although he was still sceptical, her enthusiasm was infectious. He decided to hear her out.

Kunti then told him about a boon that the great Sage Durvasa had given her long ago. A sacred mantra that she could use to summon a devata of her choice to impregnate her.

Pandu couldn't believe his ears. 'Is this even possible?' he wondered. With mounting excitement, he begged her to continue.

Encouraged by his response, Kunti proceeded, 'My Lord, listen to me carefully! When I'm in season, I will chant the mantra and invoke the chosen devata. The summoned devata will descend from the heavens and possess you. You will then come to me. We will unite to produce progeny for the Kuru clan.'

Hearing this, Pandu's excitement died, instantly. 'Really? Your plan involves me? You very well know my vows. How can I…' He fell silent mid-sentence, dejected and ashamed.

Kunti reached out to him, and lifting his chin, said endearingly, 'My Lord, you have taken an oath not to touch a woman out of desire. For the sake of pleasure. But this will not be an act of pleasure. And you will not be Pandu.'

Pandu looked up at her with renewed interest. He wondered where she was going with this.

'When I chant the mantra with devotion, the summoned devata will arrive and take over your form. You will perform the maithuna as the devata himself. Throughout our act of union, it will be the devata with me, and not you.'

'This will not be an act of love or carnal pleasure-seeking. Neither of us will give in to the enjoyment. It will be a calibrated act of procreation, the sole purpose being to create progeny,' she finished, and looked up to him eagerly for his approval.

Pandu turned over the pros and cons of the idea in his head for a long time. He then looked up and smiled at Kunti. 'My dear wife,' he said, 'you've convinced me. I realize that I'll only be a tool in the process of creating a child, nothing more. And if this is how Hastinapur is destined to have an heir to its throne, then so be it!'

'Now tell me how we proceed with our plan.'

Thrilled with his approval, Kunti continued in a more confident tone. 'My Lord, what we have set out for ourselves is a solemn act seeking not just progeny for ourselves but descendants for the Kuru lineage too. It's like the sacrifice of the Brahmins, seeking the goodwill of the gods in the heavens. It has to be executed flawlessly to have the desired effects. We will need to condition our mind appropriately so that neither of us gets excited and let ourselves be carried away during the act.' On a more pleasant note, she added, 'Don't worry, my Lord! By our own efforts, the grace of our ancestors, and our gods in the heavens, everything will turn out fine.'

Indeed! Everything did turn out fine.

Soon enough, with the grace of Dharmaraj—the order keeper of the world—a son was born to Kunti. Pandu was thrilled. The wise old men of the forest had been right in their predictions. He had become a father! He had not belied the expectations of his ancestors or the people of Hastinapur.

He named his son Yudhishthir. What made his son's arrival on earth sweeter was the fact that Yudhishthir was the eldest born of the Kuru princes. Even though Dhritarashtra's wife had conceived much before Kunti, her pregnancy had been stretched and delivery delayed. So, Yudhishthir came into the world first. This meant that as the eldest of the princes, he could make a genuine claim to the Hastinapur throne.

For Pandu, this was a big consolation for his own aborted sovereignty. After all, wasn't an heir to his throne the greatest wealth for a king?

Moksha: At the Elusive End of Desire

Pandu woke up with a pleasant feeling. He looked out through the adjoining window to find the early stirrings of dawn. Far away, he could see the golden glint of the sun's golden rays teasing the snowy peaks of the Himalayas. The effect was dazzling.

As if a treat for the eyes were not enough, the smell of the fresh bloom from the flowering plants that surrounded his little dwelling gently wafted up to him and caressed his olfactory senses. Spring was at her blooming best! The whole forest would come alive now. A million meandering streams would erupt on the mountain sides as the hard snow melted under the passionate clutch of the sun's warm rays, like a lady who succumbed to her lover's firm, amorous embrace.

Pandu's spirits soared. Today, his worries, too, strangely seemed to melt away like the snow. He realized he had not felt so good in a long time and wondered why.

He looked around. The cottage was empty. Everyone seemed to have started their day already. Though he could see no one, he could hear the distant voices of Kunti and his children.

After Yudhishthir, Kunti had borne him two more sons, Bhim and Arjun. She had also helped Madri invoke the twin gods, the Ashwini Kumars, to bear him two more sons, Nakul and Sahadev. In all, he had five sons, as gifts from the gods.

Several years had passed since then. The infants were now a bunch of boisterous boys brimming with energy. They exhibited all the auspicious signs of royalty. Even as young lads, the princes showed extraordinary strength, courage, skill, and wisdom. Pandu was extremely proud of them all.

What more could a man ask for? He had got more than he had ever imagined. His sons were the greatest wealth he would ever have.

Abruptly, the shrill voice of Kunti brought him out of his happy reverie to the present. Pandu realized she was extremely agitated over something. He could sense anger in her voice. It must be Bhim up to some mischief again, he thought.

This was turning out to be an everyday issue. Bhim would eat up most of the available food, leaving mere morsels for his brothers. After all, he was Vrikodar, the boy with a wolf's appetite.

Visualizing the scene brought a smile to Pandu's face. The face of a delighted father. He also realized that his boys were growing up fast and needed both good nutrition and better training that befitted Kshatriyas.

The sound of Kunti entering the cottage broke Pandu's train of thought. On seeing him up and about, she greeted him cheerfully. Her smile told Pandu that Bhim's shenanigans were already forgotten. Anticipating Pandu's question, she said, 'Madri has gone to fetch water for your ablutions. She should be back soon.'

Ever since moving to the forest permanently, Pandu had adopted a routine life of austerities. Although his wives and children were with him, he tried to spend most of the time in the company of the wise men who roamed the forest. He would spend hours listening to their discourses and followed several ascetic practices prescribed by them.

He tried his best to exercise control over his mind and body and remain focused on the pursuit of moksha—that state that would liberate him from the desires of the flesh and the mind and break the circular trap of karma. 'Every action has a reaction, oh King! No mortal can get away from that,' the ascetics had repeatedly told him. 'As long as there is karma, there is no escape from samsara.'

Bringing one's senses and emotions under control was the first step towards breaking the karmic chain, the wise men had told him. Of course, it was easier said than done. His mind was still not his slave. On the contrary, he was its. He was still a creature of impulse, a victim of emotions, as he had always been.

Even as bitter thoughts from his past threatened to envelop his mind and tip it into a cesspool of remorse, he resolutely pushed the negative thoughts aside. He reminded himself once again to be grateful for all that he had.

He then decided to find Madri and help her with the water pots. Taking his bow and arrow, he set out on the path that would take him to the waterfall.

On the way, he saw his sons. They were playing a game. How handsome they looked, he thought, his eyes washing over them with fatherly affection. He felt lucky to have such fine children.

His mood lifted once again, and he proceeded on his path to the waterfall.

The path to the waterfall was strewn with flowers from the trees above, as if they had paved a path to welcome him, knowing that he would tread that way. Pandu could hear the chirping of the birds, and they seemed to be exchanging words of love.

Indeed, the entire forest appeared to be putting together a symphony of love for him.

Pandu suddenly felt the stirrings of a strange feeling bubble up inside him, a sensation that he had not allowed himself to feel, an emotion he had suppressed for too long…

Desire!

Desire was everywhere. All around him. In the blooming flowers beckoning the bees, the mating call of the birds, in the cool breeze that touched and teased his body, and in the sun's rays streaming through the branches of the forest trees and lighting up the world around him…

Nature was playing the role of a wicked seductress to the hilt.

He was smitten! His spirits soared. His heart beat faster. His face broke into an involuntary smile. Joy overflowed within him.

That was when he spotted Madri, his favourite wife, walking towards him after her bath, carrying a huge pot of water on her waist. She was wet from top to bottom, and he could see her damp cloth cling to her body which, he remembered, had once offered him untold pleasures.

Almost at once, the thick, heavy chains of self-control that had kept his emotions shackled for so long gave away. The dam of desire broke, and the waters of lust gushed out…

Madri was, by now, only an arm's distance away from him. In a second, he dropped his bow and arrow, and with a swift gesture, seized the dumbstruck Madri by her arm and locked her in a tight embrace. The pot of water she was carrying slipped from her grasp and broke, the water drenching both of them.

As Madri realized what was happening, she made a furious attempt to resist him. But he wouldn't let her speak, as he pressed his hot, hungry lips on hers, snuffing out all her cries. He pinned her down on the bare earth and forced himself upon her, when suddenly something snapped inside him.

The melancholic images of a dying deer and doe flashed before his eyes. Realization struck as Pandu remembered a sage saying, 'And the hunter becomes the hunted. That's the cycle of life, O Rajan! To break the cycle, you have to conquer your emotions, your desire, your actions.'

He had tried. Tried hard, but…

Pandu fell off Madri, a look of unhappy comprehension in his eyes.

Far away, Kunti could hear Madri's screams rent the heavens…

9

Shalya

Battu Sri Charan

The city of Sakala looked as strong as ever, with a large chain of mountains for walls and free-flowing rivers for moats. This seemed like an ideal city—a fortress buried within natural and man-made defences, brimming with wealth gathered from the deep mines of the lapis lazuli. But everything must have a taint, and so did this fortress.

The strong mountainous walls that protected the city also threw strong winter winds and breezes cold enough to freeze the rivers from surface to bed. No one dared to walk in the streets before the sun patrolled the sky. Yet, a man walked alone along the rajaveethi, almost naked save for some loose cotton trousers, towards river Iravati for his morning bath. He looked strong and sturdy, like a bull. One might confuse him for a middle-aged wrestler, but a close examination of his bald head and the white hairs coming from his ears showed that he was almost one hundred years old. He was the king of Madra and Lord of Sakala. Close associates would call him Narasoma, but he was best known as Shalya, the spear.

The cold breeze bit Shalya on his cheeks and chest like a mad dog. He let it dig its teeth deep into his skin. The breath of Mother Madra would only make him stronger.

The rajaveethi started from the palace of Sakala, ended at the river Iravati, and extended as a stone bridge to the other side. Shalya freed himself of his cotton trousers and uttariya. Only a loincloth clung to him as he walked into the thick mud and cold water. It was as if he were going into the mouth of a crocodile, with its jaws catching hold of his feet first and then his thighs, trunk, and head. The cold pain would cleanse him of the pride, greed, and gluttony that came with royal affairs every day.

The sky turned pink as the first rays of the sun bounced off the icy but liquid surface of Iravati. Shalya took three dips and offered his salutations to Surya. He would usually swim for a mile towards the south and back after his bath every day. Today, he longed only for the calmness of the river.

'What should I do, Mother Iravati?' Shalya whispered to the water. 'A call to war came today from the Kauravas and Pandavas. Whom should I back?' The river remained calm. It answered with a gentle nudge of water towards him, but he could not understand its sweet, watery language. 'I have kin on both sides, so I answered with neutrality in the war. Why am I being punished to watch my friends and relatives kill each other, Mother?' A tear rolled down from each of his eyes and merged into the river. The king of Madra showed his weakness only to it. His blood mother was separated from him when he was adopted by his maternal uncle as heir, as the custom of Madra decreed that no biological sons of a king could succeed their father to the throne. River Iravati had filled that void for him.

The rising sun brought the noise of the waking city with him. A rooster from some corner of the city crowed, and a shepherd passed by alongside the riverbank. The shepherd seemed to have not recognized the king, or else he would have bowed. Soon, the river would be filled with naked men and women, and the calm river would assume the form of the goddess of love, bending their hearts to her will. This was all a sport for the mother river, and it would not look good if Shalya became trapped in her mischief. He left the river quickly and put on his trousers. He bowed to the river one last time and walked towards the palace on the other side of the road.

Two sleepy guardsmen were guarding the gateway to the palace this morning. Blue Madraka banners flapped from the poles on the outer wall all around the fort. Mother Madra stood in the form of the goddess of the harvest on the banner in her bright red shawl. Several gargoyles, in the form of deer heads, looked down from the battlements, as if judging the entrants as friends or foes.

The guardsmen recognized Shalya and opened the gates, bowing to the king several times. The outer bailey hosted sparring grounds for wrestling and sword fighting. There were not many soldiers practicing during this peak winter, but he could see his sons, Rukmaratha and Rukmangada, practising a duel with their swords. A young soldier struggled to balance the spear in his hands. He must be a recent recruit, for Shalya had his soldiers excel in spear craft before they moved to take on a particular weapon of their choice.

'Keep your right hand in the rear, and hold it firm.' Shalya moved towards the young soldier to adjust his position. 'And move your right leg a little on the rear side.'

The boy understood and exchanged the positions of his arms on the shaft. 'Yes, sir. Feels right. Thank you, sir,' he said.

'You may as well address him as Maharaj, soldier. He is the best spearman in the entire Bharatavarsha.' Rukmaratha seemed to have been watching the interaction. He bowed to Shalya before the soldier could comprehend what his words meant.

'I am sorry, sir … Maharaj.' The soldier was shaken.

Shalya nodded and continued on his path to his quarters. Well past the inner wall, he intercepted the morbid stenches of the butchery and the sweet scents of the winery, as he made his way up the central hill in the inner bailey.

The royal quarters consisted of a huge circular structure on the slope of the hill that surrounded the summit like the petals of a lotus. The summit of the hill was crowned with the marble dome of the royal court. The quarters hosted individual apartments for each member of the royal family and were connected by a single corridor running through the centre.

To make his way to the quarters, Shalya had to climb the hill through the carved steps on the slope. The hill tired him easily and reminded him of his age. 'It is the court that tires me,' he thought, looking at the dome on the hill crest. 'I must crown my nephew Nakul after the Pandavas win this war. I can retire to spend the rest of my days on the riverside.' He pulled himself onto the steps. He might be old, but he was still stronger than most young men in the country. He hated to be carried in a palanquin like an old wretch.

By the time he reached the royal quarters, the sun was well above the eastern mountains, and the delicious aroma of the spices and food filled the entire royal household. A full-day feast was being arranged for the messengers from Aryavrata, who came with war invitations. The other three kings of Madra were invited as well.

Servants carrying large vessels walked frantically in the corridors from one kitchen to another. Shalya had to tread carefully in the corridors to avoid clashing with the busy servants.

His wife, Pujawati, a tall and slender woman, supervised the main kitchen, tasting the delicacies and instructing the chief cooks on what was lacking in the courses. As Shalya passed by the kitchen, Pujawati left her work and trailed after him.

'You are not dressed yet, Narasoma. The kings of the Madra and the messengers are already seated in the feast hall.'

'They did not leave yet?' Shalya feigned surprise. 'I thought they would leave once I made it clear that I did not intend to join their war.'

'They will not give up easily,' Pujawati said. 'An akshauhini is too valuable to be lost.'

The corridor twisted in different directions, and they followed the west side, where Shalya chose his bedchamber to enjoy the sunsets in the evening. They passed by the guest apartments and other residential apartments of his sons and grandsons.

'They have half of an akshauhini from the other kings. That should be enough,' Shalya said, once they reached his bedchamber. He looked Pujawati in the eye and asked, 'Tell me the truth, Puji. Am I doing the right thing? Should I have taken a side in this war?'

'Why do you ask this, Maharaj?' Pujawati said. 'You have decided to not take part in the war.'

'My sister, do you remember her?' Shalya asked. Pujawati nodded. 'When Madri died, I took a mental vow of protect her sons. Am I not abandoning them now? What did I do for them when they were driven into the forests by their wretched cousins? I should have slayed the Kauravas with my spear then. But I stayed quiet. And I stay quiet now.'

'For our daughters, Shalya. Would you have made our daughters, who married the Kauravas, widows?'

Pujawati took Shalya's hands into hers. 'You are in agony, Maharaj. Be calm, and let the storm in your heart retreat.'

Shalya took a deep breath. He stayed quiet for a moment. 'The love of a father binds my feet from moving towards dharma. I am being torn asunder by the duty of a king towards dharma on one side and love towards my daughters on the other. I confess before you, Pujawati. I have mocked others throughout my life for being cowards. How will they all mock me now for running away from my duty?'

The bedchamber went quiet. The curtains of the bed stopped moving for a while, as if they had run out of words to comfort their king. The crossed swords and spears on the wall had not moved before, but even they seemed to have gone into a forced silence. The portraits of the Madraka cast piercing looks at Shalya as if to judge his merit as a king. Only a cold wind brushed Shalya's hair as it glided through the window into his room.

'What is done is done,' he said firmly. 'I'd rather regret the consequences of my decision than torment myself with indecisiveness. Neutrality in war preserves my people and my soldiers. Let the world laugh.'

Pujawati kissed the king on the cheek. 'It is for the best, Maharaj. Perhaps you want to get dressed and attend the grand feast you threw for your guests?'

Wine flowed in the dining hall that day. The servants of the palace sat in neat rows on the hard rock floor, chatting with Shalya's sons, brothers, and their sons. The raised dais was for the host and his guests—the messengers and the kings.

Dancers clad in colourful garments of the western Madraka style occupied the back of the stage, facing the raised dais. Shalya's daughters-in-law led the catering party on the floor, serving food, while the queen's maids rushed from one corner to the other with pots of the boiling liquor called Gauda, as its malty fumes filled the hall.

'The soma of the mountain kingdoms,' Shalya's now-departed father used to call it. 'Cheaper, but quicker to dim your wits. Drink it only when you want to look like a fool.' Shalya avoided it and took madhu, the sweet wine. The other kings of Madra had no qualms about emptying the pots of Gauda, one after the other.

The messengers dug into the soma like flies. They looked with squinting eyes and hidden grimaces when the kings chewed the succulent lamb. Shalya passed lamb loins to the messenger from the Kauravas. He saw the messenger lick his lips, but he politely refused. Shalya knew that the culinary culture of Madra and Aryavrata did not agree with each other. The Aryavrata tradition specifically prohibited messengers from eating wine, sheep, and a few other animals. 'Odd rules and ridiculous customs. A man has the right to take pleasure in food,' Shalya thought. He pitied them that they would never feel the crunch of the roasted beef and garlic or the tenderness of a youthful lamb. They did have the peacock joints, though that could have been because of a lack of other options for them.

The feast was the best Shalya had had in years—since Madri's wedding, in fact. The messengers brought spices and cooks adept at working with them, and the kings brought their own cooks as well. Too many cooks enrich the broth. Sometimes.

'I am impressed with your excellence,' Shalya applauded from his seat. 'The cooks may ask anything they desire.'

A huge cheer from the floor followed, but he didn't miss the queen's disapproving looks. 'What if someone asked to become the king?' He knew she would ask this, as she had done a hundred times before. Shalya smiled sheepishly at her, not knowing what to do.

The cooks, all sweaty, lined up in front of the dais. Some asked for jewels, some asked for rich houses, some for land. None asked to become king, he noted.

A sharp and rough voice cut the hall as the Kaurava messenger stood up from his seat beside Shalya. 'I ask for a boon too, O King of Madra,' he said, putting his wine glass on the table.

It was clear that the messenger was drunk. The servants and the attendees of the feast donned a face of concern and began to whisper. The kings seemed amused by this and set aside their wine goblets to watch.

Shalya smiled at the messenger from his seat. 'Sit, my honourable guest,' he said calmly. 'It must be the king's word that initiates an offering. It must be I who should give away boons and gifts, not the other way around.'

The messenger did not hide his wounded pride. He picked up the wine glass on the table and flung it onto the floor where the royal members sat. 'Why do we need this tribal feast, O King, when you do not come from your safe haven like a coward?'

Whispers erupted into roaring voices. 'Arrest that man,' the minister at the end of the table commanded the soldiers near him. Rukmaratha got up from the floor, grabbed a sword from a soldier nearby, and pointed it at the Kaurava messenger.

'Enough!' Shalya's voice cut through the chaos of the hall like a spear. It echoed for a few moments until the noise faded into empty space. He waited till everyone sat in their allocated places. 'My guest shall not be harmed. My personal guard shall escort the honourable messenger to his bedchamber, while the feast continues as before.'

The messenger did not object. He followed Shalya's guard and exited from the hall. He must have realized that Rukmaratha would not hesitate to kill him if he stayed there any longer.

'The people from Aryavrata have always been like this,' King Dyutimat noted once the feast resumed. 'They see us as uncivilized brutes and thieves. Now, I must fight beside these people in that damned war.' The other kings nodded in agreement. Shalya could not disagree.

The Pandava messenger quickly fell on Dyutimat's feet. 'It is a great honour for the Pandavas to fight beside you, O King of Madra. It is never our intention to dishonour the great Madra. The Pandavas admire the rich Madraka culture, and the nephews of King Shalya often remember fondly the time they spent in their uncle's house.'

Dyutimat raised the messenger from his feet. 'This is the difference between the associates of the Kauravas and Pandavas. No need for apologies, O Messenger. I love my daughter and her husband, Sahadev. Consider this war won.' He turned to Shalya. 'Although, I would like my brother Shalya to join this war on our side.'

'You will not need an old man in this war, brother,' Shalya said. 'I just want to live the rest of my life in peace. I am tired,' he sighed.

Dyutimat nodded. 'I understand. I hope I will see you again with the pride of victory and one hell of a smile dancing on my face.'

It was almost midnight when the feast ended.

The attendees soon took leave for their chambers. Only Shalya and Pujawati stayed till the servants cleaned the hall.

The silver crescent of the moon was above the dome when they retired to their bedchamber, tired and drained. Pujawati freed herself from her jewellery and prayed to the gods as she did every night before she slept. Shalya envied her gods—Indra, above all. Indra's Airavata, the five-trunked elephant, fascinated him the most. 'A mendicant wants to be a king, and a king wants to be God,' he smiled at his petty fancies.

'Why do you smile, Narasoma?' Pujawati asked, her hands on her hips. She was one of the few who knew Shalya's true name. 'Do I look awful without my trinkets?' she asked.

'Those trinkets look dull before your radiance, Grey Hairs,' Shalya remarked. A faint smile played on her lips. *Damned smiles. She always got her way with those faint smiles. How many years had they been married? Eighty? Maybe more.*

'Sleep well,' Pujawati kissed his head and went to bed.

Shalya unwrapped the cannabis powder that the royal physician gave him for good sleep. He heated it near the torch at the door and absorbed the fumes as much as he could until his eyes burnt. Too much. He sneaked to the bed and pulled the woollen blanket over his head. Pujawati was already snoring lightly, so he did not disturb her.

Soon, he felt his eyes drop and his ears push away the cold air that slipped through the slits of the blanket. He floated in a deep, dark void, ecstatic and unwilling to move, as his skin lost touch with the world.

A sweet, rushing song trickled in his ears, mingling with the short melodies of parrots and cuckoos. The song was of Mother Earth, uninterrupted and uninhibited by the deficits of human abilities. The sweet scent of Sami and Pilu leaves tickled his nose. His eyes would not open easily, but when they finally did, he saw dirty yellow trees with grey trunks, blurred and blunt, with their canopies brushing each other. The singing river ahead of him appeared dark blue, oddly clear amidst the grey mountains behind it. He could see those mountains and the river as far as the horizon on either side without turning his head. Was it the cannabis causing illusions, or had he become colour blind?

He realized he had been chewing at a sharp bitterness all along. His throat burnt as the bitter stuff slipped inside. 'A dream,' he thought.

Shalya had to drag his legs when he tried to head for the river. He licked at the water absently till he saw deep into the blue depth.

A pair of hollow, dark slits stared into his eyes, mimicking the ripples of the still and shining water. He pulled himself back, surprised. *Am I a blackbuck?*

He tried to make sense of the ambience. There were indeed a few blackbucks, all female, nibbling at the leaves and crunching the thorns of the sami trees. He was a female too. A majestic male, stood far away, its curling black horns longer than any he had ever seen.

Plop.

What was that noise? Shalya's ears stood erect, as his eyes searched around. Too late. Jaws, like hot iron, crushed the bones under his throat as he growled in pain. He tried to pull back, but the jaws would not let go. They only dug deeper into muscle and bone, as he growled some more. *Pain.* He shook his head and tried to hold the ground as the vicious creature began to drag him into the depths of the waters. *Pain.* The deep blue of the river turned grey as his hind legs tried to cling to the last bit of land. The world blurred, and the yellow screen blackened. There was no longer any pain. Only a deep void coming closer. *Death.*

The pain returned. A loud roar emerged from the creature, as its jaws loosened on his throat. He ran clumsily from the waters, no longer blue, to the safety of the ground and fell on his knees. Blood dropped like wine, darkening his pale legs. He grunted in pain and lay still on the ground, panting and giving in to the burns under the muzzle.

'Fear not, child.' A voice whispered from the river. A soft touch brushed Shalya's throat, as the pain receded. He opened his eyes in gratitude as the world turned to yellowish hues again.

A woman, clad in water—yes, water—was sitting by his side with his head in her lap. She smiled kindly and kept brushing his muzzle. *A goddess.* The male buck stood beside her, its curling horns now dripping in blood.

'This one has blinded the crocodile,' the woman said. She had a strange accent that Shalya did not recognize. Almost like the rush of a river.

He looked with gratitude at the male buck, but it ignored him and hopped to its position away from the river where it had stood guarding its herd.

'You think you know the water, living with the rivers all your life,' the woman said. 'Such familiarity drives away the usual caution. You must not forget that vile creatures hide under the disguise of the water.'

Shalya nodded at the wisdom and stood up. 'Who are you, divine one?' he asked.

The woman smiled and rose. 'You don't remember me, child? You bear me on your banners. You pray for me every morning. I wash your crops like river Iravati. Do you recognize me now, Shalya, son of Tejowati?'

He bore the emblem of Dhanya Devata, a form of Madra Devata herself. He trembled in her presence. A deep sense of warmth and cold permeated his blood. He tried to fold his hands in salutation, as humans do, but he was in animal form. So, he bowed his head to touch her feet.

'You have graced this old man with your presence now, Mother?' Shalya asked. 'Order this child of yours. What am I to do?'

'He raises, child,' Mother Madra's voice turned into the heavy flow of the river. 'He attempts to lead the kings of Bharatavarsha and win the Great War.'

'Who, Mother?' Shalya asked, confused. 'What Great War?'

Mother Madra shook her head. 'The eternal enemy of Dharma. The Herald of Darkness, Decay and Disease. The incestuous child of Krodha and Himsa. The dweller of Dice. Heinous of all creatures. Kali.'

A cold twitch passed through his nerves at the trepidation in her voice. Kali Purusha was the evil incarnate, who was believed to be the ruler of the next age of the universe. Shalya had not believed those legends till now.

'The Great War that is to come, decides the fate of Madra, of earth, and of time itself. Its outcome will shake the pillars of the cosmos: dharma, artha, and kama. How humanity balances these three Purusharthas will change. Men will be the weapons in the hands of Dharma and Kali in this war. Be the spear of Dharma. He protects those who protect him. Protect that Divine dharma that has protected you now from him.'

Shalya looked at the male buck, standing tall despite its broken legs. 'That is Dharma?' he asked, surprised.

Mother Madra nodded. 'And the crocodile is Kali. It waits for Dharma to be its prey. Let that not happen, child. Protect Dharma. Aid his son in the war to come.'

Shalya knew what she meant. 'I will aid Yudhishthir in this battle, Mother. I will lead the armies of Madra to the battle and win whatever it takes to win,' he said, amazed at the confidence in his tone.

'Beware of the demon Kali, Shalya. Keep your eyes wide, for he can lurk beyond the corners of your eyes. Beware of what you listen to, for it can distort the sweet words of a friend into threats from an enemy. Beware of what you taste, for he can cloud your perception of poison and nectar. Beware of what you smell. Beware of what you touch.'

Before Shalya could speak, the river flooded the ground in fury. Mother Madra became the river Iravati. He drowned in the depths, gasping for breath as his eyes filled with water.

He opened his eyes to the soft snores of his wife. Sweat dripped over his skin and hair under the thick blanket. He hesitated to slide the blanket down for fear of the cold, but when he did, the breeze sang him to sleep. He slept peacefully that night after what felt like an eternity.

'Must you leave tomorrow?' Pujawati asked desperately. Two months had passed since the messengers left Sakala. Madraka armies had arrived in the meantime and burdened the city with their sheer numbers.

'I see ill omens,' Pujawati added.

Shalya smiled and cupped her face in his hands. 'Like what?'

'Camels and asses braying at night. Don't you hear them?'

Only a deaf man could bear the noises from the royal sheds in the outer complex. They had been braying since dusk. 'They are fed sparsely these days,' Shalya said. 'Like the rest of the city. The armies of the entire Madraka were here for a month. That's reason enough we should move quickly.'

'I heard the women curse me for taking their sons and husbands,' he said, hoping to cheer her up again.

'And fathers and brothers,' Pujawati said.

'Did you ever curse me for killing your father?' Shalya asked. He had fought with her father, Anggana, for her hand in his youth. Anggana had died that day.

Pujawati frowned. 'I don't remember those days anymore,' she said with disinterest, as she pulled back from Shalya's hands. 'And yes, the servants curse you. And don't smile. Their chances of becoming widows are a little less than certain. Speaking of widows, I want you to grant me a wish if I am ever widowed.'

Shalya frowned. 'Do not speak ill, Pujawati. I pray to gods, even your gods, that all our men return home safely.'

'Then the gods take you for a fool,' she said harshly.

'No, no. Did you forget that I can suck half of my enemy's strength when they fight with me in anger? Men always fight in anger,' Shalya jested. He did not know who had created such a ridiculous notion, but this gossip had travelled far beyond Madra.

The queen did not smile, much to Shalya's disappointment. 'Perhaps their strength does indeed decrease by half when they believe in all your supernatural stories, but I'm sure you don't gain it all. How could Bhim defeat you then?' she asked, as if to wound Shalya's pride. 'You know, when you went to prove your old strength to marry that poor Draupadi? I was forever thankful to him for showing you what would happen if you tried to marry another woman.' It was Pujawati's turn to chuckle now.

Shalya kept quiet for a moment, searching for the right sort of answer. 'She was too young for me, and I knew it was my nephew,' he lied. He had been so embarrassed that day when he lost twice—in hitting the fish at Draupadi's swayamvar, which was a narrow miss, and the second defeat when he lost to Bhim in wrestling, his stronghold sport. In his defence, Shalya was older and slower, while Bhim was younthful and agile.

'Anyway, will you promise me that you will grant me whatever I wish for before going to war?' Pujawati asked.

'Yes, yes. Of course, why not?' Shalya was more than eager to give her whatever she asked for, partly because even he was afraid of his death in the battle. And partly because he wanted to cheer her up. 'I promise.'

'Let me follow you in the fire if you die in the war.'

Shalya's throat choked as she spoke. A barbaric tradition in the Vahika lands. Even his sister, Madri, had sacrificed herself in fire after her husband Pandu's death. Her death still haunted him.

'No, you won't,' he said sternly. 'You aid the future kings, Nakul and Sahadev, in their rule, and, if they die, their heirs.'

'You promised me this,' Pujawati said coldly.

Shalya beat his head. This was on him. 'You had always warned me against the consequences of my reckless promises. Why do you do this to me, Pujawati? Make another wish. A promise cannot be taken back and must be defended with life.'

'Then come back alive.'

'Damn you, woman,' Shalya cursed and turned away from her to lie on his side. 'Do as you wish.'

He woke up to the shaking blows of the conches, as armies began to position themselves on the outside of the royal complex. The sounds blew as if to wake the sun himself. Pujawati woke up at the same time and prayed to her gods. Shalya prayed to the river goddesses. 'May the rivers bring out the spoils of our soil and reward the farmers' toil.' He was still upset with Pujawati, so he did not look at her when he left.

The Prabhadrakas, the mercenary allies of the Panchalas, were stationed outside the royal complex on the streets, armoured in leather and metal and with swords in their hands. The mountain tribes stood with their wooden bows and bony arrows. The armies of the five kings were aligned in five columns, with their coloured banners flying high in the wind. An akshauhini of an army. The chariots were stationed behind them. Behind them were the horses, and behind them the war elephants. They all extended beyond what his eyes could see.

'Victory to Madra!' Shalya's war cry moved as a wave from his end to the last and died with the trumpets of the elephants.

Dyutimat and Shalya were to lead the army to Matsya. The elephantry and infantry were slow and could not compete with the cavalry and chariots. And so, the army was split. The slower group was to take shortcuts through the mountains, where chariots and horses could not travel. The faster group would take a sophisticated but longer highway of the Uttarapatha and was expected to reach the destination around the same time as the slow group. Shalya volunteered to lead the slow group through the mountains and the rivers.

They had started at noon after Dyutimat's party had left for Uttarapatha. Shalya prayed for Mother Madra one last time and sought her blessings mentally.

It soon proved difficult to manage a huge caravan. The generals did their best to make sure that no one slowed down. Yet the older soldiers tired easily, and sometimes the elephants refused to move. There was so much hiking, and it only made the journey worse as they had to take more frequent breaks than on plain ground. Many small rivulets could be crossed easily, but the elephants would start playing once they saw water, and that slowed them down even more. The water froze at night and would only melt late in the morning. When it came to the large rivers of Iravati and Shatadru, the elephants took to the waters while the soldiers crossed the bridges.

The food made things worse. His men were used to meat and wine, but when they were served wheat cakes and rice puddings, some of them suffered from indigestion, making them weak. Some men used nets to catch fish in the rivers, and when fortune smiled, they got some fish. But the winter made it hard to find the fish in the ice-cold water. And most of them craved some wine. Even Shalya. He remembered Pujawati's warm embrace and chided himself that he had not talked to her properly when he left.

As they passed through hillside villages, people looked at them with excitement and wonder—some with hostility, as the elephants and men trampled the mountainous crops and destroyed their water ponds. They did not mean to do it. It was the sheer magnitude of the numbers that caused such destruction. Shalya wondered if the number of villagers who had cursed them could affect their victory in the war in some way. The only comfort in the journey was that they had not had any encounters with the robbers and rebels who lived on these mountains.

On the tenth day of their journey, the Saraswati River, which stretched as far as one's eyes could see, appeared in the light of the golden moon. Its cold waters, although still, stung Shalya bitterly when he tried to step into them. They had to wait till dawn for warmth.

'Rest for today,' Shalya instructed the generals. But before they could put down their load, a thousand red globes appeared, gliding over the dark waters. Not the reflections of the stars that hung in millions from the sky roof. Real globes. They grew in size as they approached, shifting from spheres to irregular shapes. Fire.

'Raise your bows,' Shalya commanded. The men scrambled to bring the archers ahead, and it was not long before the bows were pointed to the sky. If whatever was coming wished to harm them, it must deal with an akshauhini of men and elephants.

Shalya soon realized that the approaching shapes were boats with torches. He waited till they came to the shore, his spear ready in his hands to pin the intruders if they meant harm.

A man, perhaps sixty years of age, climbed down from the first boat. His eyes were drooping, and his bare body was covered in a plain green silk uttariya. A couple of servant men, their chests bare, stood behind the elderly man.

'Pranam, Madrapati Shalya,' the elderly man greeted with the accent of the plains of Ganga. 'I am Mitra, servant to the true heir of the Kurus and the protector of dharma. Indeed, I am. He welcomes you to Aryavrata, Maharaj.'

Shalya thanked Yudhishthir mentally for his concern for their comfort. Yudhishthir had sent them boats to carry the men across the river and servants to look after the elephants on this side. Apparently, the luxuries of silk beds and hot food were waiting on the other side.

The dishevelled soldiers were eager to get into the boats, and Shalya empathized with them. Bland food and tough ground had worn them all down. They all sang happy songs, and even Shalya laughed cheerfully as they crossed the vast river onto the other side. He owed it to them to allow them at least this moment of joy. The war that followed would steal any joy, if not their lives.

On the other side, hundreds of maidens waited to offer them water. There were a large number of pavilions arranged neatly. Madraka soldiers rushed into them, forgetting all dignity, and before Shalya could push some sense into them, Mitra ushered him into a larger pavilion that towered over those around it.

A throne, although not as grand as the one in Sakala, stood at the far end of the pavilion, and a large, smooth bed, spread with even smoother blankets, welcomed him.

Mitra clapped, and a string of servants appeared with bowls of food in their hands. First came honeyed milk and barley cakes. Then came the spiced lamb, roasted and laden with garlic. Boiled peacock soon followed, seasoned with corn and lemon. Even gravy beef was brought, to Shaya's surprise. Tigress joints were roasted and fried in garlic oil. Camel curd and butter came last, to compensate for the heat of the meat. The food was prepared as preferred by a Madraka.

Shalya belched at the end of his dinner and struggled to get up. A servant brought a goblet of black wine, warmer than usual and whose flavour he did not recognize, although it smelt familiar. He did taste a hint of malt, though. It tasted funny—a mix of sweetness and pungency—but he had already had five goblets before he realized.

'Your elephants look gigantic, Maharaj. Indeed, they do,' Mitra said as Shalya sat on the throne. Mitra kept his head bent throughout, as if the king was going to strike him if he raised it.

'Trained in the northwest, but born in the east,' Shalya said. 'But none can match the might of Airavata that the fool Indra had. He is unworthy of that giant beast.'

'Indeed he is,' Mitra nodded in agreement. 'You can handle spears better than Yudhishthir, match Bhim in mace fights, embarrass Arjun in archery, teach the twins to fight with swords, and beat Krishna in driving chariots. No mortal can challenge Indra. None indeed, save you.'

'You give me too much credit, my friend,' Shalya smiled. He shook the goblet in his hand as a sign to the servants to serve more wine, and they obeyed.

Mitra did not talk for a while. He often opened his mouth to say something but did not speak, as if he were waiting for the right moment.

'What is it, Mitra?' Shalya said. 'Speak out.'

'Your host waits outside, Maharaj,' Mitra said slowly, without raising his head. 'Are you satisfied with his service?' he asked, worried and doubtful.

'Of course, I am. Why not, why not?' Shalya assured him. 'The king will get whatever he wants, this I promise. Let my nephews in. I have not seen them for a long time.'

Mitra went out as Shalya swallowed down another gulp of wine. Shadows entered—six shadows, all of different stature. The five Pandavas and Mitra, he counted. Physical forms emerged as he moved his eyes from the shadows to their conjurers. One moment he looked in confusion, and the next moment his heart skipped a beat. He coughed as the wine choked his throat.

Those were not Pandavas. Shalya recognized all the six figures as they bowed before him.

Duryodhana entered first, and his brother Dushasana followed with a crooked smile. Then came the old Shakuni, his wrinkles mimicking the scars on his face, followed by the tall Karna, feigning a lack of interest in the affairs. The last one that followed Mitra was short and walked with a bent posture. Shalya recognized the Kaurava messenger immediately as he smiled and bowed.

'It was the messenger's work,' Shalya thought. 'I should have cut his tongue then.'

'Welcome, Uncle,' Duryodhana mocked. 'Are you refreshed?'

The taste of malt receded on his tongue as Shalya returned to his senses. 'Ask what you want, and let us be done with it,' he said with irritation.

'Straight to matters then,' Duryodhana smiled. 'What gives me more pleasure than you aiding me in this battle for dharma, Uncle?'

Shalya knew there was no bargaining with Duryodhana. He must go against the collective decision of the Madraka kings and aid the Kauravas. His throat ached for a moment as a sharp pain sparked, like hot iron crushing his bones. His father's words echoed in his ears. 'A true king will never back down from his promises. He will even fight God to keep his vows.'

'Forgive me, Mother.' Words without voices escaped Shalya's heart. 'Forgive me, Dharma.'

10

Janak and Sulabha: The Royal Umbrella and Stick

S. Anuradha

Sulabha took her stick to pull up the creeper that grew between two trees and blocked her way. As she tried pushing up the creeper, she saw a spider web connecting the trees. Any more pushing would destroy the web. She brought back the stick and decided to crawl underneath the creeper to walk further into the sandalwood forest. A few days ago, a villager had told her about the forest.

'Once you reach the sandalwood forest, take the upward route from the stream. There will be some caves. Go there before the rain starts, or else you will face competition from the animals,' the villager said, on the last day of her seeking alms in the place.

Getting up from underneath the creeper, she placed the staff gently on the ground. Neither the earth nor the animals were meant to be hurt. An ascetic didn't compete with anyone for food or shelter.

There was a rustle of dry leaves behind her. By now, she was used to the sounds of the forest. The jungle had a rule—never turn back. No one interfered with the jungle's rules and cycle. She continued to walk. There was movement ahead of her. For a brief while, she could hear the sound of the leaves being trampled upon, and then it stopped. Although she had no intention of examining the jungle and its inhabitants, her eyes fell on the object in front. It was a doe with a small belly and frozen eyes.

Something leapt, and its impact sent leaves up in the air. It took less than a second for Sulabha to turn around with a growl and stand in the way of the tiger. It growled back.

'Forgive me, my four-legged friend. I shouldn't snatch your meal, but I just wanted to remind you that the death of an about-to-be-born baby can create severe bad karma. Take me if you want to,' Sulabha said.

The tiger growled back—a fraction of a second was enough to lose the prey. With the deer disappearing, the tiger jumped over the stream to go over to the other side. Sulabha continued her walk, and, in a short while, the pregnant deer came out of the bush and stood next to her. Up close, Sulabha saw that the belly was quite big. The deer was still shaking. Sulabha ran her hands over the deer's head, ears, and neck. Every time Sulabha stopped, the deer would headbutt her softly, and she would continue to stroke the scared animal. The clouds were gathering. It was time to find a cave. The deer started moving ahead of her and led her to a small cave. Sulabha waited for the deer to go in first, but it didn't. It waited for her to sit, and curled up next to her. After some time, the deer got up and walked around her several times. Sulabha went out, collected some fresh leaves, and made a bed for the animal.

The deer slowly went and sat on the bed of grass and leaves. She licked her protruding belly and went into labour. The two legs which were facing her started moving but she didn't take her eyes away from Sulabha. With each grunt, her womb started pushing out the baby. The legs came out first, and then the whole body. The mother immediately got up and started licking the fawn. Once she was satisfied that it was all clean, she turned, her eyes inviting Sulabha to have a look at her newborn.

Sulabha petted the baby and placed her hand on the mother's head. The time had come to leave. A mother and her newborn were not conducive for an ascetic to stay in seclusion. They were serious distractions. Without turning back, she kept walking in the direction she had come, as large drops of water fell on her head.

The queen's hair covered Janak's face. His nose could catch their fragrance, one part coming from the flowers, another part from the herbs with which they had been washed, and a final part from the sweat that carried in it the flavours of the food she had eaten. His tongue felt the soft hair, and his eyes opened to the beauty of those curls. The queen's legs had locked him and were not allowing him to get up. 'The sun is not yet in the sky, and you belong to me,' she whispered into his ears.

'Go ahead, I am your slave,' he said with a smile.

The queen tied her long hair around his throat and tried to throttle him. 'Now croak like a frog, and say you love me,' she said.

He uttered the words and pretended that he was being suffocated. 'O Aruna, O Surya, come reclaim my husband, who is my slave every night and dies in the morning. Let me bring him back to life so that he can serve you.' Saying this, she kissed him on the lower lip first, then on the upper lip, and then both lips together.

'Thank you, my master,' he said, getting up from the bed. He placed one leg at a time on the floor, the earth from which Sita, the daughter of one of his ancestors, had appeared and into which she had disappeared. Janak, which was the name given to all the kings of the Mithila kingdom, paid his respects to the earth. After drinking water from the earthen pitcher, he paid respects to that element and prayed for enough rain to fill up all the lakes, ponds, and wells. In a crevice on the eastern side of the bedroom wall, there was a small, swan-shaped silver lamp. The lamp was always lit, reminding him of the fire god, Agni, who purified all and connected humans and gods. He bowed down before it. He slowly opened the door in the southern direction, and let the gentle breeze in. 'O Vayu! Help everyone achieve all their desires quickly, and give them the strength to absorb both the good and bad as effortlessly as you do.'

Standing in the southern direction, he looked at the sky—the space, the very Brahman. He drew water from the well, washed his hands and face, and waited with a pitcher of water for the sun. It was an auspicious day. There was no cloud blocking the arrival of the sun. Janak poured the water in the eastern direction, chanting Vedic hymns. After a short passage of time, the first rays of the sun emerged. This was his favourite moment of the day, reminding him of the valiant Suryavanshi who had married Sita. The sun was the perceptible Ishwara who nurtured and purified everyone through his sometimes gentle and sometimes harsh rays.

Sulabha was leaving the forest as the monsoon season was going to end in a few days. The rains were heavy this year, and most of the time, she took refuge in trees for the caves had been taken by the animals.

The forests ended, and the common land was now approaching—the land on which wanderers, gypsies, nomads, and sadhus could pitch a tent, the land on which the landless could grow one crop to sustain themselves or cut wood to sell as fuel.

Sulabha decided to sit under a tree in the common land for some time before deciding where she would next go. As she walked towards the tree, two men approached her.

'Greetings, sadhvi! Please take this food from us, and bless our king and the kingdom,' they said.

Sulabha smiled. 'That's very generous of your ruler. Let there be all-round prosperity there,' she said and asked them to drop the food in her pot that she held out. The men did as they were told but didn't leave. Sulabha decided to walk on; however, she could hear them following. The men were panting, trying to catch up with her.

'Sadhvi, we forgot to give you this,' they said, handing her a silver coin.

'Don't you know that the matted-hair one has no use for silver or gold?' Sulabha said.

'We invite you on our king's behalf to come to his court and discuss with him the highest truth,' they said.

The men were officials of the Kashi ruler, Ajatshatru.

'Why is the king so keen on dialogue?' Sulabha asked.

'He is a seeker of truth,' one of the men said. Sulabha was not convinced by the rehearsed reply. She had to give only a second look to the men for them to rattle out the truth. 'Our king, the great Ajatshatru, has a rival. A rival who hasn't snatched away his land, cattle, or women but has attracted more scholars than him.'

The situation was so bad that none of the scholars were coming to his court. All were lining up for an audience with King Janak.

Sulabha laughed. 'So, you catch anyone who is walking around and take him to your court?'

'We are not that foolish, sadhvi. We have heard about you,' one of the men said.

'Okay, I will definitely come to your king's court, but for now, I need to go somewhere urgently.'

The men looked crestfallen.

'Alright, give me the silver coin,' Sulabha said. One of the men gently dropped the coin into her palm.

'Take it,' she said, returning the coin to the men. They moved back, reluctant to take anything from a matted-hair person. 'Please take it. This silver is no compensation for the gem you are helping me to discover.'

The men didn't understand what she said, and with bent heads and folded hands, asked her to visit the Kashi court in the near future.

Janak commenced the morning fire sacrifice in the central courtyard of the palace for the welfare of the universe. Before starting the ritual, he asked the minister in charge of the forests, rivers, and mountains if the standard pack of wooden sticks, ghee, and herbs had been dispatched in all the households of the kingdom. In Mithila, it was the practice that all communities conducted fire rituals.

Those who knew the scriptures well could conduct these rituals at home, and those who didn't know any mantras could participate in the community fire sacrifice that was conducted just after the king finished his prayers.

Janak himself chanted the mantras and performed the fire sacrifice. As the smell of ghee mixed with burnt wood and herbs filled the air, he had faith that the atmosphere was purified, and the gods who presided over the sense organs and natural elements allowed them to function properly.

After this ritual, Janak spent the morning checking if the army was fully prepared. He was assessing the reports on the weapons and soldiers. Just before midday, he performed another fire ritual, specifically to protect his soldiers.

Lunch was usually shared with a visiting diplomat and, on some occasions, a king. Today, the lunch was being shared with the king of Kalinga in his private chamber.

Janak welcomed the king with a namaste. Neither of them bowed to the other, but they just smiled politely. The king was not his ally and had come to Mithila to visit the birthplace of Sita. Janak followed the kingdom's principle that access to pilgrimage spots and temples would never be curtailed, irrespective of whether the visitor was from a friendly or hostile land. All precautions were taken so that no one created any trouble.

The Kalinga king deferentially handed over the prasad from the temple and offered a plate of fruits, flowers, and sweets to Janak. A similar set, but with many gold coins, had been offered at the temple for Goddess Sita.

'I pray that the goddess protects you and your people,' Janak said.

After a short nap, Janak attended to revenue matters. 'The festival season is coming. Let us not increase the tax this quarter,' he told the treasurer.

'But we need funds to build the new roads, my Lord,' the treasurer said.

'Let us raise the taxes after the harvest season.'

An hour was spent meeting various messengers, scribes, merchants, bards, and historians who updated him on what was happening in his kingdom and outside. What were the new things people were singing, eating, playing, and praying? He would eat dinner with his queens only once a week. The rest of the weeknights were spent in making rounds of his kingdom in disguise. He wanted to know first-hand what the citizens and enemies of his kingdom thought and felt.

Today's discussion with the scholar had been boring. The quality of the scholars was falling. They repeated whatever the king liked to hear. These coached scholars were not stimulating, and the annual gathering of scholars was still many months away.

Sulabha was on the outskirts of Mithila. Her brown, unstitched cloth had collected so much dust that it looked no different from the earth on which she walked. Her nails had grown and were discoloured. The lips were chapped, and the heels had blisters. She was not going to present herself in court like this. She cleansed herself and her cloth at a nearby stream.

As she entered the city, she could smell the smoke—a smell she had forgotten after staying in the forests and hills for years. It was the smoke from the sacrificial fire that had been raised in the ground at the entrance of the city. The smell was a combination of burnt sandalwood, nutmeg wood, dried herbs, cow dung, and ghee.

Just ahead of the ground, there was a huge water stall on the right, and, on the left, a common kitchen was serving meals that comprised two chappatis, a fistful of cooked rice, lentils, vegetables, and a sweet. Those who wanted to sit and enjoy were offered a proper meal, while mendicants like Sulabha could get the food dropped into their vessels. Sulabha was in no mood to eat, but the woman serving the food addressed her, 'Sadhvi, come and eat some food. Our king doesn't like guests to be hungry.'

'Not today, I am in a rush to meet the king,' Sulabha said. The woman was surprised to hear this and tried not to laugh.

'Did I say something funny?' Sulabha asked.

'Sorry, sadhvi, you need not approach our wise king for a single piece of cloth, a begging bowl, or a staff. I am qualified enough to give them to you. Don't tire yourself.'

Sulabha laughed. 'My dear woman, I want to meet him because I want to know his view on the supreme soul, Atman.'

'Yes, please go. Our king is very wise and has had discussions with self-realized men like Yagnavalkya and Ashtavakra. The one and only Ved Vyas sent his son, Shuka, to learn self-knowledge from our king. Learn to frame the questions well,' the woman said, this time not making an attempt to stifle her laughter. Sulabha thanked her and left the place.

As Sulabha walked towards the palace, some bowed before her as soon as they saw her. Some didn't even look at her face and just fell at her feet, while others asked for her blessings. Some, though, turned away the moment they saw her from afar.

She reached the moat surrounding the palace. There were four entrances to the palace. Men and women were queueing up to present their credentials so that they could be directed to the correct part of the palace. Before she could join the queue, a man approached her. 'Sadhvi, of what service can the state be to you?'

The engagements for the day were over, and Sulabha was asked to rest for one night before meeting the king the next day. A special tent, resembling a cave, was recreated. From the transparent, fabric roof, Sulabha gazed at the beautifully lit-up sky.

The list of potential visitors was shown to Janak. As was the practice, sadhus and scholars were second only to diplomats in gaining the king's audience. The royal priest had told him in the evening that a sadhvi wanted to meet the king. Janak could not sleep the whole night. He had never had a discussion with a woman scholar. He had heard how Gargi would pose many questions to all, including the very venerable saint, Yagnavalkya.

The king was seated in a meditative pose when the queen entered the bedroom. Tonight was the night to leave the king alone. Still, she couldn't resist taking a dig at him. 'The king is summoning up all his powers to meet the matted-head one,' she said.

The courtier announced the arrival of the king, and all the ministers stood to attention, except the royal priest. Janak accepted the greetings of his ministers and bowed before the royal priest. The court's schedule for the day was announced. The sadhvi was third on the list, but Janak asked her to be presented first.

The first thing that struck Janak about Sulabha was her mane. She walked in like a lion with her waist-length matted hair. A single golden-earth-coloured piece of cloth was wrapped around one shoulder, leaving the other shoulder and arm bare. The arm had the strength of a woodcutter, but it was not an eyesore as it was beautified by her shapely fingers. Her wooden padukas announced her confidence. Her big toe and second toe firmly held the knob, showing that she had mastered her senses.

Janak got up from his seat and said, 'Welcome, sadhvi, to Videha.' His kingdom had many names, his favourite being Videha, which meant bodiless. His real nature, the nature of Atman, was indeed bodiless. Atman couldn't be limited to a body.

After offering her a seat, Janak poured water over her feet and dabbed them with a soft, silk cloth. Without turning his back, he returned to his throne.

Sulabha examined the king—a towering man with the strength of a wrestler and the sharpness of an archer. He had tied a blue silk dhoti, which went between his legs, highlighting his householder status. On his head was a diamond-studded crown, and each part of his visible body was covered with jewellery. His hair had been collected on the right side and formed into a bun. From his ears hung two trident-shaped earrings. The cartilage that separated his nostrils was pierced. On his neck, he wore several gold chains studded with precious stones that were only partially visible because he had adorned a garland of blue lotuses. There were golden bands on his wrists and slip-on anklets around his ankles. A slight fragrance emanated from him and became stronger when he moved away from her. The perfume was a combination of tulsi and jasmine. When he spoke, his mouth smelt of cloves and cinnamon. Surrounding him were ministers of various races, genders, and appearances. Sulabha thought either his kingdom extended far and wide or his influence was so strong that he was able to attract talent from afar. The court was adorned with delicate carvings and paintings. On one side of the higher floor, his wives sat, and, far away from them, other women, such as dancers, singers, cooks, garland makers, hairdressers, perfume makers, prostitutes, and servants. Everyone was allowed entry into the sessions where the king discussed spiritual matters. 'Never deny anyone the opportunity to hear about the Self,' he had told the royal priest when the latter protested the presence of the masses in the court. 'The pursuit of self-knowledge is the birthright of all. It is the greatest purifier.'

Sulabha was not sure a man living openly in such opulence was capable of knowing himself. She had to ascertain the level of the king's understanding. Using her yogic powers, Sulabha entered the mind of Janak and bound him up such that he could not stop her from reading his mind—the outer mind that could give instructions to the sense organs, and the subconscious mind that was storing up all the said and unsaid desires of several births, some waiting to fructify in this birth.

Through his austerities, Janak knew that Sulabha had entered his mind, and he blocked her from penetrating into his subconscious. He was ready to play her game. In the palace of their minds, they were both without their current identities. He was without his royal umbrella and sceptre, and she was without her stick. But, in court, they were ready to debate, displaying their outward symbols.

Janak asked Sulabha who she was, what her lifestyle was, where she came from, why she had come to Videha, and where she was planning to go.

'No one can, without questioning, determine another person's proficiency in the scriptures, age, or order of birth. You are worthy of my respect. I wish to know you completely for, like me, you are a seeker of the highest knowledge, that of the Self.'

One of the court singers gave a side glance to the king's second wife and said with a hint of sarcasm, 'The king is so interested in the matted-hair woman. He will soon forsake his wives. Remember, Yagnavalkya gave the most valuable self-knowledge to his second wife, Maitreyi, and only the perishable material riches to the first wife, Katyayani.'

Sulabha answered only one of his questions. 'I heard that you are committed to the knowledge of the Self, but, seeing you surrounded by worldly things, I am doubtful if you know yourself. Clarify this doubt of mine, and I will answer all your questions.'

Janak loved the question because it allowed him to explain the qualifications required to understand the Self. 'Yes, listen to me on how to acquire this knowledge for there is no one better qualified than me to explain this.'

Janak said he had learnt the highest knowledge of the Self from Panchashika, a mendicant belonging to Parashara's family. Janak said there were two lifestyles available for those seeking the Self and establishing themselves in it. One was the path of contemplation called Sankhya, and the other was the path of action, Yoga.

'My mendicant guru stayed with me for four months during the rains and taught me the highest knowledge of Brahman. He, however, did not order me to give up my kingdom,' Janak said and waited. He was not one of those who were so fragile in their understanding that their line of thinking could be broken when encountered by a question.

In a sweet, gentle voice that was not capable of disturbing anyone, Sulabha said, 'Renunciation is the greatest qualification to be cultivated for attaining self-knowledge. Please explain to me the things you have renounced. Where do you observe dispassion?'

Janak smiled. He had to use apt words to explain to the ascetic that the highest form of renunciation was through knowledge, and not through actions and material possessions. 'Like a fried seed incapable of sprouting, my attachment to any sense object does not bear fruit.'

'Oh, generous king, do you lack the courage to give up these objects? Are you holding on to them as backup, in case you are not able to understand this knowledge? Have you renounced even a pair of slippers and stayed without a roof for a night?' Sulabha asked with a laugh.

In the audience was a Kapalika ascetic, carrying a skull head, and he started laughing. 'The lioness has caught the fox in her mouth and will throw him into the ground.' The guard glared at him, but he didn't have the guts to tell him to shut up. The king's standing instruction was never to meddle with the audience. 'They learn by hearing the discussion, and I learn by studying their reactions,' the king said.

Janak was not flustered by her ridicule. He was going to reiterate that one needed to renounce the fruit of action, not action itself. He could be doing thousands of actions and be completely detached. Moreover, real renunciation is freeing oneself from the pair of opposites.

'I never experience love for my wife or hatred for my enemies. I regard both in the same way—the one who smears my right hand with sandalwood paste and the one who wounds my left. I regard a piece of stone and a lump of gold as the same. I enjoy the beauty of the world because they don't bind me.'

Sulabha shook her head, and, before she could say anything, Janak continued. 'Lady, you are very proud of being a renunciate, but I can tell you that if householders exercise self-restraint, they become the equals of sannyasins. On the other hand, sannyasins who exhibit desire and aversion are like householders.'

Sulabha asked the king's permission to interrupt him. She would not let him build an argument based on subjective standards. 'O King, don't run down what you have not been able to achieve. This restraint of the mind, mastery of the senses, and endurance of the extremes prove that you really have these qualities. Saying that you have an understanding of these concepts is not enough.'

Sulabha commented that if Janak had really attained the highest happiness, he would not be seeking joy in finite pleasures, such as fine clothes, delectable food, and attractive women. The smell of the ghee-mixed smoke around the palace was proof that the king had not yet understood the defects of karma.

Janak wanted to break the woman's pride in her external symbols—the staff, water pitcher, matted hair, and ochre robes. What made her think that it could only be achieved by those with the staff and not those with the royal umbrella!

'Pleasant lady, you are confusing knowledge with lifestyle. Knowledge of the Self is more important than external symbols. Let me tell you, poverty is not liberating, and neither is wealth binding. Using the sword of the scriptures, I have set myself free from the fetters of wealth and emotional attachments. Freedom is the final proof of having understood the Self. I feel great freedom, although to you I appear to be toiling in the twin fields of bondage—kingdom and family.'

Sulabha softly said she was not convinced by his arguments. 'Tell me what you mean when you say you never experience love for your wife. So, when your wife kisses you, do you let her do what she wants, or do you exercise your choice? Is that choice not based on like or dislike? How are you then saying that you are free from the opposites? To me, you are a hypocrite. You do one thing, say another, and mean something else. You should be a role model, both as a king and as a seeker of truth. I am afraid you are a very poor one. Those around you will be confused. I don't know whether I should call you a hypocrite or a cheat.'

The ministers were looking at one another nervously. Had the ascetic managed to trap the king with her arguments? Given that the kingdom had the rule that a person vanquished in a religious debate had to adopt the lifestyle of the victor, would they now have to start preparing for a successor? The prime minister visualized a bald Janak and immediately closed his eyes.

Janak could sense the nervousness in the court and stood up. The ministers also moved up from their seats, but Janak gestured for them to sit down and raised his right hand in abhaya mudra. The time had come to completely uproot the ideas the lady was holding on to. 'Look, who is calling whom a hypocrite and a cheat,' he said.

The court was stunned. The battle of ideas was heating up.

Janak had restrained himself for a long time, taking into consideration that Sulabha was his guest and, more importantly, a seeker of the truth. Now was the time to nail down the argument.

Without raising his voice, Janak told Sulabha that he knew that through her yogic powers she had entered his mind to read his thoughts. 'That act of yours is not in keeping with the symbols you wear.'

Janak said he was beginning to doubt the intentions of the sadhvi. 'You have entered my gross body without my permission. That is violence. You have abused me.'

Janak accused Sulabha of committing many transgressions—a woman of Brahmin origin trying a physical union with a Kshatriya and a renunciate committed to liberation seducing a grahasta. 'If your parents are alive, they will be outraged just in case you and I turn out to be from the same gotra. And, by chance, if your husband is alive, he will be outraged at this attempt at adultery.'

One of the prostitutes hooted and lifted up her skirt in front of the sadhus. 'We have nothing to hide, but it looks like you and your ilk hide many delicate desires under coarse clothes.' A sadhu who had covered his whole body, including his mouth, in white cloth got up in rage and was about to pull out the white mask from his mouth but held back when the friends of the prostitute covered her mouth with their hands.

Sulabha sat still with her head held high, even as Janak continued to pile charges upon her. 'From what I understand, you want to claim victory over me, my court, and the learned men in this sabha. Intoxicated by the power of your austerities, you want to test whether I am liberated or not. I am not going to request it anymore. I am commanding you to leave my body. But before you leave the court, reveal to them who you really are, to which family you belong, which guru initiated you into sannyasa, and who taught you self-knowledge.'

Sulabha was not disturbed, despite the barrage of harsh words. She began replying in a manner that was more beautiful than her physical appearance. Before replying to the questions put forward by Janak, Sulabha decided to explain to him the qualities of proper speech. 'The words uttered by me will be free from ambiguity, harshness, and difficulty of comprehension. I will not let anger, fear, desire, shame, mercy, and pride taint my replies.'

Sulabha asked Janak why he was interested in knowing about her antecedents. 'You say you are free from duality but are not able to see your body in other bodies and your soul in other souls. You still talk about caste, gender, and power, the factors that only strengthen duality.'

The renunciate asked how Janak could consider himself liberated if he could not look impartially at someone who had a view different from his. 'Your attempt to acquire liberation is like the use of medicine by a patient who indulges in all sorts of forbidden food and practices,' she said.

Sulabha explained to Janak how the role of the king was not conducive to the attainment of the highest knowledge. A king was always attached to the duties of rewarding and punishing subjects. There were many limitations on the king. He was always bound by the advice of his counsellors on the clothes he wore, the food he ate, the women he enjoyed, and the time he slept.

Sulabha gave more examples of how a king is always afflicted. An enemy at the door, a drought, or the outbreak of a contagious disease could completely shatter one's internal peace. 'Where are the moments of calm for you, oh brave king? The highest knowledge is not a fix for the sick. It works only for those who want to achieve nothing more. But you can't have enough land, gold, and women. I can mention countless faults of kingship, but let me stop for that is not my purpose.'

Janak sat with his back erect, paying attention to everything the sadhvi said. 'You have an interesting perspective, though I may not agree with what you have to say.'

Sulabha smiled. 'I have not yet finished, and there is no need for you to pass a decree. The truth doesn't need a stamp of approval.'

The renunciate lowered her voice, and even the fan-bearer started to slowly move the fans. They wanted to hear everything the sadhvi was going to say and didn't want to be disturbed by the rustle of the wind.

Sulabha told the king that she had entered his mind through the power of yoga, and her mind had not in any way touched him or altered his thinking. Her intention was not to have a physical relationship with him. 'It was a private transaction between you and me. Why did you need to make it public? By doing so, you want to cast aspersions on me. What harm have I done to you? Renunciates are always looking for empty spaces in which to meditate and reflect. It looks like your mind is really an empty one, devoid of the knowledge you are famous for.'

Sulabha asked Janak why he should assume that her presence in his mind would taint him as king, as a man, and as a Kshatriya. 'On the one hand, you claim that you are untouched by the joys and sorrows of royal life, and on the other, you think my presence has stained you. How can I believe that the great mendicant Panchashika indeed taught you the knowledge of liberation? Have you really heard the scriptures pertaining to Brahman or have you heard some other texts and considered them scriptures? You have strayed away from the life of a householder and have not yet attained liberation. You are caught in two worlds but pretending to be liberated.'

Sulabha knew it was her duty as a guest to answer the questions of the king. 'You asked me about my caste. I am not a Brahmin, Kshatriya, Vaishya, or Shudra. I belong to the family of the sage Pradhana, who was found in the forest by the rishis. My ancestors include sages, kings, soldiers, traders, and craftsmen who performed fire sacrifices that were attended by the gods themselves. I am telling you this because you asked. As for myself, I have no identity other than someone who is moving on this earth, seeking the highest truth, clarifying all doubts, and establishing myself in it.'

Janak was carefully listening to what Sulabha was saying. The mendicant said her purpose was not to glorify herself or humiliate others. 'Those who know themselves never flaunt their knowledge or claim any superiority. I have only one commitment—the knowledge of Brahman. A mendicant doesn't stay for more than one night at a place. You have honoured me with words and other offerings. I will leave now.'

Hearing these words, Janak chose not to reply.

As Sulabha left the palace, the sadhus, whose garment was just their matted hair and sacred ash, cheered her all the way till she left the city. This sadhvi had to be protected because she was safeguarding the highest teaching of Brahman from those who were trying to dilute it.

In the court, the relieved ministers and courtiers applauded the king. The chief priest placed a garland of sandalwood flowers on his neck. Their ruler was a great role model for householders. He was proof that they were also eligible for the highest level of knowledge. While the householders discharged their duties, took care of the dependents in society, and paid all taxes, they were mocked by the renunciates and considered ineligible for self-knowledge.

The fan-bearers slowly started moving the fans. The younger girl said she was confused. The naked sadhus outside were claiming that the sadhvi had won, while the court here was declaring that the king had won. The older girl said there was no single winner for hadn't the dear cowherd God himself said, 'In this world, there are two seekers of Self. Those who seek the Self through renunciation and others who seek the same, taking the path of selfless action.'

And the debate continues.

11

Subhadra: The Forgotten Princess

Shambhavi Tripathi

Part I: Innocence

I was getting ready to attend the festival of Raivataka. I wore the beautiful red sari embroidered with a golden thread that my mother, Rohini, had gifted me.

'You have to look the prettiest princess there, my daughter,' my mother had said while handing me the sari. I put on the golden necklace and bangles. My braid was decorated with beautiful white flowers and colourful jewels.

I was putting on my earrings when my elder brother, Krishna, came. 'You are looking beautiful as ever, Subhadra! I bet many princes are going to fall for you tonight,' he said teasingly. I smiled shyly, looking at him. He continued, 'Dau is already looking for a suitable prince for you. I guess you have not told him about that one man you adore a lot.'

I was already aware that my eldest brother, Balaram, had decided that I had to be married to the crown prince of Hastinapur, Duryodhana. Balaram considered him to be worthy of me—he was, after all, his favourite pupil. I, on the other hand, had someone else in my mind and heart.

'I don't adore him, Dau. I respect him as a human being and a warrior.' I lied about not adoring that one man Krishna Dau was talking about.

There was not a single thing about me that my elder brother, Krishna, did not know. I was adored by both my brothers. They loved me the most. But my relationship with each of them was different. I loved and respected Balaram a lot, but he was like a parent to me. Krishna, on the other hand, was my friend. He knew me as no one else did. 'You are my Yogmaya, Subhadra! You think I cannot see right through you?' he asserted proudly. 'Be on time, little sister,' he said smiling widely as he walked out of my room.

Krishna told me many stories about his friend, Arjun. The best archer in the world—handsome, kind, respectful, and righteous, these were just a few of the many adjectives that my dau used to describe Arjun. He told me stories about his archery achievements. How he shot right through a bird's eye when his teacher, Guru Dronacharya, asked him to aim at the thing he could see. The story about Panchali's swayamvar in which candidates had to aim at a moving fish's eye while looking at its reflection in the water. How his kindness had captured the hearts of his elders and teacher. How his charm had captured even Menaka. All these stories created an image of him in my heart, but I had never seen him with my own eyes.

The festival of Raivataka was organized every year to worship the mountain Raivataka. The whole place was lit up with earthen lamps. People would talk and laugh, and delicious dishes were made and served. I reached there with my friends right before the puja was about to begin. I attended the puja, said my prayer, and took blessings from the priests. That may have been the occasion when Arjun saw me for the first time, and it did not take long for Krishna to understand what the look in his eyes meant.

I was painting when Krishna came to meet me in the evening. I had been working on this painting for more than two weeks but just could not figure out what was missing from it. It seemed rather plain and shallow to me, unlike my other paintings. It was important for me that my paintings convey a message or tell a story, but this one just could not come across.

'How about adding a moon there?' he said peeking over my shoulder.

'But it's a moonless night, Dau, with only lamps and stars to provide some light. That is how I imagined it,' I replied.

He considered it for a while, then said, 'Sometimes, little sister, a thousand lamps and stars combined cannot rid the universe from the darkness that envelops it. The moon is required to guide the night towards the dawn.'

I smiled at him and started drawing a moon over the clouds. He watched me paint for some time then said, 'Are you ready to marry Duryodhana?'

I was surprised at this sudden question. The question brought back the pain that I had been trying to ignore for the last few days since the talks about my marriage started.

'No. I'm not. But Balaram dau wants me to, and I am not going to defy him,' I said without looking at him.

'What about Arjun then? What if you get married to him?'

I quickly turned to face him, my eyes wide open, and my mouth at a loss of words. 'Is it possible?' I asked after some time.

He looked at me with his usual bright smile, 'Anything is possible, Subhadra, if you have enough courage to stow your chariot.'

He told me to meet him at the temple of my palace at midnight when everyone was asleep. When I reached there, the sage who I was serving for the last few days was sitting at the stairs of the temple. He stood up quickly when he saw me coming. I was about to touch his feet to seek his blessings when he stopped me. 'Please, princess! I am already ashamed of lying to you about my true identity.' I was surprised at this comment—'true identity'—what did this young sage mean by this? I looked at him in bewilderment and opened my mouth to reply to him, but before I could do so, Krishna dau came down from the stairs of the temple.

'I knew you would not be able to lie for long,' he said laughing. 'Little sister, do you want to know who he is?' As if I would say no! Of course, I wanted to know more about this young, charming sage.

'He is the man whose stories have bewitched your mind. My dear friend, the son of Pandu, Arjun,' said Krishna in a proud tone.

I stood there, too surprised to say anything. I could not believe what my brother was saying. Was he trying to prank me? But why would he do that? While I was trying to contemplate all this, Krishna snapped his fingers in front of my face, bringing me out of my thoughts. 'What are you thinking, little sister? Do you think I am lying?' he laughed.

'I do not understand. What is happening, dau?' I asked him in a feeble tone.

'He has come here to take you with him,' he replied cheekily and turned to look at the sage or, rather, Arjun. 'Do you want to marry her?'

'Only if you allow it, Krishna, and if she feels the same way about me,' answered Arjun. Both of them looked at me, the surprise in my eyes must have outshone the blush of my cheeks because Krishna dau asked me, 'Why are you looking at us like that? Tell us! Do you want to marry him? We must take a quick decision before somebody gets to know about our plan.' Suddenly, Krishna looked at Arjun and said, 'Ask her yourself, and as long as my permission is concerned, I know you would treat her nicely. However, Balaram dau has some other plans for her marriage,' Krishna told him.

Arjun approached me carefully, as if weighing his words and actions. 'Princess Subhadra, please listen to my story first, and decide for yourself,' he said to me. He then told me who he really was and what he was doing there dressed as a sage. He had been exiled for breaking the rules of the marriage pact agreed between the brothers and Panchali, according to which no other brother was allowed to enter the chambers of Panchali for the year when she was residing with one of them. So, Arjun was punished with twelve years of Brahmacharya and exiled to the forest. 'You can tell the rest of your story later. We don't have much time right now,' Krishna said coming towards us. 'Do you trust us now, little sister?' he asked me.

'I never doubted you, Krishna dau. I was just surprised. And I know you only want the best for me, and I want to be with him. But what can we do now? You know Balaram dau has different plans for me,' I said in a single breath. Krishna smiled and said, 'So, here's the plan.'

We listened carefully to his plan. The plan of my abduction. Arjun, however, had his apprehensions regarding Krishna's plan and rejected it flatly. 'Aren't you the one who told me to follow my dharma? Wouldn't it result in adharma? How can you, of all people, suggest the abduction of your little sister?' He projected many such questions towards Krishna.

'Of course, it would have amounted to adharma had Subhadra not been already in love with you. Do you think I would go against her wishes? Am I wrong, little sister?' he asked me kindly. I nodded my head in agreement.

'If she loves me, then why do I need to abduct her? I can simply ask Balaram to marry Subhadra!' Arjun protested.

'Because he wants her to marry Duryodhana, and there is no way he would choose you over his favourite pupil,' answered Krishna. When Arjun did not say anything, he continued, 'To marry a woman, a man has to win her through swayamvar. However, if a woman already loves him, then it's befitting for that Kshatriya to abduct her.'

Krishna was telling us the plan, but my mind was somewhere else. I was torn between two very different thoughts, one thrilling and the other frightening. Thrilling because I was about to get married to Arjun. Frightening because I wondered what consequences this marriage would entail. While planning the abduction, he told me to stow the chariot, so that it would appear that I had abducted him. Suddenly, I understood what he meant by courage when he came to my room last night.

The next day, also my wedding day with Duryodhana, I went to the temple and sought blessings from the Goddess Durga. As planned by Krishna, while returning from the temple, Arjun came with a chariot that Krishna gave him for my abduction. He lifted me in his arms and put me on the chariot. I immediately took the reins of the chariot into my hands. After driving it out of Dwarka, Arjun asked me to stop the chariot. He asked me to sit at the back and started driving the chariot himself. On our way to Indraprastha, he told me that Gada dau, my older brother, used to study with him in the same gurukul and often visited him. 'She is a beauty. And the intelligence, I cannot even praise her intelligence enough. There are no words to describe my sister, Subhadra. I have heard that when she was born, the priest said she would be involved in a magnanimous event that would decide the turns of the future. Can you believe that?', Arjun mimicked Dau so well that I chuckled in delight, and then suddenly I was overcome with sadness over the thought of missing my brother.

He already had several wives, he told me. His main wife was King Drupada's daughter and Panchal's princess,

Krishnaa. Another was the Naga princess, Ulupi, who had fallen in love with him and threatened him that if he did not agree to marry her, then she would not let him go back to his family. His putrikadharma wife was Manipur's princess, Chitrangada. I wondered if I would be able to find a place in his heart, and, more importantly, if he would ever respect me the way he respected Panchali and thought so highly of her. I would have to work very hard to make my place in that palace, I thought to myself. The first obstacle in front of me was already there, pleasing Panchali.

Arjun said to me, 'To please Panchali, you have to assure her that you are not here to snatch her husband away from her.' I nodded my head in agreement. I assured him that I would do my best. 'It's not going to be so easy. I suggest you remove all your jewellery and wear a simple sari. Go to her as a servant, not as a princess.' I looked at him surprised, lost at words.

'But I am not her servant. I can be her friend or sister. You are asking me to please her by putting my dignity at stake,' I protested.

He looked at me with his kind eyes and put his hands on my shoulders, 'You are always going to be the queen of my heart, my dear. But Panchali is the one who you have to win over.' Finally, I agreed and removed all my jewellery, my fine red sari, and all other royal finery, and donned a simple sari without any decorations. Soon, our chariot reached Indraprastha and the beautiful Palace where the five brothers resided.

Panchali was looking out at the chariot standing on a balcony, as if searching for answers from the moon that the night asked her. She was beautiful in every way. Her dusky skin shone brighter than the moon highlighted by the beautiful golden ochre garment she was wearing. Her welcoming eyes sparkled like the lamp lights reflecting the beautiful jewels that adorned her body. Her long black hair in many interlaced strands was gathered in a neat plait with white jasmine garland wrapped around it like a vine climbing up a long tower. Grace and elegance danced around Draupadi like her friends. A devi, indeed.

I went to her and fell at her feet, touching my head to her feet. She got startled and took a few steps back.

"What are you doing?" she asked me.

'A servant is touching her queen's feet to seek her blessings,' I replied quietly.

'You are not my servant. You are the wife of Mother Kunti's third son, Arjun, whom you seduced very cunningly,' she replied bluntly. I was on the verge of crying, protest and anger welling up in me, but I knew I had to keep my composure. If I failed this test, the coming battles would destroy me completely.

'I may be one of Arjun's many wives. But to me, you are my only queen and an elder sister. Krishna dau told me about your struggles and sacrifices, and ever since then I have looked up to you as an elder sister,' I replied honestly. She did not say anything, so I continued, 'Krishna dau has always treated you like a friend. He calls you sakhi. Please allow me to treat you like my elder sister and call you jiji.'

The look on her face softened. 'You are after all Govind's sister, so naturally, you know your way to people's hearts.' She finally smiled, pulled me up, and hugged me. I felt relieved that I had been able to win Panchali's heart.

After her approval and blessings, a huge wedding ceremony was held in the palace of Indraprastha. Panchali dressed me up with her own hands and looked after everything from food to decorations, arranging musicians and dancers, and hiring a priest. I never thought I would find an older sister in her. The thought of her treating me like a sister filled my heart with immense love and respect for her. I promised myself to serve her in any possible way I could, and I would keep that promise till my last breath as I considered that my dharma.

Part II: Dignity

I listened to Arjun's war stories when I was pregnant. He told me about various war formations, and I remember him telling me once about one such war formation known as Chakravyuh. I listened to the details about the whole formation very intently—how to enter the Chakravyuh, how to make your way through the various levels, how to reach the centre unscathed, and how to beat the layers of soldiers to make your way through. It was all so fascinating. However, after a while, I started feeling a little sleepy and fell asleep.

'And that is how you come out of the Chakravyuh, isn't it magnificent? I was the one only in my class to learn this technique. Hey, are you listening?' Arjun was asking me in my dream, or was it reality? I could not tell the two apart. 'Hey, are you listening?' Arjun said again, and I saw him, he was standing in middle of thousands of soldiers. 'I was telling you something so important, and you fell asleep?' he questioned me.

I was about to call out to him, but suddenly he disappeared, and now where he was standing, stood a young boy, hardly fifteen or sixteen years old. His head was turned away, so I could not see his face. 'You should not have fallen asleep, Mother,' the boy said, turning his face towards me. I saw his face, grotesque, bloodied, and distorted. His body was full of stab wounds and arrows. I screamed. A scream so loud that screeched through all the heavens and hells. I woke up screaming, sweat dripping from my forehead, tears in my eyes. Arjun was calling out to me, 'Subhadra, it was just a dream. Calm down. I am right here, look.' Seeing him, I realized I had been screaming in my dream for a while. Crying, I fell into his arms. I did not realize then how important the information about the Chakravyuh was, not for me but for my only son. The lecture about getting out of the Chakravyuh would cost me the biggest treasure of my life. I remained unaware of that until it was too late.

During my pregnancy, Panchali and the others took great care of me. Panchali's little boys always kept me entertained for hours with their stories. 'When is the baby coming, Chotima?' Soon, I would say. Finally, the baby came. Holding him in my arms and looking at his face, I knew there was nothing more precious to me than this tiny human being. Eyes as kind and warm as his father's and a smile as mischievous and charming as his uncle's, Krishna.

'He is going to be the greatest warrior, Subhadra, just you watch,' Arjun chimed holding the baby.

'What should we name him?' asked Panchali looking at me. Krishna, who was playing with his baby nephew, answered quickly, 'Abhimanyu.'

Months went by. All was calm and peaceful. But a storm was stirring in the distant horizon, and all of us were unaware and hence unprepared. The storm came as an invitation. An invitation from Hastinapur.

'It is for some event that they are organizing there. A game of dice, if I heard right, is being organized there. They want to mend the differences between us,' Arjun told me that night.

I had a feeling that this was bad news. 'I don't think you should accept the invitation or go there. They have never been good to you till now. What makes you think that they are inviting you with good intentions?' I said in a concerned voice.

'It is the king that accepts the invitation. We have no say in that. Besides, brother Yudhishthir will never reject an invitation from King Dhritrashtra,' Arjun explained to me. My opinion and protest were not going to change anything.

We reached Hastinapur a week later. The city was marvellous, twice as big as Indraprastha. Huge markets, beautiful temples, colourful gardens with plants and trees across the lands. 'This city is beautiful, I know. But Indraprastha was just a barren land when they gave it to us. I was hopeless when I reached there the first time. But look now, the palace of Indraprastha is the most beautiful all around Bharatvarsh,' said Panchali proudly. She was in the palanquin alongside me.

I clasped her hands into mine. 'Only you could have done that, jiji.'

Panchali and I stayed in the same chamber for the three-day event in Hastinapur. The first day was all about festivities, full of feasting, music, dance, and entertainment. On the second day, things started stirring. Yudhishthir, the king of Indraprastha, the eldest of the Pandavas, indulged himself in a game of dice with the crown prince of Hastinapur, the eldest of the Kauravas and my ex-fiancé, Duryodhana. Alongside him was his uncle, Shakuni.

'He loves gambling, especially with the game of dice. He plays with me as well. He was quite shocked when I defeated him in our first game,' laughed Panchali.

'Gambling? Don't you have to put something at stake to play the game?' I questioned.

'Yes, money and other valuables,' answered Panchali.

Isn't 'valuables' a bit too vague a term? I wanted to ask her but decided otherwise.

The game had been going on for more than two hours. All the ladies in the chamber were chatting with each other when a guard came.

'Greetings to the queen of Indraprastha. You have been summoned to the assembly hall right away, Queen,' the guard said, bowing down.

Summoned to the assembly hall? But women were not allowed to enter the assembly hall when the men were playing games, I thought to myself.

Panchali asked the same question to the guard. The guard explained what had happened in the assembly. King Yudhishthir had lost everything, including the kingdom, the army, his brothers, himself, and even Panchali. He had justified putting his brothers and wife at stake by saying that they were valuable to him, and he was very proud of them.

I looked at Panchali, tears welling up in my eyes, and grasped her hand tightly. 'You don't have to go there. We are leaving right now. And if anyone tries to stop us, I know Arjun and the others will protect us. Let's go, jiji,' I pleaded to her. But she was stiff as a statue, her face red with anger, and tears rolling down her cheeks because of the great sorrow that had befallen her—or maybe it was embarrassment. What kind of man bets his wife in gambling? What is the point of having a great warrior and righteous king as your husband if they treat you like property that can be gambled? What were the elders of the family—the great Bhishma or the intelligent and kind Vidhur—doing when their daughter-in-law was being treated like that? All these questions were rising inside me. I did not need answers to them—right now I just wanted to do something for Panchali. She said something to the guard that I could not hear in my anger and confusion. The guard left. I hugged her tightly, tears rolling down our faces.

We were waiting for the guard to come back with answers, but he did not come. Instead of him, Dushasana, the younger brother of Duryodhana, came. He grabbed Panchali's hand and started dragging her with him. I ran after them, but the guards stopped me. I called her name and begged Dushasana to stop, but nothing worked. I fell to the ground weeping. I had never felt this helpless before. I kept praying to the gods for her well-being. 'Why aren't you here, Krishna dau?' I whispered to myself.

By the time she came back, I had lost track of time. Had it been one hour? Two hours? Thirty minutes? I didn't know, but it felt like an eternity. I ran towards her, but she stopped me, 'Not now, Subhadra. I want to be alone.' I looked at her, all her ornaments gone, her hair open, her face bruised, her sari askew. I clasped my mouth with my hands. I wanted to say something to her, but I couldn't. So, I left. I felt guilty for leaving her alone in this condition, but I knew she wanted that.

I ran to the men's chamber. 'Call Prince Arjun. Tell him his wife is here,' I ordered the guard.

He came out a few minutes later, his face unable to hide his embarrassment, his head hung low, and his eyes not looking into mine. 'What happened in the assembly? How can King Yudhishtir do that to his wife? Why didn't you stop him? You should have protected her.' Rage was building up inside me. He didn't answer, or perhaps he couldn't answer. I grabbed his shoulders and shook him. 'Answer me!' I yelled.

Finally, he told me. King Yudhishtir kept losing every game, and in the hope of winning his losses back every time, he kept betting. After he lost Panchali, the Kaurava brothers tried to disrobe Panchali in front of the entire assembly. Panchali, enraged, cursed the assembly with destruction and death. King Dhritarashtra begged Panchali to forgive them and assured her that all that was lost by King Yudhishthir would be returned to them. 'If they want all of that back, then they have to win it from me, Father,' declared Duryodhana. Another game of dice had been scheduled the next day to give a chance to King Yudhishthir to win everything back.

When he was finished describing the events, I stood there, stunned. 'Another game? What else does King Yudhishthir have to bet this time? And how are you planning to get Panchali's respect back, O great warrior?' I said to Arjun, unable to hide the sarcasm that came with it.

That night I couldn't sleep. I kept dreaming about the assembly and Panchali standing there, trying to protect herself. The walls of the assembly were burning, but nobody cared. They were all laughing and enjoying the scene, unaware of the fire that was soon going to engulf them all. Then I saw Krishna there, standing beside Panchali, covering her in bright, red light, a light so brilliantly bright that nobody could look at her.

The next day, another game of dice took place. This time everyone was present—the men, the women, the servants, and the sages. I was sitting right next to Panchali, holding her hand. But perhaps fate had already been decided by the gods above, for good or for bad. The Pandavas, or, should I say, King Yudhishthir, could not win back whatever he had lost the previous day. Prince Duryodhana laughed at their defeat and declared proudly, 'I wanted my cousins to win back whatever they had lost yesterday. But, as you can see, they could not. So, here's what I propose. The Pandavas and their wife Panchali go into exile for twelve years and spend one more year in Agyatvas. If they spend their Agyatvas undiscovered, they shall be given back their kingdom and army. On the other hand, if we find them during the Agyatvas period, they will be exiled for another twelve years and one year of Agyatvas.'

The entire assembly started whispering. Panchali's grip on my hand tightened. She wanted to protest. I wanted to too, but I knew it would be futile. How was an assembly that couldn't protect a woman from getting disrobed going to stop this unjust treatment?

'I accept your proposal. We will leave right away,' declared King Yudhishtir.

I looked at Arjun. 'What about me? Our son? You cannot accept your defeat this easily.' I looked at him and pleaded silently. He understood. He had a sad smile on his face and looked away. I would go wherever my husband went, I decided.

As soon as the assembly dispersed, I ran to catch Arjun. He saw me first and grabbed my hand to pull me into a quiet corner. 'I know what you are thinking, but I cannot allow you to come with us,' he said without even listening to me. Panchali always used to tell me that Arjun could understand what was going on in my mind just by looking at my face. I would just laugh it away. 'And with me, even if I tell him word for word, he would still mess it up,' she had said once, laughing, but I had sensed a tinge of sadness behind her laugh.

'But I want to. If Panchali can go with you, then why not me? I am not as weak as you assume me to be. I promise I won't be a burden. I know how to defend myself. I even know how to wield a sword. I know I would be helpful to you,' I said, my voice cracking.

'I know you are not weak, and that's exactly why I need you to stay here. I need you to take care of our sons, educate them, and train them for the upcoming war. And that cannot be done in a forest. I need you to give them a proper education, and Krishna and Dau Balaram to train them in war tactics,' he said holding my hands.

Upcoming war? Why would there be a war if the Pandavas fulfil the conditions of exile? I wanted to argue more and convince him to take me with them, but I also knew that no matter how hard I tried, Arjun would never let Abhimanyu, who was less than a year old, go through the hardships of exile. He loved Abhimanyu the most and wanted the best for his son. All my pleadings fell on deaf ears. Arjun did not allow me to go into exile with them. I stayed back with our sons and promised myself to give them the best training and education. And I promised to Arjun, in my heart, to wait for him. No matter how long it took, I would always wait for him.

The Pandavas and Panchali, dressed in simple clothes, were ready to leave for their exile. Panchali came to me and as we embraced, we both broke down. 'Take care of my sons, little sister. I request you,' she said.

'They are my sons too, jiji. Don't worry about them,' I assured her.

Arjun was busy with his brothers and talking to Bhishma. He looked at me from his corner and smiled at me brightly. Everything was going to be alright, it said. They were following their dharma. I had to follow mine.

After they left for their exile, I asked Bhishma to arrange for my departure to Dwarka. 'But why Dwarka? You can stay here. You are our daughter-in-law. I assure you that you and the children will not have any problems here,' said Dhritarashtra after he overheard my conversation with Bhishma.

'How can I stay with the same people who destroyed my happy family? And I also know how you treat your daughters-in-law. I would not stay at this place after knowing the reality of the Kaurava clan,' I jeered at him. I regretted talking to the old blind king like that, but my anger knew no bounds. Angry or ashamed, I did not know exactly what, but Dhritarashtra did not say anything further.

The chariot for my departure arrived soon after. I carried Abhimanyu in my arms and Panchali's sons walked beside me. I asked the charioteer to start driving. Thus, we left for Dwarka to spend the next thirteen years there. We reached Dwarka a few days later. When I got down from the chariot, Krishna was already standing in front of the Palace gates. I ran towards him and fell in his arms, sobbing miserably.

'Why did this happen, dau? What wrongs did I commit to be condemned to such grave misfortune?'

He caressed my hair with his palm. 'No, Subhadra. It is not your misfortune. You are leading this entire generation to its salvation. You are not yet aware of it, but it is for the greater good.'

Greater good? Salvation? I didn't care about those things. I only wanted to spend my entire life happily with Arjun and Abhimanyu.

Krishna probably understood what was going on in my mind. He said in a very calm voice, 'You are kind and courageous, and I know you will come out of this test stronger than before.'

Part III: Sacrifice

The days in Dwarka went by very slowly and very hurriedly at the same time. This was probably because the kids grew so fast or the war was coming, and I wanted it to arrive as late as possible. But, at the same time, I also wanted to meet Arjun. I wanted him to meet Abhimanyu and see what a great warrior he had become. He was kind-hearted and brave like his father and mischievous like Krishna. He called me Chotima, just like Panchali's sons, and loved his brothers more than his own life. I loved all these things about him,

I have raised him very well, Arjun, I whispered in my heart.

Twelve years had passed—one last year of Agyatvas, and it would be over. I spent my days reading, painting, and meditating, while the kids were away training with their uncles, Krishna and Balaram. When they came back from training, I would cook for them and spend time with them, telling them stories of their gallant fathers, the brave Panchali, and the birth of Krishna and his battles.

Finally, the last year was over too. The Pandavas finally came back to Dwarka. I welcomed them with proper rituals and introduced them to their children. When Arjun met Abhimanyu, he started crying and hugged him tightly.

'And who could you be? Making my husband cry like that?' Panchali asked teasingly.

'I am Abhimanyu, your youngest son, Mother. I will be the sword of my fathers and shield of my brothers,' he replied politely. Panchali smiled proudly and embraced him.

My beautiful, humble, and brave son, Abhimanyu, made me proud to be his mother. We spent the day talking and feasting. The Pandavas were sharing their stories of exile with their sons. Arjun came and sat beside me and told me he missed me every single day. I told him I missed him too. While I had suffered the pain of separation for thirteen years, this single thing he said to me made all the pain disappear, and I felt whole again.

The next day, the Pandavas sent word to Hastinapur that they were coming to claim what was rightfully theirs, but Duryodhana declined to give back their kingdom to them. He had found them before the Agyatvas was over; hence, they had to go back into exile again, he claimed. The messenger came back with this gloomy news.

This time, the Pandavas were sure that no matter how many more exiles they went through, Duryodhana would never give them back what was rightfully theirs. Hence, they consulted Krishna, and he told them that he would go to Hastinapur and try to convince Duryodhana. Duryodhana would not listen to Krishna either. As a last resort, on the advice of Krishna, the Pandavas started preparing for war.

While the war preparations were going on, King Virat came to pledge his allegiance to the Pandavas with his family. The Pandavas had spent their Agyatvas in King Virat's kingdom. Arjun had helped their son, Uttar, in protecting the kingdom from the army of Hastinapur while King Virat was away. However, the king and his wife had not come to just pledge their allegiance—they also wanted their daughter Uttara to marry our son Abhimanyu. So, the preparations for the wedding started.

Uttara was a sweet girl, kind and humble. She was perfect for my son. The wedding ceremonies were great distractions from the preparations for the upcoming war, but all good things come to an end—the wedding was over within three days, and everyone was back to war preparations.

The next few weeks went by fast. The men were busy with war tactics, acquiring weapons and allies, and strategizing their attacks and defence. The women, on the other hand, spent their time cooking favourite dishes for the men, doing puja for their well-being, and planning their course of action in case the Pandavas lost the war.

The war was due to begin in two days. Camps were being set near the warzone, where women and children could stay during wartime and welcome the warriors back in the evening. Panchali, Mother Kunti, Uttara, and I shared the same tent. Uttara was talking to Panchali, and I was watching her from my bed. How similar she was to me. My husband had to leave after a year of our marriage, and her husband, my son, was leaving her for the war within a month of their wedding. Both of us were carrying the burden of being the wives of the greatest warriors of the era. So, naturally, we were not supposed to be weak or emotional, but we still could not help but be worried about their safety and the outcome of the war. Panchali was worried too, but her desire for revenge surpassed her worry.

The war finally started. We could not see what was happening because our camps were at a safe distance, and every night the men would come and tell us about the war. A day felt longer than a year. What news would the evening bring with it? One week after the war had started, Uttara started feeling uneasy and nauseous. The healer came to check on her and announced that she was pregnant. I kissed her forehead and blessed her. A new life was growing inside her amid the horrifying dance of death. My son was going to be a father, and I was going to be a grandmother. My happiness knew no limitations that day. For a while, I even forgot about the war. I couldn't wait to tell Abhimanyu and Arjun.

After sunset, when the warriors came back from the battle, Panchali and I went running out of the tent to meet them and give them the good news. Their faces were dark and eyes red, cheeks stained with dry tears. It seemed they had aged several years within a day. I went straight to Arjun, unable to hide my excitement. 'You are going to be a grandfather very soon. And our lovely son is going to be a father.'

Arjun's eyes widened, and he fell to the ground wailing, a cry so horrible that I felt my heart would drop to the deepest trenches of my body.

'My Abhimanyu, my precious boy, they killed him,' he started screaming.

'No, that is not possible. Stop it. Where is my son? I need to tell him that he is going to be a father. Bring him here,' I cried.

Bhim, Arjun's elder brother, came forward, carrying a limp body. I could not recognize who the person was. His body was all bloodied, with wounds inflicted by sword, mace, arrows, and who knew what. His face was completely distorted, unrecognizable. Only a small gold ring that Abhimanyu had been given on his wedding day made me realize that the limp and distorted body was that of my son. They told me how he had been killed—that he was killed by treachery and deceit. When he entered the Chakravyuh, all of the Kauravas and their allies were waiting for him inside the vyuh and attacked him at once, a clear violation of war rules. I could not listen anymore. The entire world started spinning around me. I gasped for air and fell to the ground. Arjun held me in his arms, and we both cried.

'I will avenge my son. I swear on my life, Subhadra. I will,' Arjun said after a while, his voice resolute and loud.

That night, Uttara went down with a high fever after she got to know about her husband. The healer came and gave some herbs to bring her fever down. After a while, she fell asleep. I came out of the tent to meet Krishna. I ran into his arms and started crying, 'How much more do I have to sacrifice, dau? Is it not enough for the greater good? I don't want to lose Uttara and my grandchild also. Please protect both of them, dau, please,' I pleaded him.

'Stay strong, my sister. Uttara needs you to stay strong. Only you can be her strength, now and in the future,' he said calmly.

That's all you have to say to me, brother? I wanted to say, but I controlled myself. He always said things that held greater purposes. He wasn't the person who would say things just to make you feel good, my brother Krishna.

The war went on for more than two weeks, and, finally, Duryodhana was felled. The Pandavas won and avenged Panchali. The women were discussing the rituals for the War dead in the Jayantipuri camp when Dhrishtadyumna's charioteer came running to ask us to accompany him to the Asandivat camp, where the Panchalas and Panchali's sons slept.

We went there, and what we saw destroyed our entire world, the last hope that we were holding on to. Panchali's sons were lying on their beds, dead with their throats slit. Panchali fell to the ground and started wailing. I sat beside her and held her in my arms. I wanted to console her, but no words came out of my mouth. All my sons were dead—mine and my jiji's—all of whom I had raised with my strength and love. All gone in an instant. The Pandavas were talking to each other in a hushed voice, and they left together. Krishna also left with them. After a while, I brought the wailing Panchali back to our tent, away from the gruesome scene. She sat on the bed with Kunti on her side.

I went to Uttara to check on her. A few moments later, a light entered the tent, a bright white light, like a shooting star, and entered Uttara's womb. She started screaming in pain, putting her hands on her belly. I ran out to look for the healer, but I could not find them. Suddenly, I saw Krishna running towards our tent. I called out to him,

'Dau, something is wrong with Uttara. Please help her. The healer is not here. I don't know what to do.'

Krishna didn't reply but went past me into the tent. I went after him. He went to Uttara who was crying miserably and put his hand on her belly. After a while, he lifted his hand, and light emerged from her womb and dispersed into thin air. Uttara went quiet and her breathing relaxed. She joined her palms to thank Krishna, and he put his hand on her head and advised her to sleep. She fell asleep in an instant. I thanked God for keeping her safe.

'It was a Brahmastra, launched by Ashwatthama to avenge Duryodhana. He was the one who killed Panchali's sons. But he has been punished for his deeds,' informed Krishna.

After the eighteen-day-long war ended, we all headed to Hastinapur. The city looked as magnificent as ever, as if nothing had ever happened here. But the families who had lost their men in the war were mourning. And I could feel their pain. I had lost everything in the war too. My husband had won the war, but I knew he felt defeated as well. Not just him, but his brothers and Panchali too. And Uttara, how could I forget her? We all had lost someone precious in the war. But this new life that was growing inside Uttara—that little person was going to be the new start for all of us. Uttara eventually gave birth to a boy, Prakshit, and the silence in our lives was filled with his laughter. With each inch he grew in height, the happiness we had lost grew back by yards and miles. The upcoming years brought all the happiness that had been snatched away from us. Prakshit would grow up to be a great ruler and even a great warrior, the replica of my son Abhimanyu—brave, kind, and respectful.

Part IV: Reward

'You fought well, little sister,' said Krishna on the coronation day of Prakshit. 'You followed your dharma till the end, even though you had to sacrifice all you held dear to you. You see how important you have been in bringing closure to the Great War?'

Yes. I could see that, and for the first time after I lost Abhimanyu, I felt satisfied and calm. The role that I had to play in shaping the future of Hastinapur and the entire Bharatvarsh was finally coming to an end. 'Yes, dau, and I think I have done a good job in painting the canvas of my life with all the shades. What do you think?' I asked with a smile. Outside the window of the assembly hall where the coronation ceremony was going on, I could see the moon making its way through the dark clouds. Soon enough, it covered the entire sky and land in its bright, white light, shimmering through the lining of the clouds.

'The moon is required to guide the night towards the dawn,' Krishna had said once.

12

Bhanumati: A Matter of Consent

Shantheri Mallaya

She was born to the fiery, valorous tribe of the Kalingas, descendants of Kalinga, the third son of Sage Dirghatama. Her birth brought great joy to the kingdom of Kalinga, in particular to her father, King Chitrangada.

It was the morning of the season of spring. Chitrangada had just returned to Kalinga from a wedding in the neighbouring kingdom of Anga. Princess Sula, daughter of his eldest brother, Virasena, had been given away in marriage. When he saw the princess, he knew he wanted a daughter above all things. The queen of Kalinga, Rujapraksha, was expecting their first child. They had been childless for several years till Sage Narada paid the kingdom a visit and blessed them. The king recalled his words. 'O King, you will have four children—a daughter and three sons, nothing less.' Chitrangada was anxious for a child—not an heir in particular—but a daughter to cherish and love. Heirs would come and could wait.

During the time of his ancestors, Kalinga—the kingdom of the entire tribes of the Angas, Vangas, Pundras, and Suhamas—had extended from the mouth of river Ganga to the mouth of the river Godavari. So, overseeing, managing the kingdom, and conquering new places was Chitrangada's rajdharma, something he relished. But the birth of his first child was going to be very joyous too—something really special. He did not want to miss the occasion.

He was waiting to hear the news. The queen was in labour. He got off his royal chariot and walked post haste to the queen's chambers but was firmly stopped by Bala, a senior aide of the queen. 'You will have to wait, Your Highness,' she said.

The newborn let out a cry from the inner chamber, as if in clear announcement of its arrival. 'It is a girl,' Bala confirmed. Overjoyed, Chitrangada rewarded the maid who had brought the news from the queen's chambers with nine heavy gem-studded necklaces.

Maids blew the royal conches with joy, drums were beaten, and festivities were organized to celebrate the birth of the princess. It was vasanta, the season of spring, and a delighted Chitrangada decided to name his daughter Bhanuvasanta—the spring of joy—and called her Vasanta, the source of his happiness.

Little Vasanta remained her father's favourite child, though he had three sons soon after—Srutayu, Ajeya, and Yajapala. It was his firstborn who captured his heart and attention. When it came to Vasanta, Chitrangada left no stone unturned—be it getting her gurus to study the scriptures or to learn archery and horse riding. Vasanta took to everything with ease.

As they were fast growing up, Vasanta and her brothers enjoyed the freedom of Rajapura, the Kalinga capital, which had wide streets and a lush landscape with both sides dotted with trees.

Vasanta was now twenty-one years of age. Tall and lissom but a girl of not too many words. Yet when she spoke or laughed, the court bards swore that her voice sounded sweet and feminine.

One day, Chitrangada summoned her. 'Vasanta, my child, come here. I have something very important to discuss with you.'

Vasanta looked at her father quizzically. She had never heard such serious words from her indulgent father. Chitrangada sensed his daughter's confusion and broke into a smile. 'I am just eager to understand if the princess of Kalinga is ready to be wedded?'

Vasanta blushed and thought to herself, 'Ah, so this.' Her father noted her silence and gently said, 'Well, with your consent, we can call for your swayamvar—the best of kings and princes will be invited to vie for your hand.'

Vasanta smiled, nodded in consent, bent her head, bowed to her father, and walked out. Her mind was like a clean slate, with nothing written on it. She was yet to write the course of her life. But she was now beginning to feel a new trepidation, a new exhilaration—emotions that hitherto had been alien to her. She was yet to untangle her thoughts, one from the other.

Without a doubt, Vasanta had been lost in thought since the day her father revealed his intention for her swayamvar. Until that day, she had had no fixed notion about love of the non-filial kind, no particular dream or desire. But something had clearly stirred within her. She kept checking with her friend and closest confidante, her handmaid, Supriya.

'Supriya, who do you think will be the best suitor for me among all the great kings who will be present?'

Supriya would smile, think for a bit, and reply, 'O Princess, look inward. Your heart will tell you at that moment.'

Vasanta wondered what her heart would tell her. It seemed like she had been given a big decision to make—one that could be life-changing—but she had no idea what to do or how to go about it. She would often go to the prayer room in her chambers and look at the calm visage of Chamunda Devi, the *kuldevi* of the kingdom of Kalinga, to seek answers for a firm decision. Chamunda Devi was her solace, her guide, her friend, and played multiple roles in all times and situations.

Could she tell her mother about her fears? Her mother, Queen Rujapraksha, seemed oblivious to her daughter's anxieties and made herself busy with the preparations for the swayamvar. She looked extremely happy at the prospect of seeing her daughter wedded. Vasanta did not want to spoil her mother's bliss and kept silent. Supriya was her only solace during this uncertain phase.

Meanwhile, Vasanta observed the preparations get underway—invitations for the swayamvar, embossed in leaves of gold, were delivered to different kingdoms and were duly accepted. The kings, who were out on conquest, changed their course to Rajapura. The invitees travelled far and wide and started arriving at their kingdom a day prior to the swayamvar, along with an entourage of chariots, carriages, and soldiers. The hospitality at Rajapura was famed—luxurious chambers, handmaids in waiting, a smorgasbord of delicacies, and musical evenings—and the guests were in a state of anticipation. They could see mammoth preparations taking place and had heard of a grand arena being readied for the event.

The day of the swayamvar dawned. The kingdom of Kalinga was bright with decorations and festooned with flowers. The streets and markets were agog with the excitement of the big event. The royal palace was decorated; the court and the chambers were dazzling. The air was vibrant with joy.

Vasanta was attired in bright red and green. She was excited, with only a tiny trace of nervousness. She went to her parents' chamber to take their blessings.

Vasanta's brothers welcomed the invitees from the different kingdoms across Bharatavarsh. The sounds of chariots, horses, and entourages filled the air.

Chitrangada assumed his seat on the throne. The royal ladies and their entourage sat to the left of the court arena, a level above. The invitees were seated all across the vast arena in multiple rows. Chitrangada rose and greeted everyone. 'Dear kings and princes from lands far and wide, I extend my warmest welcome and sincere gratitude to all present here for honouring my invitation. Today, the princess of Kalinga will choose her partner from one among you, and it will be our privilege to give her away in marriage.'

Cheers followed this welcome. Vasanta caught a quick glance in her father's direction, could see Chitrangada beaming, and intuitively sensed that he was inwardly hoping for a quick decision on her part.

Suddenly, there was a loud chant of 'Narayan, Narayan.' The chant was unmistakably that of Sage Narada's.

Chitrangada rose, stepped down from his throne, and rushed to greet the divine sage, 'O Narada, we are blessed to have you here!'

Narada greeted him in return, 'O King, may the gods and rishis shower their blessings on you and all in your lineage. I was passing by during my sojourns, and I heard about Princess Vasanta's swayamvar and thought I should come by and bestow my wishes upon her. It has been years since I last came to Kalingapura.'

On hearing this, Vasanta made her way towards Narada and bowed down to him with respect. She was accompanied by two of her handmaids. Narada took one look at the princess and said gently in a paternal voice, 'Ah, here she is. She is indeed beautiful, a Chandramukhi, as in the stories that I had heard about her. May she choose the best man here.'

Chitrangada beamed and Vasanta smiled demurely, the trepidation in her heart concealed. She exuded the composure that was expected of a princess. As she turned to make her way back, the sage turned, leaned, and with a cryptic smile, whispered into her ear, 'However, O Princess, be wary of the arrogant. They will try to coerce you.'

At that moment, the hall stood still for the princess. Vasanta's heart raced, while she scanned quickly for the faces she saw as the suitors for her hand—the huge assembly right across the other side of the area. Nothing seemed to register amid the sea of faces. Supriya held her hand reassuringly to calm her down. The celestial sage left the hall, calmly chanting 'Narayana' on his way out. Vasanta felt a strange sense of foreboding.

She stood rooted to her place till she heard her name being called by her father. He was beckoning to her to step into the arena. Conches were blowing, and it was time for her to make a decision. Taking a sharp breath, she walked out into the open with Supriya and her bodyguards in tow. She walked slowly, taking her time. It was still morning, but the rays of the sun were strong on her face.

The bodyguards were slowly telling her the names of the kings, princes, and their lineage as she passed each person. Vasanta could hear the names of the mighty kings—Shishupala, Jarasandha, Bhishmaka, Vakra, Kapotaroman, Nila, Rukmi, Sringa, Asoka, and Satadhanwan being called out. The guard described each of them as proud, brave, and strong. She was processing the descriptions while she looked at each one of them and wondered if they were really brave, valorous, mighty, and strong. What qualified for such descriptions or eulogies for these men, she thought to herself, as she slowly made her way past the assembly. Was it the fact that they had huge kingdoms to rule? Or was it because they were brave hearts who went to war without a second thought? Or was it their physical strength that was being celebrated as 'valour'? She was mildly amused at her own train of thought during such an important moment. 'Wait, was she imagining the downcast faces of these grand names as she crossed them? Was rejection a tough pill for them to swallow?' she thought to herself, but these were just vague tangles within her mind.

She had to choose someone, and that was her big challenge. Sage Narada's words kept coming back worryingly to her mind, and she tried to turn them away. The sage was known for his sense of subtle, naughty, and sometimes wicked humour. *Was he trying one of those famed tricks on me? Yes, that is what it is.* Vasanta convinced herself but in vain, as she kept walking slowly.

As she moved further, she could hear the guard's voice reeling off names like he was reading out from a leaf. She kept advancing as she caught glances of kings and princes looking at her expectantly, as she was nearing them and then with disappointment as she walked past them. She thought to herself, 'What if I were to reach the end of these vast arrays of suitors and choose no one?' Fear and trepidation gripped her heart.

Vasanta kept moving on, her face so calm that no one had an inkling of what was going on within her. It was then, she heard a name from the bodyguard. 'O Princess, this is the Prince of Hastinapur, Duryodhana, the eldest son of King Dhritarashtra and Queen Gandhari. Mighty and valorous, he wields the mace as if he were born with it. The yoddha next to him is his bosom friend, the King of Angada, the invincible Karna, who has accompanied him to the swayamvar.'

Vasanta heard this and raised her head slightly to see the face. She saw the face of a man, handsome she felt, but exuding arrogance and gazing at her with desire, and the man next to him, equally striking in looks but with a nonchalant air about him. Her head bent and her cheeks burning mildly, she started to walk away when she heard a thunderous voice. Her heart beat wildly, and she turned back to see the Prince of Hastinapur, Duryodhana, his voice bellowing and eyes glazing with anger. Before she realized, he held her by the wrist in a vice-like grip. She couldn't bear to meet his angry gaze. This was a face that had been filled with desire just a few minutes ago. She found herself being pulled, much as she was resisting him. Supriya was also pushed in along with her by the King of Angada, Karna. The crowds that had gathered broke into chaos, and the other invitees were pulling out their weapons. She could see Chitrangada's and Rujapraksha's faces wrought with panic. There was consternation in the air. Vasanta could perceive the nonchalant prince of Angada, shielding her, Supriya, and Duryodhana, and challenging the august gathering, 'He who dares to step forward to prevent us from leaving the place will have to face me.'

Several kings came forward. Karna rained arrows that created a shield, preventing the assembly from coming towards them. The four of them reached Duryodhana's chariot. Duryodhana commanded the charioteer, 'Let's leave. Rein in the horses!' Vasanta found herself lifted by Duryodhana and, standing beside him, Karna followed suit, lifting Supriya, but he was also busy keeping the hordes of people running behind the chariot at bay. There were a few more carriages attached to Duryodhana's—all vigilant, led by Duryodhana and Karna, the fiery Kuru army showering a rain of arrows at the crowd chasing them. People sprang up from everywhere. Rajapura was not going to let its princess go away so easily.

She saw her brothers chasing them in chariots for a very long time. Ajeya was livid, and Yajapala looked like he would kill Duryodhana in an instant. She had seen Srutayu engage Karna in a fierce arrow duel, till Karna managed to stop the Kalinga prince's chariot midway by stringing an arrow to his chariot wheel, damaging it beyond repair. She saw, with unending dismay, her brother's angry, panicky look, and wrung her hands in momentary despair. 'This cannot be happening! What will befall me now?'

She could vaguely register Karna and Duryodhana showering arrows, ably supported by the Kuru soldiers. After what seemed like endless time, the crowds began to disappear. Many were lying injured by arrows that had been aimed at their feet; others were bidding their return back home, once they realized that their chase was futile.

Soon, the fleeing carriages picked up pace, gathering clouds of dust along the way. Vasanta and Supriya were in a daze. It dawned on them that they had been abducted by the prince of Hastinapur, Duryodhana, and his friend, Karna. Sage Narada's words had come true—the arrogant had indeed achieved their goal by coercion.

The sky was overcast. There was a long journey ahead. Vasanta was silent. After the initial shock, she regained composure. She was observing the two men and could see Duryodhana looking stoic but a little guilt-faced. Karna appeared calm and unruffled.

Her thoughts were a quagmire. Should she have challenged her abductors to a duel? Would that have been pragmatic? Or would that have helped her escape their clutches? There were no easy answers to the questions that welled up in her exhausted mind. Challenging the two warriors would have meant further humiliation to her father. However, silently submitting to the abduction was also hurting her pride. She wondered if her brothers would ever have to think and analyze so much if they had to face a similar situation. She could visualize Srutayu, Yajapala, and Ajeya retaliating without a care. Her mind already knew the answer. She was steadily realizing that women had to face their circumstances a little differently despite all the privilege, love, and care they might have received. She sighed, as she knew that she had to accept the situation and behave accordingly. She was a princess, and now was her time to show her abductors that she was not a mere little girl from Kalinga who was afraid. 'No, I am tougher than that,' she said to herself inwardly.

The carriages journeyed through day and night. She was tired and fell asleep on the carriage seat. Supriya stood all the while, stoic in her silence too. Duryodhana then arranged for one of the carriages in his entourage to be made into a small chamber and turned to Vasanta, 'O Princess, you may make yourselves comfortable in this chamber.' Vasanta nodded, and walked slowly into the chamber carriage, followed by Supriya. The Kuru carriages had spare food supplies that kept the group going. They passed through fields, water, jungles, roads, and small villages. Vasanta could hear Duryodhana's rough voice commanding one carriage to go ahead to Hastinapur and relay the message of their impending arrival and the events that had taken place. Her mind was filled with an emotion that she knew she had never experienced in full measure: anger towards the conceited prince. But the wave of resentment receded, and she soon became calm again.

Vasanta lost track of time, seated inside her makeshift chamber, her thoughts in a race beneath the calm she showed. What would be her future? While she had had no particular ideas about her life or the man she would wed, she had not expected to be lifted off like this. She had taken one look at the face of Duryodhana and decided she would not wed him. It was instinctive. But, strangely, there was a pull she felt towards the face. Had it been less arrogant or had the man been gentler, perhaps she would have chosen him in the first instance. Anyway, there was no looking back now. If she had to marry Duryodhana, then she knew what had to be done. Supriya held her hand, their unspoken word a pact of silence. Vasanta closed her eyes in silent prayer to Chamunda Devi, her force of strength.

The carriage was journeying north for days, stopping by villages and towns of various kingdoms for refreshments. They were treated with respect wherever they went. Vasanta sensed people knew their identity. She was trying hard to keep her sense of direction. They were heading to Hastinapur, she knew. The long journey was scary. She had never set foot outside Rajapura before. Supriya's constant presence was soothing and gave her a sense of equilibrium. 'All is not lost,' she thought. She hardly spoke to Duryodhana and Karna during the journey. They were respectful and seemed to keep out of her way. Vasanta and Supriya were hosted in the royal guest chambers of visiting kingdoms. Different lands, different people. Vasanta felt drained at times trying to understand the nuances of the diverse places, the clothes, the dialects, and the food. Other times, she was excited. All that she had learnt with her gurus was standing her in good stead. She was able to cope since she was trained in the art of studying direction. Hence, she could keep track of the course of their journey.

When they reached Mathura, Vasanta particularly enjoyed the warmth and hospitality of the Yadava king, Sakhasena, and his queen, Rukma, where they were stationed for two nights. The senior aide to the queen taught Supriya the art of braiding hair, and soon Vasanta had her hair braided in a long loose plait. The queen gifted her with gems, clothes, and a fruit case for the journey. The queen also gave her some parting maternal counsel. 'O Vasanta, you have come this far with a man you know nothing about. The prince of Hastinapur will make a good husband. Accept this as your destiny. Every woman in this position does.' Vasanta listened to her quietly and smiled as she walked into the carriage that was to be her abode till they reached Hastinapur. Yes, the queen was right—she had made a long expedition with a man she knew nothing about. The very thought sent mild shivers down her spine.

Two more days passed by as they crossed dense jungles, stopping by a small village only during one of the nights. She had become used to the sounds of the wild animals in the jungle. Karna's presence made her feel safe. She could not fathom the reason for her affinity towards the king of Angada. It was not a romantic attraction. It was a strange deference, an emotion she was not experiencing for Duryodhana. Perhaps it was Karna's calm bearing and a sense of mystery about his birth, the stories of which she had heard. Or perhaps it was his loyalty towards Duryodhana. Vasanta's curiosity was piqued. She whispered to Supriya quite often during the weeks, 'Angada raja is no ordinary man. I would like my brothers to blossom into warriors like him.'

Soon, as the hours passed, she got the sense they were nearing their destination. She was not wrong. After what seemed like a month by her count from the time they had left Kalinga, the carriages started slowing down again and appeared to be entering onto more even roads. She looked out and saw that the path led up to a grand-looking palace. Supriya peeped from the makeshift chamber window and asked the charioteer, 'Where are we?'

The charioteer responded, 'In Hastinapur, the land of the Kurus.' On hearing this, Vasanta nodded. She felt a sudden longing for her natal realm and felt a twinge thinking of her parents, brothers, and her people. She had travelled several thousand miles away from them. Would she ever see them again? Would she ever feel the warmth of the love of her people? The words of Queen Rukma had reverbated in her mind since the days she left Mathura. The moment was dense with unanswered questions and decisions that threatened to overpower Vasanta, but she held herself together with a deep breath and a knowing gaze at Supriya. She had been trained in breath control and exercised the skill now.

Vasanta heard the chamber door open, and her name being called. Duryodhana was standing outside the chamber and looking at her. Her gaze towards him was unwavering. He was trying to look unresponsive, and not succeeding too well. Beside him was Karna, still and calm. The two men did look war-weary but still very alert and strong.

She could see a huge palace in front of her. Hordes of sentries dotted both sides outside the palace entrance, and an array of maids was approaching her. They bowed to Duryodhana, Karna, and her in unison. Duryodhana commanded, 'Take the princess and her companion to the finest chambers in the palace and take care of their comfort.'

The maids accompanied Vasanta and Supriya. The princess walked once again with a slow, measured gait, never losing her composure. She could not let herself, or the Kalingas, down.

The chambers were exotic—the walls were made of granite, marble, gems, and rubies. Large paintings adorned the walls, huge lamps of gold opened up from the ceiling, and smooth veils—functioning as curtains—separated the inner chamber from the outer. Her tired eyes were slowly taking in the splendour of her surroundings. Rajapura was quite austere in comparison to Hastinapur, she felt. Strangely, she was too fatigued to feel overawed.

There was a huge bathpool ready for her. The maids helped her get ready. She was adorned in rich bottle green garments and jewellery to match. She looked at herself in the mirror.

A maid walked in and announced, 'O Princess, the Queen of Hastinapur, Gandhari, mother of Prince Duryodhana, wishes to see you. You may please step out, and we will take you to the queen's court chamber.' Vasanta's heart beat fast—this was the moment she was waiting for. She nodded to Supriya, and the maid led them through a maze. There were turns and twists to the route. She was no stranger to palace architecture, and during these weeks, she had come across many palaces, but this was different and magnificent, a little intimidating. Vasanta restrained herself from wanting to touch the walls, the curtains—there was a girlish curiosity to feel everything, but her royal deportment prevented her from doing so.

They reached the queen's court chamber. Vasanta's name was announced, and she was led in by a couple of maids who appeared from inside. As she walked into Gandhari's court chamber, she saw a lady, with streaks of silver hair, in loose royal robes. Vasanta felt she looked very elegant as the lady approached her. She was blindfolded in a rich silken scarf. Vasanta bowed, thinking to herself, 'Ah, so here is the famous queen, who had blindfolded herself because she did not want to see or enjoy a world her husband could not see.'

Gandhari sensed her presence and came forward to greet and bless her. Vasanta was amazed at her steady, unwavering steps. She spoke in a tongue whose vowels were slightly alien to Vasanta, but she comprehended the language. She reflected, 'The people of Kalinga speak in a slower tone, while the people of Hastinapur speak in a faster tone. Queen Gandhari belongs to the land of Gandhara, which is again a land far away, and her voice still carries the distinct flavour of her birth land.' Vasanta was discerning in languages and the use of words based on the various places she had crossed over the weeks and was pleased that she had learnt something after all. A month was a long time.

Gandhari's voice broke into her thoughts, 'O Princess of Kalinga, it is our pleasure to have you here. I apologize for my son's haste and conduct. Please accept my sincere apologies for his behaviour.'

Vasanta was not expecting this. She marvelled at the grace of the older woman. She replied softly but firmly, 'O Queen, I thank you for your words and the hospitality of the Kurus. A deed once done is done. But I have a wish—I seek the audience of the famed elders of the Kurus and the presence of the prince who brought me here. I will speak to him in the presence of everyone so that there is no assumption about my acceptance or rejection of my situation.'

She noticed that Gandhari was struck by the firmness in her voice. The queen sighed, and replied, 'O Princess Vasanta, you shall have your wish fulfilled.'

Gandhari asked all the Kuru elders—Bhishma, Drona, Vidura, Dhritarashtra, and Prince Duryodhana—to assemble in her court chamber.

They came into her chambers post haste, barring Duryodhana. It was not every day that the reticent Gandhari called for people into her chamber.

On seeing the presence of so many stalwarts, Vasanta's heart lurched with nervousness, if only for a split second. She drew a deep breath and was back to being placid and composed. She knew she could not allow any signs of weariness to take over.

Vidura broke the silence and brought her out of her momentary reverie 'O Princess of Kalinga, please accept Vidura's welcome to you. I hope your stay here has been comfortable so far. We hear you wished to speak to all of us.'

Vasanta looked at the man who addressed her. His eyes seemed to brim with wisdom, deep as the ocean. Strangely, she felt she could trust him. She bowed to all, starting with Bhishma and ending with Vidura, and said, 'I bow to you all and thank you all for the welcome and for making time to meet me. But I await the Prince of Hastinapur. I desire to confer with him in your presence.'

She looked at Bhishma, grey-haired, but dignified with an aloof air about him. She could not gauge his thoughts. She could see him watching her in a detached manner. There was a movement outside the court chamber. Duryodhana and Karna walked into the chamber. Duryodhana glanced at Vasanta and smirked, 'I hear the Princess of Kalinga has called for our presence. And so, here we are, present before you.'

Vasanta looked at him, facing him squarely, her gaze unflinching. Her eyes were calm but unwavering, a gaze that made Duryodhana squirm a little, or so she felt. Karna appeared indifferent as if saying, 'Do not hold me to anything that happened—I have done nothing.' She looked at him a little puzzled and disappointed, unable to understand this studied nonchalance from a man who had fought so valiantly for his friend while abducting her. She thought, 'Am I expecting too much of an emotion or reaction from this man? Why would he talk on my behalf anyway? We are not related in any way.' The rationale gave her a sense of balance. She turned her gaze swiftly back to Duryodhana and asked him in an unruffled and clear voice, 'Prince of Hastinapur, what was the provocation for the act you committed? Is it honourable for a prince of your stature to abduct a woman and bring her to a strange land to wed her against her wish?'

Vasanta was watching the prince closely. Duryodhana was evidently stunned by the boldness of the princess. He could feel her questioning look, almost accusing him and coercing an answer. Vasanta could see the nonplussed expressions of the others present in the chamber, all trained on Duryodhana. He had to respond. He looked at his friend, who calmly nodded at him. The prince gathered his wits and looked straight at Vasanta while responding, she felt, with a touch of his quintessential arrogance, 'Princess, I kept with the tradition of the Kurus. I did no wrong in bringing a woman I desire along with me. I have not touched you even once. I will wed you and make you my queen. I will honour our dharma.'

Tradition of the Kurus! Dharma! All eyes went to Bhishma now, including that of Vasanta. Duryodhana continued, turning to Bhishma with a dramatic flourish, 'My great-granduncle, Bhishma, who you see standing there, set an example to us when he brought in the princesses of Kashi for his brother. Rajamatas Ambika and Ambalika set foot on this soil to wed grandsire Vichitravirya. So, I have just carried out what was expected of me.'

Vasanta could hear the small gasps that followed Duryodhana's words. Gandhari looked stricken, and so did Dhritarashtra. Vidura became thoughtful. Drona looked away. Bhishma was thoughtful but calm. Vasanta smiled and responded, 'Well, that was a great analogy to give in order to justify your action. But do you recall what befell their sister, Princess Amba?'

The people in the chamber now realized this was no ordinary girl who was in their midst. She was a wise, spirited young woman who was very clear about what she wanted. She did not want to be married to Duryodhana, not without a true reconciliation of the past.

Vasanta caught Karna gazing at her with admiration—the indifference had turned to a look of genuine respect. She felt a keenness to know him better and was tempted to draw him into a conversation, but her better sense told her to save any possible interaction with the king of Angada for the future. *There is time for this, but I am going to talk to him undoubtedly.*

Meanwhile, she saw Bhishma flinching, his face contorted into sadness. He had been reminded of an event he wished to forget.

Vasanta continued to stand her ground, calm and demanding an answer. Supriya was by her side, smiling victoriously, evidently proud of the princess and her stance. Duryodhana did not seem to have an answer. The chamber was still, eerily quiet. Bhishma's booming baritone broke the silence, as he turned to look at Vasanta. 'O Princess of Kalinga, the daughter of Chitrangada, it is true that I did bring the princesses of Kashi here against their will. And it is indeed true that Princess Amba resisted the move and asked to go back to the man she loved. And when he refused to marry her, she came back to me and asked me to marry her. How could I? I am under an oath of celibacy. So, when I refused her, she consumed herself in flames. Yes, I regret what happened to her. Princess, I do not wish for any of that to be repeated again, ever.' His eyes were moist, as he recalled the past. It was as if he were uttering the rhetoric to himself.

Gandhari let out a soft sigh. She seemed to be speaking to herself too. 'No, this cannot happen again.' With a sense of urgency, she rushed towards Vasanta and clasped her hands. 'O Princess, do not, do not repeat the actions of Amba. I beseech you.'

Vasanta's eyes softened, and she looked at the Queen calmly. 'O Queen, I do not wish to humiliate anyone here, nor will I consume myself in flames. I want the Prince of Hastinapur to come up to me and ask me if I wish to marry him by my will and consent. I will answer him.'

While her gaze remained steady, Duryodhana appeared dumbfounded. Vasanta could see Vidura, Bhishma, and Drona, in turns, subtly signalling to him to accede to her request.

Vasanta waited. Her eyes were fixed on Duryodhona. His dilemma was quite unmistakable. His ego battled with his longing for her. The princess of Kalinga had won his heart with her fearlessness, sense of propriety, and fairness. The prince seemed to be in a different mood altogether. He finally turned towards Vasanta and said evenly, 'O Princess of Kalinga, I realize I brought you here against your wishes. I was bewitched by your presence and angered by your rejection. I regret my deed. I still desire to wed you. Will you consent to be my wife?'

Vasanta smiled. One part of her was expecting an angry walkout by the prince, but here was the other part—the part that she wanted. He was actually asking for her forgiveness and in an amicable manner! It was then that Vasanta made up her mind—all her misgivings dissolved with his charming honesty. She could feel his struggle while he let go of his ego. She turned to face him and responded with a full smile.

'Prince of Hastinapur, I appreciate your apology and the fact that you have asked me for my consent. I would be very happy to wed you and become the princess of Hastinapur.'

The others were overjoyed. Duryodhana gazed at his wife-to-be and said, 'I will take your consent for one more thing. Your face radiates the warmth and loveliness of the sun. Hence, it is my wish to call you Bhanumati, the sun-faced queen of my heart.'

Vasanta nodded in agreement and said, 'O Prince, it is my heart's desire that my parents and my brothers should be present at the wedding. If they could be invited to the occasion with all honour…'

Vidura stepped in and assured her, 'It goes without saying, Princess. We shall send word to them immediately. It will be our good fortune to have the royal family of Kalinga take part in the grand wedding.'

The palace was soon abuzz with the news that Prince Duryodhana and Princess Vasanta were to wed. As Vasanta desired, Chitrangada, Rujapraksha, and the princes of Kalinga came and partook in what was one of the finest wedding festivities Hastinapur had ever seen. The streets were filled with banquets, flowers, and token jewellery for all the people—rich and poor alike. Kings and princes from far and wide came in attendance. No one had completely forgotten the excitement or the humiliation of the abduction drama that had happened right under their noses. But, when a wedding was announced by the mighty Kurus, all rancour dissolved. Some of the kings had already opened their kingdoms to Duryodhana during the journey from Kalinga to Hastinapur. Allegiances were strong; no one wished for uncalled-for enmity with the Kurus.

As the day of the wedding dawned, Bhanuvasanta was bedecked as a Kuru bride ought to be. After a magnificent wedding ceremony, she became Bhanumati, the wife of

Duryodhana. She was also doubly happy that Supriya continued to be her chief maid-in-waiting and soon wedded Viloma, the chief of the Hastinapur palace guards. Bhanumati stepped wholeheartedly into her new life, as the princess of Hastinapur and as the queen of Duryodhana's heart.

13

Malayadwaja: The Story of a Forgotten Warrior

Rajesh Ramachander

It was a luminous nightfall over five thousand years ago, and Prince Malayadwaja stood gazing at the banks of the Tungabhadra River. Standing on the shore, he watched the waves roll in and break without piling up on the bank. He noticed a long glitter trail glistening in the water. Above the lake, the waxing moon gleamed and shone with such purity that it brought joy to his soul. The night before an oncoming battle and the beautiful scenery offered an excellent provocation in the prince's mind. Should he bask in the splendour of the scene, or should he be contemplating the next day's conflict on the battlefield?

His thoughts were interrupted when Duta arrived beside him. The forty-year-old charioteer of the prince also doubled as a trusted advisor.

'Prince, pardon my interruption. I want to share the king's final decision on your war participation,' said Duta.

Taking a deep breath and turning slowly towards Duta, the prince said, 'Duta, I can already foresee the message you carry. The king has deliberated on it since we marched off from Madurai. I believe he does not want me to go into battle with him tomorrow. Isn't this what you want to say to me?'

The prince noticed the composure on Duta's face. But, at the same time, Duta saw the disappointment on the prince's face.

Duta said, 'Yes, the king's decision after much considerations must also be for the good. Significantly, one cannot disregard that you are the only heir to the throne. Furthermore, you are inexperienced in actual combat. In contrast, the Yadava prince, Krishna, is skilled in the art of war and is renowned for performing sorcery on the battlefield. Until now, no one has been able to trounce him on a battlefield. So, one cannot fault the king's judgement in this matter.'

Hearing the words of Duta, Malayadwaja felt a glorious battle victory snatched away from him. Frustrated, he turned back to look at the moon again. But, unfortunately, it had disappeared into the clouds, hurried by the wind. By then, Duta also left the place.

Malayadwaja, the Chandravanshi prince of the Pandyan kingdom, was twenty years of age, long-haired, with sunken cheeks, tall, solid, and well-built. He was the spitting image of his father, King Kulasekhara Pandyan, but a younger version. He had undergone rigorous training as a warrior. However, he had never been in a real battle before.

The Pandyan army battlegrounds were on Kishkinda, bordering the northern banks of the Tungabhadra River. The place, a neutral territory, was agreed upon as the site for the war by both sides. The Pandyan army was gearing up to fight a war against the Yadavas led by Krishna the next day.

The next day, the prince woke up too early for there to be any light. Mornings were his alone time when he could practice martial arts, bathe, dress up, and worship the rising sun on the eastern horizon. He left his quarters every day only after performing his religious routines at daybreak.

Duta drove the prince in a chariot towards a large canopy amid the camp to meet the king. On his way, the prince noticed a sea of modest shelters and legions of soldiers ready in battle gear. They were cheering and praying to their gods. Next, the prince saw his father, King Kulasekhara, mounting a giant war elephant that had kneeled. He always admired the warrior in his father. His father looked splendid to him in full battle gear as if fully set to annihilate the enemy.

'Son, I am off to the battlefield and intend to crush the enemies. I will capture Prince Krishna before the day ends,' said King Kulasekhara, smiling at his young son.

The prince's eyes lit up, and he spoke to the king.

'Father, that would be an astonishing sight indeed. But unfortunately, you have denied me the joy of witnessing the destruction of our enemies,' said the prince.

As soon as the prince said this, his father's smile disappeared.

'Son, this battle can go either way, as we have a formidable foe. I have already lived fifty summers in my life. If God forbid, I perish in this war, I can go away with some peace knowing that Madurai's future is safe in your hands,' said King Kulasekhara.

Malayadwaja, on the chariot, gazed up at his father, King Kulasekhara, who was seated on his war elephant.

'Father, I know that you always have my security and the well-being of Madurai uppermost in your mind. However, If I am not going to the battlefield, I prefer not to be idle in the camp. So please give me orders for any other assistance I can provide,' replied the prince.

'Son, you need to promise me that you will not leave the camp until the war ends. Take care to ensure that our war supplies reach the frontlines. Our armies will return to the base every day at sunset after the battle. So, nurse our injured soldiers with medicines and help cremate the fallen as if you are their son and their brother,' said the king before instructing the mahout to march ahead.

Malayadwaja stood there watching the king, his commanders, and the enormous army marching into the battlefield on elephants, horses, and foot. After nearly an hour, he heard distant battle conches and looked up to see the turquoise heavens turn ash grey. He sensed right away that the war had begun in earnest. Prince Malayadwaja ensured arms, food, water, and weapon supplies reached the soldiers on the battlefield. The first day of the battle was over, and there wasn't any breakthrough for the Pandyan king. Malayadwaja nursed injured soldiers and attended to cremating many fallen soldiers after sunset. It pained him to see so many in the Pandyan army lose their life on the very first day.

Before departing for the battlefield on the second morning, the king summoned his only offspring to meet him privately in his camp abode.

'Today, son, I'm going to give it my all. If I don't return, the war ends at that point. You will inherit my kingdom.'

'Father, please do not so much as utter such unfortunate words. I have prayed to God, seeking His blessings for your success in this war,' said the prince.

The king said, 'This is a war where I am not on the side of dharma. Therefore, even asking for God's blessing for victory is disgraceful, as I invited this war on myself by summoning Krishna to fight here.'

A surprised Malayadwaja looked at his father in disbelief as he heard this admission of the king.

'I did this to fulfil a vow made to a dear friend and the emperor of Magadha, King Jarasandha. Krishna is the archenemy of my old friend, King Jarasandha. Jarasandha, endowed with riches, strength, and greatness, wants to retake Mathura and slay Krishna to avenge the death of his wicked son-in-law, King Kamsa,' said Kulasekhara in a low voice.

The prince looked at his father intently, as if asking why he had to take the side of Jarasandha, even knowing that his friend was not on the side of dharma.

Sensing the unspoken words of the prince, the king said, 'I can guess your curiosity. My promise to Jarasandha binds me. Not even the gods can stop me from fighting this war. I was once a fellow student at a gurukul along with Jarasandha. I had unwittingly given him the oath to fight on his behalf whenever summoned. So, Jarasandha invoked my vow to him, and he has asked me to fight Krishna now.'

The prince felt like a giant boulder was crushing him, and he thought, 'Is the impossibility of victory staring at my father?'

'Krishna is invincible and is dharma himself. He could have won the war yesterday, but he spared me so that I live for another day. One thing I am certain of is that he wouldn't annex our kingdom even if he slays me,' said the king.

The words now sounded very ominous to the prince. The king got up to leave for the battlefield. However, the prince still stood frozen.

It was late afternoon that day, and Malayadwaja became restless in the camp as he strongly suspected something grave had happened to his father. A squad of soldiers returned to the camp at that point and bowed before the prince. 'We have some awful news for you, Prince. The war is over. The king is no longer with us. Long live the king!'

Malayadwaja's worst fears had come true.

'No!' He let out a sorrowful cry. 'This can't be true,' he cried in disbelief.

He decided to enter the battlefield. So, he mounted his chariot, drew his sword, and Duta steered the chariot towards the battlefield.

The hard realization that his father had passed away pained the prince to the core, and his body trembled. He wanted to see his father and began to recall their time together. All the times they had been together raced through his mind. But, as Duta drove the chariot nearer to the battlefield, the prince was already welling up with tears. He saw a bloody sight on the battlefield. Loud groans of injured soldiers and sounds of pain and sorrow all around filled the air. Duta skilfully manoeuvered the chariot amidst the corpses of soldiers on the ground, bringing it to a slow halt in front of a small band of Pandyan soldiers standing guard over the fallen king in a large ring formation. Malayadwaja's heart sank when Duta stopped closer to the ring. He saw his father's torso inside the circle, with the severed head lying adjacent to it. King Kulasekhara lay dead, slain by Krishna. Malayadwaja alighted from the chariot and walked towards his fallen father. Then, choking with grief and pain, he kneeled and screamed in pain, holding his father's head on his thighs.

The prince's grief turned into a rage. His eyes became bloodshot red. All he could think of was now to take revenge on Krishna. The surviving Pandyan soldiers quivered upon seeing the prince's wrath. Malayadwaja then rose and climbed back onto the chariot. He furiously blew his war conch, challenging the retreating Yadava army to turn around and fight.

The victorious Yadavas walking away would not turn around to fight unless their supreme commander, Prince Krishna, ordered them. Kritavarma, a seasoned warrior and confidant of Krishna, looked at Krishna, who was on a chariot, watching the unfolding scene on the battlefield.

'Kritavarma, counsel the grieving Prince Malayadwaja against fighting a battle that might result in his destruction,' said Krishna.

Nodding his head towards Krishna, Kritavarma drove forward his chariot towards Malayadwaja. After reaching Malayadwaja, he said, 'Prince Malayadwaja, I am Kritavarma, the general of the Yadav armies, next only to Prince Krishna in the Yadava army camp.'

'I am in no mood for introductions, Sir. I need to avenge my father's death. So, ask Krishna to fight with me,' yelled prince Malayadwaja.

'Prince, you are too young, and I have passed your age long ago. I know your blood must be rushing like an unbridled warhorse. I met your father before the conflict and counselled him against waging war. However, your father did not relent. Keeping up with Kshatriya dharma, Prince Krishna had to respond to the war call of your father. After all that has happened until now, Prince Krishna graciously does not want to annex the Pandyan kingdom despite winning this war. He has ordered our armies to head back to Mathura and leave the reins of the Pandyan kingdom entirely with you,' said Kritavarma.

'Prince Krishna should respond to my war cry. He mustn't retreat and instead fight with me too. Is that not Kshatriya dharma to respond to my challenge, too, General?' said Prince Malayadwaja in a rising voice, seemingly unable to control his anger.

'Calm down, Prince. Our Prince Krishna is unconquerable by anyone in any fight. Recall that your father never let you be in this battle to safeguard your life. Your father went down fighting like a brave man, and his plan of protecting you mustn't go in vain. Therefore, I suggest you give some time and think about the next course of action, whatever it might be. However, now is the time for you to grieve for your father. This war is already over,' said Kritavarma.

After hearing these words, Malayadwaja, numbed with pain in his heart, controlled his rage, threw down all his weapons, got down from the chariot, and walked back to his dead father's body. He was overwhelmed with emotions and cried inconsolably over his father's corpse. Kritavarma retreated from the scene. A heartbroken Malayadwaja gave up the thought of taking instant revenge and headed back to the camp. The remaining Pandyan soldiers followed Malayadwaja in silence, carrying their dead king's corpse to the base.

The prince performed the last rites for his father on the banks of the river Tungabhadra. He promised himself that he would make a difference in this world and carry his father's legacy forward. The Pandyan prince decided to return to Madurai and instructed his armies to do so. The journey to the capital was a month away, and the march back was most saddening for the prince and the defeated soldiers of the Pandyan army.

Soon after returning to Madurai, the royal preceptor of the court anointed Malayadwaja as the new king of the Pandyas. After his coronation, Malayadwaja began touring the entire Bharatvarsh. He collected powerful astras and the knowledge needed to launch them. He undertook training in martial arts directly from the great warrior Brahmin Parashuram himself. In every direction he went, he earned powerful weaponry from notable warriors. Even the godlike Bhishma blessed and gifted his weapons. Drona and Kripa also instructed Malayadwaja on the science of archery on the battlefield. Except for famed archers such as Arjun and Karna, no other archer could rival the knowledge and weapons that Malayadwaja began to possess. He gradually rebuilt a vast army, owned the best artilleries, and felt the time was ripe to seek revenge on Krishna.

Then, a chance meeting with Maharishi Agastya at his hermitage changed the course of Malayadwaja's vengeance.

'Maharishi, I seek your blessings to be successful in my life quest,' said Malayadwaja with hands folded to Maharishi Agastya inside his ashram.

'Oh, young king, you now possess great strength, military skills, and determination. However, do not ever forsake dharma to settle personal scores, as all the skills you have earned this far will also forsake you someday,' said Agastya.

Malayadwaja was taken aback by the words of the maharishi, as he did not wish anyone to know and foil his secret plan. He was stunned that the maharishi had divined his thoughts instantly as soon as he met him for a private audience. He wondered how he knew of his quest to seek retribution on Krishna.

After a brief silence, Malayadwaja said, 'Gurudev, my pursuit of martial arts training and acquiring weapons are for a particular purpose. I want to slay Krishna to avenge the death of my father.'

Maharishi said, 'A king following dharma mustn't be vengeful against anyone, and it is ominous to think of revenge on a person born to re-establish Dharma. Unfortunately, your father mistakenly made a vow to King Jarasandha above dharma and thus ended up siding with evil. He neglected to protect and adhere to dharma, and the decision cost him his life. O you young valiant king, give up the mindset of retribution and always uphold dharma and dharma alone. If you disregard this advice and press forward with the mindset of revenge, it will have disastrous consequences for you.'

Malayadwaja said, 'Gurudev, forgive my impudence, but I want to avenge my father's death. I am not embarrassed to admit that I don't understand dharma fully well now. But I have the training and the might, and possess the best weapons in the world to defeat Krishna in any war.'

Maharishi Agastya smiled upon hearing this and gently said, 'Your plan will do more significant harm to you than any good. Your birth is for a much nobler purpose, so sacrifice the thoughts of hate. Learn about dharma, focus on your subjects, and make your kingdom celebrated again. Your steadfast devotion to Lord Shiv would bear fruit in some years, and the great Lord would reward you when you follow your life journey.'

Malayadwaja was baffled after hearing this. He knew a catastrophe would occur if he went against the maharishi's wishes. Still, at the same time, he did not know how to let go of his plan. Moreover, he could never forgive Krishna for killing his father. Yet he followed the advice of Agastya and decided to return to Madurai after nearly five years of pursuing weapons and undergoing severe training to battle with Krishna.

Many good things began to happen once he returned to Madurai. Soon after, he won the hands of Kanchanamala, the beautiful princess of Kuntala, in a swayamvar. Madurai city flourished anew under his rule. There was happiness all around in the kingdom, the crops were plentiful, the city was protected by a grand army, and the town acquired a golden aura of prosperity and plentifulness. Malayadwaja began to study and contemplate more on dharma. He made dharma the cornerstone of all his future actions. As time passed, he realized that being with the kingdom and serving his subjects brought more joy than vengeance ever could.

Nearly two decades had passed since this incident, and the political circumstances in Bharat had changed. King Malayadwaja, like other kings of Bharat, also got drawn into the Kurukshetra war. He instantly supported the Pandavas, as he felt dharma was on their side. Malayadwaja led his army of one akshauhini, consisting of warriors mounted on 21,870 chariots, 21,870 elephants, 65,610 horses, and 109,350 foot soldiers. He also brought immense war supplies and chariots for the services of the Pandavas. His army reached the forests of Kishkinda on their upward northbound journey to Kurukshetra. Wise old Duta, a septuagenarian, still charioteered the king, skilfully steering through the woods on the banks of river Tungabhadra. The air was filled with the fragrance of wild forest flowers and the sounds of the fast-flowing river waters. The landscape slowly unravelled, seemed familiar, and brought back painful memories to Malayadwaja.

'Duta, stop the chariot here for some time,' said Malayadwaja.

Duta did as he was told and turned towards the king with astonishment, wanting to know what had suddenly happened.

Malayadwaja, looking at Duta, said, 'Everything is fine. It is memories tethering me here, as this is the same spot where my father laid his life down fighting Krishna many years ago.'

'Indeed, this is the same place where the great King Kulasekhara battled and lost his life,' said Duta.

Malayadwaja descended from the chariot and knelt on the ground before clasping a handful of the forest soil. He smeared the red mud on his forehead.

Afterwards, the king rose and gathered his composure. Looking at Duta, Malayadwaja said, 'Ah, today, my father would be smiling from the heavens for my decision to fight on the side of Pandavas. Moreover, he will be pleased with my small efforts to help win the crown of Hastinapur for Yudhishthir, the epitome of dharma,' said King Malayadwaja, his voice trembling with emotions.

Duta noticed the king's eyes welling up and knew that even after many years, he still missed his father and was yearning for his father's eternal happiness. So, he said, 'Certainly, King, your father would surely be happy and proud of your determination to fight for the protection of dharma.'

'Duta, a lot has changed inside me since my father's war with the Yadavas. As you might know, the revenge I wanted to take on Krishna also melted away as the years rolled on.'

Duta said, 'Ever since you returned to Madurai, only good things have happened to our kingdom. Dharma prevails everywhere in our vast kingdom, and your rule is popular as a most dharmic reign across Bharat.'

Malayadwaja smiled and said, 'It was only a chance meeting with Maharishi Agastya that slowly extinguished the fire of revenge inside me. However, before it could completely dissolve, a part of it transformed and spurred me to pursue being the mightiest king of this world. So, as you know, I embarked on yagna after yagna to please the gods and bless me with unlimited shakti. Eventually, I conducted the Ashwamedha yagna so that various lokas would fall under my command.'

Duta said, 'How can one ever forget that moment when even Lord Indra swiftly arose from the glowing fire of the yagna, looking splendorous in his shining armour?'

Malayadwaja said, 'If you recall, in all his brilliance, Lord Indra asked me to withdraw from the Ashwamedha yagna as it would be futile and instead perform the Puthra-Kaeshti yagna and beget a powerful child. He said Queen Kanchanamala, because of her strict tapasya from several earlier births, has been blessed to give birth to an avatar of Parashakti. So, Indra said that I must do the yagna he suggested. Then the mother of all shakti, the Parashakti of this universe, will be pleased and assume the avatar and come to my home as my daughter.'

Duta responded, 'Yes, I recall those moments vividly, after which Lord Indra disappeared into thin air.'

'I stopped the Ashwamedha yagna midway and followed Indra's advice. The Puthra-Kaeshti yagna took weeks to finish. When the yagna reached its culmination, the crimson coral flames changed colour and turned into sapphire and emerald. Emerging from the majestic fire was a three-year-old girl. Her eyes were beautiful and comparable to that of a fish. So, I named her Meenakshi, one with eyes that resembled a fish,' said Malayadwaja.

Duta said, 'It is an unforgettable moment for us. The sages present blessed our princess and proclaimed that she was born to do great things for the world. Princess Meenakshi is now only fifteen years old, yet she is already popular among the citizens. She has mastered the Shastras and rajdharma, been militarily trained in the art of warfare, and is cherished and admired in the entire Pandyan kingdom.'

Malayadwaja's chest swelled with pride on hearing these words. He then said, 'Meenakshi is the apple of my eye. She will make a great queen of Madurai someday. I know that after my time, Madurai will be safe in the hands of Meenakshi.'

Duta wondered if the king was foretelling something. The moment then seemed to him wrapped between joy and sadness at the same time. Malayadwaja climbed back on the chariot, and they resumed the journey towards Kurukshetra.

The Pandyan army marched through the Vindhya mountain ranges, and after more than a hundred days since they had started, they finally reached Kurukshetra. First, King Yudhishthir, his brothers, and Lord Krishna greeted King Malayadwaja when the latter arrived at the Pandava camp. Then, after the customary welcome ritual, the men continued their discussion inside the Pandava camp.

Yudhishthir said, 'O benevolent king, the bull of the south, our forces are now stronger through your support and generous supplies of war materials. Even before Arjun and Duryodhana started their separate journeys to your kingdom for your support in the war, Krishna was already sure that you would surely cast your support on us. Such is the fame of your steadfastness to dharma.'

Malayadwaja Pandyan smilingly looked at Yudhishthir and said, 'O noble king. On whichever side Krishna is present, there is dharma present. So, wherever dharma exists, there is strength already on that side. I feel blessed to battle on the side of those fighting for dharma.'

A smiling Krishna said, 'O the great warrior of the Pandyas, the war will dawn very soon, and history will recall this place as the one where dharma got re-established.'

Malayadwaja smiled at Krishna, the foe-turned-friend. He said, 'O Janardhana, it is an honour to be here and meet you.'

Krishna said, 'O king of Dravida, you have chosen to protect dharma. The sons of Pandu and myself will always be grateful to you.'

'Janardhana, you put me on the path to knowing dharma, for which I am eternally grateful. Two events altered the course of my life. The first was when you dispatched Kritavarma to counsel me to give up my thoughts of fighting with you on the battlefield after you had killed my father. The second was when Maharishi Agastya urged me to give up revenge on you altogether and adopt dharma. If not for these experiences, I might not even be here today,' said Malayadwaja.

Krishna smiled and said, 'The wise counsels that appeared as if by chance were indeed fruits of your good karma in past lives. You then decided the course of your life's journey, which has now brought you here to Kurukshetra today.'

Malayadwaja said, 'Listening to your wise words now is my good fortune. You speak the truth with full authority and yet with such sweetness simultaneously. Blessed are those who know you.'

Krishna smiled at Malayadwaja and said, 'You have come a long way in this life, O king of the Pandyas. It is a sheer joy to see your total transformation from a restless, hot-headed youth to a wise king devoted to the cause of dharma.'

Malayadwaja paused for a while as tears of joy flowed from his eyes, hearing the words of Krishna. Then, he said, 'My fury borne out of ignorance has waned, and the revenge mindset on you has faded entirely. With each passing moment, I have constantly devoted myself fully to the cause of dharma, in which I find more joy than anything else. I am ready to make any sacrifice for dharma. Thus, I am here today at Kurukshetra to fight on the side of dharma.'

Krishna said, 'O great king, your time has come. Now fight with all your courage in this war for this is a mahayagna for establishing dharma. Your life journey, courage, and devotion to dharma will inspire the men who discover you in the future.'

Malayadwaja soon left for his abode in the war camp as a contented man after this heartfelt conversation with Krishna. The cloud of war was looming over Kurukshetra. Malayadwaja had just one mission—to fight for the cause of dharma. He knew his time to show courage and bravery on a battlefield was just a night away.

On the following day, the Kurukshetra war began. Malayadwaja showed his astuteness as a warrior with every passing day on the battlefield. With him on the side of the Pandavas, Yudhishthir knew he had a reliable ally. Every day, Malayadwaja fought valiantly and wreaked havoc on the Kauravas army.

The sixteenth day of the war dawned, and there were vital changes to the Kauravas' army's combatants. The powerful Bhishma had fallen. Guru Drona had perished in the battle, and Karna was now the Kauravas' army commander.

The Pandyan king's energy had never wavered since the beginning of the battle. Malayadwaja tore through the Kaurava army like a thunderstorm on the sixteenth day. He effortlessly slayed the enemies with his arrows and many other weapons. Further, as his chariot rode through the Kaurava flanks, it seemed like a missile-spewing machine, resembling a glowing fireball. The sight was so breathtaking that even Lord Krishna paused his chariot and prompted Arjun to watch Malayadwaja in action. One could see the corpses of elephants, horses, and Kaurava soldiers falling like ninepins as Malayadwaja's chariot waded through the sea of the Kaurava army.

A troubled Duryodhana, looking at the havoc caused by Malayadwaja, then said to Karna, 'Mate, why are you letting this happen? At this rate, the Pandyan king will destroy much of our remaining army.'

Karna looked at Duryodhana and said, 'Malayadwaja is unstoppable. Remember, on the eleventh day of the warfare, he single-handedly pierced through the defence of Guru Drona and struck his arm with an arrow. King Malayadwaja is no ordinary warrior, imbued with immense strength and excellent bows. Such might, skill, courage, and adherence to the code of war are spectacular to behold in him.'

A furious Duryodhana raised his voice and said, 'You are the army's commander! Do not forget this. Stop admiring the enemy, and instead devise a plan to kill him.'

'He is a maharatha and powerful as several hundred warriors put together, and he is not an easy target. So, no one else besides myself or Ashwatthama can engage with him and slay him,' said Karna, looking at Duryodhana.

'Send a word for Ashwatthama to come here immediately,' said Duryodhana impatiently to Karna.

Karna dispatched a soldier with a message to Ashwatthama, asking him to meet immediately. When they all met on the battlefield, Karna described to Ashwatthama the devastation to the Kaurava army caused by Malayadwaja.

Now, looking at Ashwatthama, Karna said, 'Only one of us will be able to slay him. I cannot move from here to chase Malayadwaja, as it will expose Duryodhana to being captured by the enemy. However, I can cut away the flanks of Malayadwaja's army if you begin engaging with him. Then, you should take the battle straight to the Pandyan king and finish him once and for all.'

'Remember that Malayadwaja pierced our Guru Drona on the eleventh day of the battle. What better tribute to your father, our guru, than slaying this wretched Pandyan king,' growled Duryodhana.

Soon, Ashwatthama rushed to face the mighty Pandyan king.

As Ashwatthama neared Malayadwaja, he roared, 'Oh, Pandyan king, turn around and fight with me.'

Malayadwaja looked back and saw Ashwatthama calling him for a battle.

Ashwatthama closed in and then said to Malayadwaja, 'O Malayadwaja, your bravery does not shine in slaying smaller warriors, elephants, and horses. So, face me, as I can give you the combat a warrior of your stature deserves.'

Malayadwaja then responded, 'So be it, Ashwatthama.'

He then shot at lightning speed an arrow that pierced the armour of Ashwatthama. Ashwatthama, stunned by the attack's rapidity, uttered a loud cry and removed the shaft that had pierced his chest armour with his bare hand. He then shot out a volley of arrows at Malayadwaja. The Pandyan king brought all Ashwatthama's missiles to the ground mid-flight. Then Malayadwaja, wielding his bow, swiftly shot a shower, instantly killing Ashwatthama's four chariot horses. Before he could even react, the next astra launched from Malayadwaja's bow broke a stunned Ashwatthama's bow into two pieces and destroyed his chariot. Rendered unarmed in this way, Ashwatthama also fell to the ground from the chariot.

Malayadwaja then said, 'I don't attack unarmed opponents. Rise, O son of the great Guru Drona. Get a new bow and fight with me again.'

Malayadwaja graciously let Ashwatthama pick up another bow to fight. Ashwatthama was seething with shame and anger. He tied his bowstrings faster and began uttering a mantra before launching his next astra at the king. The astra destroyed the chariot of Malayadwaja, and Duta too perished in the attack. Malayadwaja jumped from the burning chariot onto the ground with only his sword in his hands. Karna, by then, had stopped Malayadwaja's army by ceaselessly shooting barrage after barrage of arrows. Thus, Malayadwaja's army could not come closer to the aid of their king. Malayadwaja now stood alone on the battleground with nothing but a sword in his hand. Ashwatthama shot his arrows aiming at

Malayadwaja, who skilfully dodged them. Malayadwaja then jumped onto a war elephant's top to take a vantage position overlooking Ashwatthama, who was on the ground.

Sitting on the elephant, he said, 'Ashwatthama, it is a shame that you use bow and arrow when I only have a sword to defend myself. Did the illustrious Acharya Drona not teach you not to fight using a bow and arrow on a warrior baring only a sword? What you committed is against the rules of warfare. Perhaps the fear of losing makes you forgo the code of war.' Malayadwaja laughed loudly, uttering these words.

From afar, Yudhishthir, who was watching the spectacle, asked Dhrishtadyumna, the Pandava army commander, to rush to the aid of the Malayadwaja.

'O King, it is tough to reach that distance and give cover to the Pandyan king. Karna is in the middle, blocking the Pandyan army as well. So, we will have to break through Karna first to reach King Malayadwaja. I will try, though.' Saying this to Yudhishthir, Dhrishtadyumna asked his charioteer to steer towards Karna.

Meanwhile, seizing the opportunity, Ashwatthama attacked with a shower of arrows that struck the elephant on which Malayadwaja was riding. The arrows broke the sword of the king and pierced his chest. Then, in another swift movement, Ashwatthama sent another volley of arrows that severed Malayadwaja's hands and head. Finally, Malayadwaja's head, adorned with a crown and large earrings, fell to the ground with a thud.

The king was dead after fighting bravely. Ashwatthama had won the fight only through adharma using a bow and arrows when Malayadwaja had just a sword in his hand. The sixteenth day of the battle was over that day. Karna was repentant, as Ashwatthama, dishonouring the code of war, had deployed a disproportionate force against a lightly armed, valiant king.

Meanwhile, in the Pandava camp, there was sorrow and gloom as they had lost a brave ally that day. Arjun lit the funeral pyre of the slain King Malayadwaja. The Pandyan army vowed to fight to the end against the Kauravas in the battle. The war was over in another two days, with the Pandavas ultimately winning.

After the war, Yudhishthir decided to send Arjun and Krishna to Madurai in honour of the dead king. The young Princess Meenakshi, the former king's only daughter, was crowned as the queen and successor to King Malayadwaja Pandyan by Krishna. The newly crowned young Queen Meenakshi was only fifteen when she took over the administration of the Pandyan empire left behind by her father. Thus, a new golden age dawned in Madurai under Meenakshi.

Malayadwaja's story is one of courage and grace and an example of a man of virtue. Though his contribution was significant to the Kurukshetra war, he remained an unsung hero. His life is a hidden gem with many lessons for men persevering in dharma.

14

Shakuni: Crossing to Light

Pranshu B. Saxena

Yashodhara Uvacha (Yashodhara States)

Born in the widespread Kuruvansh, I opened my eyes on the left bank of river Yamuna, whence my father, Durmukha, one among a hundred and more sons of the blind king, Dhritarashtra, served as his father's representative.

I was named Yashodhara—the preserver of glory—by Queen Draupadi, the real head of the clan on that side of the riverine divide of years of hate and envy, a name my Guru Ashwatthama strongly believed should have been the opposite, always insisting on calling me, Yashohara! Sankar (hara) instead of Vishnu (dhara) during my formative years.

Assigned to the Anakini of Varnavata, after that day of Dyuta, the only victorious Kuru brigade since Great grandsire brought my great-grandmothers to Hastinapur, I served under Taat Yuyutsu and had the fortune of learning Indrajal from my granduncle Shakuni whose confidant I became. One of the thousands of grandsons of the king of Hastinapur, I accepted the duties of maintaining law—the dharma, here at Hastinapur.

Human memory, even eye-witness memory is subject to error. Investigating a routine incident witnessed by among others, yours truly, I noted the details as I perceived them. Later my colleagues and other witnesses had quite a varied set of perspectives on the same mundane incident.

We are living through an age of momentous events that are changing the face of itihasa, dharma, artha, kama, and moksha on this earth. Trivial actions a mere few hours back can be in question, let alone the events that would affect our society for the ages.

That is why I write this humble offering of my experiences in the worship of Devi Sarasvati and Devi Kalka. After all, writing is in my blood—you might have heard of my great-grandfather, Krishna Dwaipayan, the Veda Vyas!

What I relate is the story of a leopard who changed his spots under the relentless persuasion of dharma. The story of my father's infamous matula, Shakuni. He would like to offer excuses galore for his past actions. The rules of Natyashastra force me to keep the tale of his redemption short. The story started like tonight, a dark night with no moon.

The Night Patrol

The dark moonless night enveloped the city of Hastinapur. I think it was a Tuesday night in the Vasant month, thirty years since the events of Khandav Vana Daha.

The second prahar of the night was over. I was about to complete my rounds near the royal palace, when the horse threw a shoe, and I stumbled on the street. The patti (platoon) with me kept their smirks to themselves.

The night may have been moonless, but the royal palace to the south was lit up like a house on Deepavali. An air of desperation had coloured the continuous feverish festivities for the past three thousand-plus nights, as if each night is the last night to celebrate. Who knows when the denouement will come.

We turned towards the royal road, the serpentine Pandupatha to the west of the palace. The elephantine palaces of Duryodhana, Dushasana, and D-company brothers, looked lively and awake, as if afraid to go to sleep lest they never wake up.

As the road turned north towards my destination, I could make out the activity in the permanent Sindhu camp where the Yavana and Kamboja wives of Jayadratha phuphaji kept a lively house and hearth.

We changed horses and decided to call it a night. My bed beckoned me. In the distance, sudden gusts of wind caused the lamps to shimmer outside the houses lined up ahead of me—the homes of night owls Vivisamti, Vikarna, Chitrasena (my favorite uncles), and, of course, my father, Durmukha!

Despite what you may perceive as my disdain for Hastinapur hoi polloi, I am part of that elite. I calculated I am 7,000 persons removed from the throne as people measure it in primogeniture. It would need a catastrophe for me to inherit the throne. It would be a catastrophe for the people, if I were to inherit the throne, my guru thundered often.

Ashwatthama's words echoed in my head as I rode past my alma mater, the large school of the son of Drona. The school that never sleeps, with dance performances, night-song festivals, and Vitandavada debates that go on through the night of an active university where the mind is shrant (trammelled by tyranny).

Behind the uproarious school, the loud boisterous celebrations of Lori in the camps of Kekayas and Avantis jarred with the shankhnaad (trumpeting) of shlokas erupting from the house of Bhurishravas, where seven yagna sacrifices have been continuously conducted since that Day of Dyuta, the day of infamy, the day Kuru family disgraced itself for all eternity.

Constantly pouring clarified butter into fire and pouring sacrificial water on himself, Bhurishravas is trying to cleanse himself of his sins of that day but failing miserably, like a man afflicted with the habit of constantly washing his hands.

I knew what troubled him! That dread enveloped Hastinapur. Reaping the denouement of the deeds of the Day of Dyuta disturbed the daily thoughts of the metropolis. That is why the Anakini of Varnavata is patrolling the streets of Hastinapur.

The House of Drona next to the palace was empty. Gurudeva was either away in his kingdom of Indraprastha or not celebrating. He did host a wide array of musicians and singers prized by the Hastinapur society. They would be out in numbers tonight plying their talents in the parties thrown by the rich and glitterati, the crème de la crème of the Kuru State.

I fought tiredness and sleep, focusing on the soothing familiar surroundings and sounds of the city that has become my home this past decade. Taat Shakuni waxed poetic about how the wide serpentine avenues of the city that never slept captured the heart of a wide-eyed youth arriving from the narrow valleys of the mountain fastness he used to call his home.

I only saw a miasma of corruption and disquiet in this city. Many blame the state of affairs on Shakuni, unfairly comparing Hastinapur to the city I spent my childhood in, on the banks of river Yamuna built by the five brothers and Empress Draupadi.

My reverie was interrupted by the sight of Grandfather as he left the palace of Somadutt in the company of visiting kings and priests. They passed me by without a nod or acknowledgement, proceeding towards the palace.

Grandson number Seven thousand, I told you!

Bharadwaj duo's musicians were among the best, but they paled in comparison to those of Somadutt's household. An aficionado of music and poetry, Somadutt collects artists like sun sucks water from lakes to return it as rain—life and culture-enriching performances.

And a blind king with no concept of day and night could arrive anywhere he wished, and so all royal houses were always alert and open for an impromptu visit by the old man.

He had also been unable to sleep for the past decade because of the depravity of that day!

I never did find my bed. An excited babble of people outside the house of Shakuni caught my attention as I recognized his personal servant running up to me.

'Babu, Mamaji is ill! Bahurani sent me to fetch the vaidya,' exclaimed Lakha as he fought for breath. I did not even need to glance at my deputy Senamukh Vinod. He had already wheeled his horse towards the house of Yuyutsu. Hypochondriac Kaka Yuyutsu has the best doctors in the city! Mamaji Shakuni has been ill quite a few times.

Jumping from the horse, I rushed into the house, washing my hands as a maid put a water bowl in my path. I forgot the feet in my hurry and heard rather than saw Lakha slip in the water the maid was supposed to pour on my feet! His squeals and scolding to the maid reassured me that he was fine as I ran to Taat Shakuni's sleeping quarters.

Shakuni Uvacha (Shakuni Said)

I doubled over in pain as I clutched the windowsill for dear life itself as my repast made a valiant effort to rejoin the soil below from whence it came. Perspiration from cold sweat bathed my body, and I shivered feverishly from the taunting cool wind—from the direction of Indraprastha, no doubt.

This was not my first panic attack. They had become a recurring theme of life over the past decade since that iniquity, but this one felt special, as it shook me out of a sound sleep with a vivid vision.

The nightmare was like a gut punch to my solar plexus, and I doubled over again in pain and retched. All the dinner had already joined the compost in Sukeshti's assiduously maintained flower beds below, and only dry heaves came. I cried out in pain as inky gloom enveloped me.

Suddenly, there were people in the room. My wife Sukeshti rushed in from another part of the house, her room for the past decade. As did the servants—quiet, dignified, and always ready. They helped me stand upright and guided me to a seat. Someone brought water, another wiped my forehead and massaged my arms. Sukeshti gave instructions for the doctor to be called as the room slowly stopped spinning and came into focus.

Yashodhara, son of Durmukha, entered the room and rushed towards us, concern writ on his face. He helped the servants lift me from the seat and brought me over to the bed.

'I have sent my brothers to Yuyutsu Kaka's bhavan to fetch his vaidya,' Yashodhara informed Sukeshti. Yashodhara momentarily looked around as his mouth curled up in disdain. Yashodhara never got along with my son Uluka, missing in action here, most likely partying away the night with his cousin Duryodhana. Uluka's wife, Sundari, caught the vibe and frowned at her nephew who sheepishly smiled back. In a family of closed eyes, Yashodhara did carry his heart on his sleeve.

Soon, Yuyutsu and the vaidya arrived and started their ministrations. Drawn by the commotion, my nephews, the night owls also turned up.

Durmukha looked at the feet of his son and gave him a slap at the back of his head. His dear uncle and guru might be dying, but a Bharata father never forgets the protocol for entering someone's house without washing their feet!

The ladies meanwhile retreated to get some refreshments for a late-night snack for the spontaneous assembly of relatives.

'What happened, matula? You were perfectly fine when we met angaraj in the evening to plan for the Dwaitavana excursion,' Durmukha asked me.

He informed the company, 'Radheya was all excited today as he informed us that 'We have a valid reason to persuade the king.' All the Kuru Ghoshas (herds of cows) are in Dwaitavana this year for the monsoon. We have not counted them for three years now. That is a valid excuse for the excursion!'

'I had a horrible gut-wrenching dream. It is a portent. We should not go to Dwaitavana. I fear Duryodhana and Radheya will escalate the conflict, and we will die,' I croaked.

I proceeded to describe the dream in detail as the attentive faces blanched and stomachs gurgled at this clear-cut communication of the coming calamity.

'In the dream, I saw someone drag my daughter, Antara, from the chariot, and she was pushed to the ground with arrows flying around. I saw Sukeshti pleading with a burly villain. Sundari was wailing with pain, joining the chorus of hundreds of the daughters-in-law and female relatives of the Kuru king. Queen Bhanumati and her co-wives were covered in dirt. The daughter-in-law of Duryodhana could not be recognized in her blood-soaked clothes as the women of Hastinapur wailed and beat their chests around me! I saw many of my nephews and their sons lying on the ground, kicked and beaten like animals without the pure strike of weapons as befitting their status as Kshatriyas. I saw bullock ropes in the hands of villains as they stuffed raw grass into the mouths of royal princes who had thrown away milk-cakes and tasty sweets in the petulance of their youth. VIVISAMTI! Don't interrupt me,' I growled in anger as my nephew raised and then awkwardly put his hand down. 'I felt great pains wracking my body as if it had just been dealt many wounds and that pain maddened me. I lost consciousness and then opened my eyes and looked at the visage of Draupadi, yes, the Queen of Pandavas! The Empress of Rajasuya poured water into my mouth. She said something to her maid nearby. I didn't hear her mellifluous voice. When she spoke in my dream, it was not her voice at all but the words of Sanjaya Gavalgani reverberating from that day of the second Dyuta. He had told us that Draupadi's eyes seemed to say that her plight on this day would be heaped a thousand-fold on the wives and females of those who have hurt us. Deprived of protection of their husbands, sons, and relatives, anathawata (having no protector), they will run around wailing like banshees, covered in blood and dust.'

Words failed me at this point, and only sobs escaped. No one moved.

I put in words what all of us had been dreading for this past decade. The dread of that very impending doom that did not allow Dhritarashtra to sleep peacefully. The terror of the future that had Bhurishravas constantly trying to worship his sins away.

The Pandavas will return. And bequeath their vengeance on Hastinapur with nothing standing in the way of the wrath of Bhim and Arjun for that wickedness inflicted on their wife—the immorality no one talked about in the city of serpent.

And in a culture seeped in presages and omens, my dream was confirming our worst fears. The room was deathly quiet as all concerned examined their mortality.

Vivisamti raised his hand again. 'Rishika Surya's mantras are used for death rituals, right?'

Yashodhara replied 'Nah! That is for the marriage ritual. For death, you use Atharva Angirasa mantras.'

Everyone looked puzzled as Vivisamti pointed at me. 'Matula didn't see me. Someone must do the death rituals for you all....' as Durmukha sitting between his brother and son, smacked both at the back of their heads.

Someone corrected, 'Yajus for marriage! I have had ten of those! But no experience of death!'

Trust Vivisamti to break the tension with his inanities. We all burst into giggles and nervous laughter.

'Chaps, eat up fast and let Matula rest. We need to go early to the court. Radheya has concocted the scheme with the leader of Ghosha and informed us of his plan. We must stop him now,' noted Durmukha, pointing to Yashodhara to stay back.

I fitfully tried to close my eyes. As the company exited, they noticed Sukeshti standing near the door, hesitant to enter, then she left. She still blamed me for the events of the Dyuta. Many rivers of misgivings separated this family.

Yesterday, Somavar, Vasant, Thirty Years after KhandavaVana Daha. Yashodhara Uvacha (Yashodhara Said)

The gathering had calmed a little after the prophetic prognosis of perfidy personified. The font of this portent was the forthcoming trip to Dwaitavana, which had been in planning since yesterday.

Yesterday, Charvaka and Subhash, our spymasters, had returned from Dwaitavana.

Charvaka with his ploys and stratagems. And people call Shakuni the wily one! The common citizen did bestow Shakuni immense powers of persuasion over the Kauravas. That was an exaggeration, what with the many factions, disparate agendas, and vested interests in this conflict-riven royal family.

Charvaka had the ear of Duryodhana. He narrated experiences of his trip to the court, painting a very sorry picture of the miseries the Pandavas faced in the forest. They were suffering from poverty and neglect. The heat, dust, wind, and weather were playing havoc with their health. Lean with want and hungry all the time, they were almost prostrate with weakness and pains wracking their soft bodies.

Sleeping on the hard floor had given aches and diseases that wracked the body of Dharmaraj and enfeebled Bhim.

Distresses faced by the Pandavas had overwhelmed Draupadi. She languished in mind and body. The learned sage went on and on, describing the travails and troubles of the king's nephews.

Anyone but the blind and their progeny could 'see' through the facade Charvaka was constructing. Enfeebled and tired all the time! Suffering in the wilds! What was this gentleman trying to sell here?

'Overwhelmed by weather and wind! Sons of Indra and Vayu! Nonsense!' exclaimed Shakuni later in private.

Draupadi tai suffering in mind and body, indeed! Subhash had just eaten a scrumptious dinner served by the Queen herself to the visitors. He might be exaggerating as he mentioned eighty-eight thousand forest dwellers participated in that repast. The Pandavas have a loyal team of well-trained officers and servants who would never leave them even in death, let alone exile. We already know that the enfeebled Pandavas had disposed of the likes of Asuras Jatasura, Kirmira, Kalasrenggi, and Sardula.

Charvaka's performance had its desired effect. Duryodhana had a totally different reaction to Grandfather as the old man started sobbing real tears for his nephews and their wife. Bless his soft heart, quick to anger, quick to forgive. He was also the man who yelled like a crazed gambler 'Did I win? Did I win?' on that fateful day of the Dyuta—his unspoken perfidy.

True to his fickle, capricious nature, the king was erratic in his moods with his fears and tears. He bemoaned his decisions that led to this sad situation. His dear beloved nephews! As candle wax and his cups deepened, he went from grumbling about the current fate of his nephews to prophesying the future ruin of his own sons. He lamented the coming fury of Bhim and the hailstorms of arrows that Arjun would bring with him.

Duryodhana was all barely suppressed chortles and joy. The Pandavas were suffering. The Pandavas were weak. The

Pandavas were in a pathetic situation. He came back to earth from cloud nine as his father's wailings turned to a prophecy of his ruin!

As Dhritarashtra went from morose to morbid in his soliloquy, Duryodhana fled the court and sought out his dear friend and spiritual guide, Radheya Vasushena.

Radheya had been the éminence grise of Duryodhana, exercising a controlling and mesmerizing influence on him for his own sinister purposes!

Shakuni, once a staunch ally, had become embittered of Radheya since the day of Dyuta.

They are two sides of the same coin. Like Radheya now, once Shakuni, the junior prince of Gandhara, tried to take a similar role for Dhritarashtra. The difference was that Shakuni had the misfortune to meet an adult Dhritarashtra, while Radheya had a wet clay pot of a child to fashion to his designs. Shakuni had to deal with competing factions and influences like that of Vidura, Kripa, Kanika, and even Sanjay. Radheya had no competition. Dhritarashtra may be mercurial, but Duryodhana is completely obedient to Radheya.

Duryodhana informed Radheya about Charvaka's report. Radheya was ecstatic on hearing the miseries afflicting the Pandavas and counselled Duryodhana that they must visit the Pandavas in Dwaitavana.

'Let us go and see the Pandavas and flaunt our wealth and good fortune in their faces and rub their noses in the dirty hovels they reside. Tortured, seeing you resplendent like King Yayati, they will curse their stars!'

'Krishnaa may have felt grief in the middle of the assembly hall. She will feel more grief than on the day of Dyuta seeing the jewels on our wives and will lament piteously! Ha, ha!'

Radheya was brimming with excitement, but Duryodhana was circumspect.

'It would give me greater pleasure to see their plight than conquering the world—nay, even having my children born. But words of Vidura from the day of Dyuta haunt me.'

Radheya's face fell like a child robbed of his toys. Duryodhana could never countenance that. Won over by his pouting friend, Duryodhana agreed to consider the expedition if Radheya could come up with a plan to convince his father and grandsire.

'Wise men do not deliberately poke a hornet's nest without intending to destroy it,' Shakuni warned Duryodhana.

Duryodhana squealed in delight.

'What an idea, Matula. We can end the conflict here and now and not wait for the fourteenth year!'

'No, that is not what I meant. Aaaahhh!' Shakuni shouted at his retreating back.

Morning, Next Day (Wednesday), Vasant. Yashodhara Uvacha (Yashodhara Said)

The dream was a clear omen. Lead by Shakuni, the night owls wanted to stop the excursion, but that ship had sailed. Radheya had found a perfect excuse. Ghosha Yatra.

The king exulted in such details, the minutiae of them. Instead of objecting, he ordered the princes to go and complete the counting of the cows. We were stuck between a rock and a hard place.

Ghoshas move around the pastures. The cows had travelled to the Dwaitavana on the borders of the Kuru and Virata kingdoms to shelter for the coming monsoon. The cowherd stations, or Ghoshas, had already been constructed.

Samanga, the chief of cowherds, was at court. As instructed by Radheya, he reported that the Ghoshas had been completed in Dwaitavana. There is an inordinate number of three-year-old calves unassigned to any labour, which is detrimental to productivity. Samanga asked for guidance.

'I do not trust these cowherds. These gwalas! We need to send someone to take a proper census of the Kuru cow wealth. It would be a good opportunity for the princes to do some hunting also,' Dhritarashtra quipped.

'But the Pandavas live there now, don't they? Yudhishthir keeps moving. Aren't they supposed to be in Kamyaka Forest?'

'Radheya is insolent and will pick up a quarrel with the Pandavas. They will burn him down with their arrows. If it is not Radheya, some junior arrogant soldier, all the Ganas (officers) are my grandsons. Young, inexperienced, and ambitious. One or more of them will end up hurting the Pandavas in some way, and a conflict will start. I do not think this is a good idea.'

In his ramblings, the blind king did not realize Samanga and Radheya were standing right there. Before Duryodhana could interject, Shakuni intervened.

'O King, you have nothing to be concerned about. The forest is vast, and we will keep miles away from the Pandavas. We would also invite the elite of Hastinapur to accompany us with their wives and children. Then it is not an armed force going for Ghosha Yatra. We will take with us singers, dancers, and musicians and create a convivial, jovial environment. We will conduct the task of census like a vana-vihara (picnic) not a chore. Small army can come to set up waystations and guard points across our portion of Dwaitavana. For far too long, Matsaya forces under Kichaka have perfunctorily violated our borders and assaulted our allies the Trigartas, Sivis, and Kekayas. We need to address these lacunae in our defence lines.'

Shakuni won over Dhritarashtra, who acquiesced to the Ghosha Yatra despite having misgivings.

If you can't stop them, join them and then affect the result. This was Shakuni's Arthashastra!

In this family, forewarned is not forearmed!

The Ghosha Yatra, a Few Weeks Later. Shakuni Uvacha (Shakuni Said)

We finally left as Jyeshtha (June) faded into Aashadha (July). The summer heat was making the citizens long for open spaces. It was not difficult to persuade them to join the excursion with their families, as the army moved out surrounded by thousands of women. Narikavacha (shielded by women) is the strategy chosen to prevent the prophesized catastrophe.

For all his faults, Yudhishthir was devoted to dharma. I had never seen him angry except for a brief second on that fateful day. Moments later, he had focused his attention on Radheya's left foot thumb and somehow dammed that volcano which would have consumed the world.

He especially respected women and would not initiate conflict with so many civilian women around. I must make sure that the trio of idiots—the limited-intelligence Duryodhana, pakya talk-too-much-do-little Radheya, and the follower-without-brain Dushasana—do not cross the line.

Traders, entertainers, and members of the high society followed us with mobile markets, gypsies, and the servants. Deliberately curtailing the army size, we reduced the area occupied by our camps—we had 8,000 chariots, 9,000 cavalry, and 30,000 elephants, most of whom carried supplies and camp equipment, joined by masses of bullock carts and other paraphernalia of the royal entourage.

We quickly set up the camp and built make-shift houses for Duryodhana and royal princes, keeping half a yojana away from the main lake, named after the Matsaya king, Dwaita, the performer of Ashvamedha sacrifices. There were enough water bodies and streams in the vicinity, so we did not really need to access the lake where the Pandavas were.

This way, I could keep the army and most of the camp away from them.

The signs were everywhere. Shakuni also means birds of portent as our ancestors believed that they, the birds, in the original language of the universe, could foretell future events. And the birds were all around us. The sky was red in the morning, the birds were screeching, and dirty, dusty godhulis were foreshadowing calamity.

The air was electric with expectation, and the buzz around the camps was that soon Duryodhana would proceed to the lake.

Yashodhara Uvacha (Yashodhara Said)

The census started, and over the next few days, most of the royal company was kept busy, engaged in doing their duties of supervising the branding of cows and assigning of calves.

Shakuni ran a tight ship. He would only allow us to go on hunts every three days. He told me, 'Yashodhara, keep the hunts simple. Do not allow them to become competitions and KEEP AWAY from the Pandavas. Brand that into your mind.'

The spies brought back the true picture of a comfortable hermitage and hearth of the Pandavas with constant visits from allies, friends, and acclaimed rishis.

Weeks went by. The Pandavas paid no heed to us. The spies mentioned that we never came up in the evening-time family conversations of the Pandavas though we were scant four miles away. Subhash joked that our ancestors invented zero to explain just such a lack of interest. He brought in some gujiyas prepared by Queen Draupadi for me, transporting me back to my childhood, memories of the self-same gujiyas prepared in the kitchens of the Indraprastha Sabha, where I was born.

Draupadi's hermitage had a heavenly feel to it, surrounded by spring flowers planted and cared for by Pandava family priests, Dhaumya and Kakshivana's daughters. The cleanliness and decorum of that longstanding hermitage were in stark contrast to our, already putrid and untidy weeks-old camp.

To pass the lazy days in the wilderness, we exchanged stories.

'Many years ago, Vidura Kaka one day rushed into the court to inform us that the Pandavas have won Draupadi at the swayamvar. "She is a fire-born goddess who will make our home a swarga (heavenly place)!" said Vivisamti. I remembered joking 'and the residents of that home swargavasi! (dead!)' chortled Dad Durmukha wiping tears of glee at the memory.

Nobody else joined in the mirth. Mother Saraswati was sitting on his tongue that day! Yeah, when a father jokes, every child must bear them and grin along.

In sharp contrast to the Pandava's disinterest, the only topic of conversation in our camp since the day we arrived had been about them. I was beginning to realize some home truths about us. We did not seem to worry the Pandavas; they did not spare a thought on us, except in passing.

We, the Kauravas, on the other hand, allocated rent-free residency in our minds to the Pandavas from the moment sixteen-year-old Yudhishthir walked into Hastinapur, carrying his infant brother Nakul and his father's ashes in his two hands.

Shakuni exclaimed, 'It is maddening to fight an enemy who does not reciprocate at the same level.'

And then it happened. The cold war turned hot when we least expected it.

There was a reason that the Pandavas had always won, and we never—because we did not learn from our mistakes. We did not learn, period.

Parashuram has described a nine-level structure of officers in the army that has been the Aryavrata standard for many years. All the leaders of the Kaurav army are disciples of Parashuram and have ignored their own guru's teachings! You can bring a horse to the sara (lake), but you cannot make it drink!

Dhritarashtra has thousands of grandsons. Ego dictates that they cannot report to someone lower in society than them, so we have a very flat, four-level structure. Thousands of ganas (sergeants) but no senior officers. Yuyutsu, my father Durmukha, Sanjay Gavalgani, and I are all ganas!

In another army, any army, an experienced set of select veteran officers would sit at command level, next to the Akshauhinipati. In our army, thousands of petulant, spoiled princes with zero experience and no impulse control—entitled, elitist brats—control our interactions with outside agents and foreign entities.

It was an open invitation to disaster!

We were informed that Pandavas will be busy with Sadyask yagna for the next few days, it would be the safest opportunity for Kauravas to use the lake for sporting activities. No interference and interaction with the Pandavas guaranteed!

The workers were ordered to prepare accordingly.

This is not an excuse, but I was bone tired. The continuous watch on the activities of my irresponsible kin, day and night, was an arduous undertaking. Unable to relax or sleep had sapped my faculties. And, anyway, my cousins never listened to me, the grandson number 7,000!

Shakuni was equally worn down by the sullen, cantankerous duo of Radheya and Duryodhana. They had been denied their lifelong ambition—a pleasure greater than having children—the humiliation of Pandavas, who simply ignored them.

Shakuni retired to his tent to catch his forty winks and thats's when contact was made.

The ganas found the gandharvas using the lake and they were tactfully asked to leave.

The Kauravas, in officious arrogance, refused to follow the traditional practice of approaching a water body with ahuti and ardhya. When stopped by gandharvas, ignoring my advice, as usual, my kin went to get confirmation from our great leader, Duryodhana.

Yatha raja tatha praja. (As the king so is the public)

Equally arrogant and pompous as his brothers and nephews, Duryodhana asked them to remove the gandharvas. The unarmed gandharvas, using superior skill and displaying better training, easily disarmed the Kaurav vanguard.

One burly gandharva caught several Kauravas and started dunking them into the water. Irritated, one of the junior princes shot steel arrows and gandharva blood was spilled. Seeing their wounded comrade, the gandharvas took out their weapons and attacked in full force overwhelming the vanguard instantly.

The Attack on the Camp. Shakuni Uvacha

Even Duryodhana should be able to handle a simple pleasure excursion. I had left Yuyutsu and Yashodhara in charge. They are of royal blood. I forgot so was everyone around them.

The quiet of the day was broken by great tumult and noise around the camp. Bleary-eyed, I rushed out to find that the camp was under attack by the gandharvas.

Gandharvas!

Where did they come from?

Our army was already in disarray and fighting for their lives inside our own camp! Enervated and relaxed by the long picnic of a sojourn in the forest, our soldiers were no match for the well-trained, cold-eyed, and steely gazed warriors.

I took my chariot out to join the fight and recognized the flag of Chitrasena Gandharva.

Chitrasena was one of the top Pandava supporters and a permanent invitee to the Sabha of Yudhishthir along with his twenty-seven colleagues. Heck, Arjun had even fought Krishna and Yudhishthir for his sake. Chitrasena's wives are best friends with Subhadra, Arjun's wife and Krishna's sister!

The gandharvas were soon making short work of the Kaurav army, and only Radheya was able to stand in front of their onslaught.

Abhitmara Gandharva easily took out the top four Kaurav maharathis, as if they were crops in a field. The gandharva, wearing the colours of Chitrarath, defeated my nephews Jaya and Bhimavikata. Gopa and Bal gandharvas blocked the gates of the camp, preventing any of the civilians from escaping to the forest. I saw Chitrarath gandharva and Kishore beating up Dushasana, Durmarshana, and the sons of Radheya. Vishvavasu and Paravasu gandharvas were showering arrows, maddening the elephants, and demolishing the Ghosha stations, forcing the cows to run helter-skelter. The cattle wealth of Hastinapur state was literally draining away in front of my eyes.

Wait! Two Chitrarath gandharvas! And that is no Kishore Gandharva.

My daughter-in-law is the daughter of Krishna's cousin Akrura. Her sister married Draupadi's son Shatanik. I was at the wedding. That is not any ordinary gandharva. That is the smartest son of Draupadi, masquerading as one. Chitrarath Gandharva was a younger version of Bhim, these are the Panchalas masquerading as and mixed in with gandharvas!

During the Rajasuya yagna campaign, Arjun had come to Gandhara with his wheel protectors, the chakrarakshakas—the ones now fighting like rakshasas and killing our cavalry and elephant troops. That is no Vishvavasu and Paravasu!

A series of curses escaped my lips!

Spycraft is played at the level of nations. Our stratagem to hurt the Pandavas would be monitored and countered by their allies like the Panchalas. *Dharmo dharmasya rakashati* (dharma protects those who follow dharma).

The Panchalas had obviously asked the gandharvas to help them out.

As the battle continued and our losses mounted, a few of us were able to set up a temporary command post and rally our soldiers. Now I was worried about the civilians—all the women and children we had brought from Hastinapur. My tattered Narikavacha strategy!

If these are Draupadi's sons and her kin, then they would keep to the rules of Aryas and not hurt the women. Suddenly, an icy fear clutched my chest.

These are the Panchalas!

And I had brought the elite of Hastinapur to the forest. I hit my head with my palm!

Queen Krishnaa was Princess Panchali before she was ever part of our family. And it was this very elite that sat motionless and silent at the humiliation of Draupadi that day of the Dyuta.

Dharmo Dharmasya Rakshati. The crowd I brought with me to act as my Narikavacha cannot claim the protection of Dharma having so callously disregarded it that day of Dyuta.

The reckoning has come due today! The humiliation of Draupadi would be paid back a thousand-fold. On the Kaurava women by the sons and brothers of the lady we wronged.

I saw the ersatz gandharvas break through to the civilians' and women's tents and then step away, their eyes cold and expressions hard as they focused first on denuding the Kaurav state of its cattle wealth.

The women would come later!

The gandharvas took the high and mighty of Hastinapur as captives and were branding number two on their heads. Slaves for the future! Two boons Draupadi asked that day of Dyuta! The freedom of her husbands and sons. She had also said her husbands will get the rest.

In the battlefield, Duryodhana suffered many wounds at the hands of Abhitmara and fell lifeless to the ground.

I was hit by many arrows from Bal and Gopal, which penetrated my armour when I tried to break out of the camp. My fingers loosened their grip on my bow. The gandharvas, meanwhile, destroyed Radheya's chariot, and he was on the ground with just a sword and shield.

Vikarna, to my right, went to his aid and picked him up on his chariot. Suddenly, Radheya took the reins from Vikarna, whipped the horses and, in the twinkling of an eye, ran away from the battlefield!

Radheya abandoned us at the worst possible time. Seeing him run like a coward, the fight went out of the army.

The gandharvas focused on the rich citizens of Hastinapur. They ignored the common market folk, traders, shopping carts, and gwalas. Seeing this, Yuyutsu rallied the commons and their vehicles into a formation and started leading them out towards the Pandava camp at the shores of the Lake. Everything I had seen in my dream was coming true.

My daughter Antara was dragged from the chariot and pushed to the ground as arrows whistled above her. I saw my wife Sukeshti pleading with a burly villain. I saw Sundari, my daughter-in-law, wailing with pain when one of the Gandharvas leapt onto her chariot, shushing her. She mouthed, 'Jijaji!'

A chorus of wailing rose from the hundreds of daughter-in-law, of the Kuru king. Queens of Duryodhana, covered in dirt, trying to escape on foot, were bound and made captive. I saw many of the Kauravas—my nephews and their sons—lying on the ground, kicked and beaten like animals. I could hardly recognize the disfigured faces of Vinda and Anuvinda. Oh, and Vivisamti!

Vivisamti was looking towards me with accusing eyes!

I saw bullock ropes in the hands of villains as they stuffed raw grass into the mouths of royal princes like Dushasana, Durvisaha, Durjaya, and Durmarshana. I saw Duryodhana being pushed around and beaten by the gandharvas like a dog.

As blackness enveloped me, Yasodhara expertly manoeuvred my chariot into the train of the common folk heading towards the Pandava camp.

The Refuge of Dharma. Shakuni Uvacha

I opened my eyes, tasting the liquid being poured into my mouth. Queen Draupadi was giving me a medicinal potion. Seeing me conscious, she asked her maid to fetch more medicine and unguent paste.

The lady who suffered the most humiliating moment of her life due to my machinations saved me in the worst situation of my life.

I suddenly remembered my wife and daughter and my grandkids. What had happened to them?

To my right, I could see Sahadev standing, looking daggers at me. Both he and Bhim were being harangued by Draupadi. Behind her, stood Sundari and Antara. Oh, some of the royal ladies made it out with the commons.

The guileless eyes of the Pandavas betrayed that they were in tune, if not in cahoots, with the gandharvas. Bless their open nature. They had never affected deceit.

How would they survive Agyatavas?

What Agyatavas? I wondered. Duryodhana is a slave of the gandharvas if he is still alive. Radheya is in the wind, and Dhritarashtra has no family left to speak of.

Turning to my left, I saw Yuyutsu and Durmukha pleading with Yudhishthir.

'The gandharvas have taken the royal family, especially the women, and they are moving out, probably making them slaves for the rest of their lives. Please save them', entreated Yuyutsu.

Bhim roared with laughter.

'We have been waiting for the day when we will be free to assemble our armies—our chariots, elephants, and horses—and meet the Kaurav army in the battlefield. Now, there is no such need! The gandharvas came from heaven and took on the pleasant burden of destroying the family of the evil king fond of the deceitful Dyuta! You had come to gloat on our emaciated bodies struck down by exposure to heat cold and wind!' Bhim mocked as he looked at me, repeating the very words Charvaka had said in the court to instigate Duryodhana to come for this Ghosha Yatra.

Bhim's look said it all—big fish from a little pond! Now, welcome to the ocean. He continued with barely concealed glee.

'We will go and rescue the poor cousins when their emaciated bodies have seen some real suffering and want for a decade or so! The sons of Kunti are not wicked. We respond to pleas for help even to the point of disturbing an elder brother in his bedroom! Visoka, what is on the to-do list?'

Visoka, son of Krishna and Bhim's trusted assistant, said nonchalantly, 'Tau, we were planning to pass some more smart comments till the cows come home!'

Yudhishthir rebuked Bhim gently.

'This is no time for cruel words. These are already frightened and dispirited people. Only taunt your enemies when they are in full battle gear and in full control of their senses. Then your taunts serve to distract them and negate their efforts against you.'

Bhim was momentarily nonplussed. Yudhishthir proved that the Pandavas were as bad at jokes as the Kauravas.

'On a more serious note, dear Vrikodar, in every house, the utensils sitting on shelves clash with each other like family members living in proximity tend to do. There are disagreements all the time. Families handle it by discussion or by force of arms. That is the nature of such disputes. Those closest to each other in family, culture, and even national mores can develop unbridgeable gaps. Then conflict may not be avoided. We can delay it; we can give chances to people to reform themselves or for the conflict to resolve itself. Even those who face the death sentence for their crimes should be allowed time to redeem their souls.' Yudhishthir was looking at me as he said this.

'The women and children are the most beloved part of the family. They constitute the honour of the clan, regardless of their spouse or parent. No outsider can interfere in that.

While fighting with each other, we are five, and they are a hundred. While fighting with outsiders, we are a hundred and five!

I cannot but emphasize this lesson. This has always been forgotten in our history when faced with an external enemy. Some look to their own interests or give in to petty jealousies and plaints. Samvarna had 2,400 brothers, but the Panchala king defeated him as they did not stand united. Let no one accuse Yudhishthir of this crime. Family and nation come above all interests. The needs of the many outweigh the needs of a few or self, Vidura Kaka advised us in the past. Chitrasena may have led this operation on account of his love for us. That is not under question. As a friend, it behoved him to come to me and share his plans. He neglected to take me into his confidence. Trust is a two-way street. People tend to break laws and ask for forgiveness later. That skirts the boundaries of dharma.' Yudhishthir looked at Arjun pointedly as Bhim chuckled.

'I was consecrated as Emperor after performing the Rajasuya yagna. The waters of all rivers and all four oceans were brought, and my hair was washed with them. That made me the supreme ruler of this Bharatvarsh. There are no term limits. I have not been defeated in battle to lose that right. As far as I understand, I am still alive, and I am the king. I am the Samrat, your Swami. You shall have no other kings before me. Only the king can punish for the crimes committed against the king. Chitrasena has no right to punish Duryodhana. Finally, I am your king. I am not the king of the Pandavas or the Kauravas. I am the king of all people, regardless of their race, varna, occupation, place of birth, and adherence to dharma. As people may not have a choice in their kings, kings do not have a choice in their people. I must love all of them equally, something the resentful may not understand. Even the criminals who assaulted my wife and tried to strip her in the Dyuta Sabha deserve my protection because the king cannot discriminate among his subjects. Dharma is subtle here, difficult to follow, but I have always followed it. Those who are powerless, I am their power, like tears are the power of little children.'

'Sadhu, sadhu! Tryartho dharma astikadi, uparicharira and sookshma! As is, higher and subtle,' exclaimed Dhaumya.

I could not help but utter, 'Chaturartho dharma, redemption and forgiveness, Paushya!'

Yudhishthir addressed his factotum.

'Indrasena, prepare the chariot of Duryodhana for Bhim and Vishoka. Chandrasekhara, prepare Durmarshana's chariot for Arjun. Vrikodara, go and rescue Duryodhana and the women from the gandharvas. Entreat them first with diplomacy. When Sama fails, take it to Danda. If they do not agree to diplomacy nor to the light skirmishing, then use the full force of your power to affect the release of Duryodhana.'

Bhim grumbled, 'So I get to save his wicked hide again! The dog's tail will always remain curled up! He will never learn. We have given a hundred chances to the hundred cousins to reform themselves.'

'You have saved him many times since that day at Kampilya when we went to collect guru dakshina. Do your deeds. Do not worry about the results,' reminded Yudhishthir.

The four Pandavas wore their impenetrable armour, picked up their weapons, and climbed onto the four chariots looking like four powerful Indras.

Shakuni Uvacha

As my nephews left to rescue my villainous nephew, Sukeshti and Antara came to my side and held my arms. I did not look at them. I was looking at Yudhishthir. I was looking at the Emperor standing before me and the versions I have interacted with in the past.

The sixteen-year-old version! The very tall, gangly youth freshly bathed, ritualistic, and solemn, presenting his father's ashes to people of Hastinapur in one hand, holding his little brother Nakula in the other, (also freshly bathed and already covered in dust and with dirty hands like all toddlers). The people of Kuruvarsha instantly recognized the King who would stand on ceremony and be flexible. I saw the demise of my sister's dreams. The one who always wears a blindfold.

The sixteen-year-old version! Quietly closing the doors of the room of his twin brothers after lulling them to sleep, as he passed me by in the dark hallway of the Hastinapur palace, he had respectfully said, 'Pranam, Matulashri.'

I snarled back, 'I am not your matula.'

Looking back in the direction of sleeping infant brothers, he quietly countered, 'I call you Matula because when I first opened my eyes in this world, Mother Madri, your sister, was holding me fast to her bosom.'

I always hated his ability to see connections in everything. Make everyone a family. Make everyone a part of his grand vision. He never looked at the reality of life! Still, it was his tranquillity that bounced him out of all problems.

Yes, Madri was my sister as well, the granddaughter of my grandfather, Kitava. Only her brothers and Yudhishthir now remember that gentle lady of mischievous smiles and delightful laughter. I hated sharing that memory with Yudhishthir.

Another version flashed before me. The young crown prince of Hastinapur inviting me—his matula—to put the toe ring on Duhshala on her marriage to Jayadrath.

'I am not your matula, Aajmidha!'

Young Aajmidha said with a twinkle of joy in his eyes, 'Matula, people call me Aajmidha not because I am born in the family of Ajamidha but, like Ajamidha's eldest son, I am also the eldest son of a Gandhari.'

I hated that holier-than-thou son of Pandu!

Every time I hurt Yudhishthir, every time I tried a ploy to bring him to harm, he calmly weathered the ruse and still referred to me as matula, as sincerely as on that first day I saw him, clutching the ashes of his father and the hopes of his 'sons', the public, a child made man before his time.

Every time I had spit on the hand of friendship and sincerity offered by Yudhishthir, he had simply wiped it away, always smiling.

One thing is very clear in my mind.

I will spit on that hand no more!

My love for Duryodhana had blinded me to his faults. Dhritarashtra and his family had done a lot for me.

I would repay that debt. And repay the debt on my soul for my sins.

I would fight the coming war on the side of Duryodhana and welcome death when the son of my sister Madri, Sahadev, uses that Panchanakha weapon to kill me and release me from my mortal coils.

I have not been a good man. But I am not evil. I will die a good man.

Other than dying for Duryodhana, I will not spend a moment's thought for his welfare or create another scheme for his benefit.

Whatever time was left for me on this earth, I will endeavour to wash my sins away.

I opened my eyes and clutched my wife and daughter close to me. It was on the night of Dyuta that Antara left the house blaming me for what happened to Draupadi.

I had ignored a lot in my blind love for my nephew who was cursed with blind parents and now, I saw myself as a blind guide! It is time for brother of Gandhari to remove his blindfold.

I had not been a good man. I would try to become one. Yudhishthir has shown the light. I will make the crossing.

Epilogue: The Journey to Hastinapur. Yashodhara Uvacha

Born of a younger son among hundreds, I always joked that I was the prince number 7,000 in some moth-eaten, forgotten register of princes.

Prince number 7,000 showed his quality on the day of the gandharvas.

I marshalled the citizens of Hastinapur and what was left of our vehicles and equipment and languidly made our way back to Hastinapur. We had lost an army equal to four Anakinis in this Dwaitavana episode. Four less for the final battle which Yudhishthir has promised.

The elite of Hastinapur who kept quiet and mute on the day of Dyuta had been given a life-changing lesson never so graphically administered as it was by the brutal gandharvas.

It was the worst day in the life of Uncle Duryodhana. He had come to Dwaitavana like a giddy schoolboy, asking throughout the journey, 'Are we there yet?'

His dreams of triumph burnt to ashes on the funeral pyre of the battle with the gandharvas. The salt on his wounds came from further twin affronts.

First, he was captured by the gandharvas. He was not allowed a Kshatriya death on the battlefield against them like his grandfather, Chitrangada. Worse, he was imprisoned and brutalized by them.

Then, even more disheartening for him, he was liberated.

Not by his best friend but by his archenemy, Tau Bhim. After his release, Duryodhana sat on the ground in front of

Dharmaraj, being counselled on how to run his life, literally burning with shame.

It was a sorry glum caravan that made its way out of Dwaitavana. I eventually ordered the animals to be stopped, and the camp set up for the night.

The next morning, Radheya returned with Uncle Vikarna. Evidently, they had been running non-stop for sixteen hours before deciding to double back and check what had happened to their families. Radheya praised Duryodhana for defeating the gandharvas, which just made him sink more deeply into despondence.

Duryodhana stated that he would starve himself to death to the shock of the assembled company.

Dushasana was proclaimed king—much to the chagrin of Lakshmana Mandara Kumara, my cousin, Prince Number One, still smarting from the kicks he received from the ersatz gandharvas. His father has complained all his life about being passed over by Yudhishthir unfairly, supposedly, and ironically, Uncle Duryodhana does the same to his own son.

Everyone tried to dissuade Duryodhana. He would listen to no one.

Then came the most iconic event of the whole trip.

'Do not foolishly abandon the high prosperity that I have won for you! Why kill yourself in this manner? This may be the worst point of your career, but you can still redeem yourselves. I have always looked upon you with eyes of love, trying to replace the love you searched for in the eyes of your parents. Let me be your true friend today. True friends always tell the truth. Like a raw clay pot in water, your character and nature cannot control sudden accession to joy or grief. So, in the depths of grief, you cannot see the coming peaks of happiness. You have enjoyed so much on this earth. Look at this as an opportunity to restart life. Think of yourself as reborn anew from the clutches of the gandharvas. Do not disgrace the graceful act of those who rescued you. Yudhishthir acted with ultimate generosity. That is his nature. You can do the same. Reward their kindness with kindness of your own. A king always pays his debts, so do not cast your life away but as a king and just ruler, reward the Pandavas. GIVE THE KINGDOM BACK TO PANDAVAS. You will win both virtue and renown by such conduct. By acting with gratitude thus, you will grace the office of the king you hold. ESTABLISH brotherly relations with the Pandavas. Be their friend, and give back their paternal kingdom.'

Shakuni thus advised his nephew.

I saw a leopard change his spots that day. Shakuni, the root of the strife among the Kurus, suggested ending the struggle and making permanent peace with the Pandavas.

Dharmaraj had always searched for the good that is there in every person, even in the blackest of souls. You kill an enemy; you increase the enmity. You convert an enemy; you get a friend for life.

Dharmaraj that day exposed Shakuni to the world! There is some good in him.

Shakuni told his viewpoint with soft hushed tones. It fell on deaf ears.

We stepped out of the tent and saw Dushasana nodding to something Radheya was saying. Another clay pot for Radheya to fashion and control to his designs.

I knew there would be no peace with the Pandavas.

But Shakuni did become truly Dwapara. Half adharma, half dharma. Neutral.

He did not participate in the hunt for the Pandavas in the year of Agyatvas. Neither did he try any stratagem during the time we collected the armies for the war.

Shakuni did not have any more panic attacks. Vaidyas moved out of the Palace of Yuyutsu and found gainful employment across the city of Hastinapur, which became an even more fearful armed camp than earlier.

Shakuni did bring his armies to fight on the Kaurava side.

Before the war, he told me that the emperor had explained the four meanings of dharma to him on the banks of Lake Dwaita. He pleaded with me not to blindly follow my kin into the conflict but to examine the truth of actions and decide.

There is a reason Dharmaraj decided not to kill all of us on the day of the first Dyuta.

Justice is deliberate, justice is unhurried, justice is dharma. Justice does not hunt. Justice will punish the guilty, but justice will, above all, protect and nurture the good wherever it finds it. Justice allows for redemption.

Dharmaraj chose to spend thirteen years in the forest in introspection, maybe to give time for us to repent and redeem.

If you continue to do good things, the good nature in the opponent, however hidden, will boil to the surface. It will manifest. Shakuni's redemption was the proof of the power of Satyagraha first explained to Demon Naga Nahusha by Dharmaraj. Relentless goodness of Yudhishthir broke the millennia old curse on Nahusha, father of Yayati, son-in-law of Shiva, Indra and ruler of the heaven, about to have Bhim for lunch. Converting Shakuni to light was nothing compared to that.

That manifest Satyagraha led me to take up arms against my own brothers and father.

On the first day of battle, Dharmaraj asked if anyone wanted to join from the Kaurava side.

Yuyutsu and the Varnavata forces moved out and took that hand of friendship.

The Kekayas and Sivis had already left and joined the Pandavas months ago.

I aimed my chariot and asked Paundraka army to follow Yuyutsu and was joined on the way by Patachhara-hanta; the son of Kratha; and Sukshatra, the son of Brhadbala, Shakuni's brother. Vishalaksha, my brother, fell in formation too, saluting me.

Dandaketu Bahalika and Prince Vrihanta made it the fellowship of seven defectors as the conches to start the war blew.

Ashwatthama shouted at me for the first time, 'Yashodhara!'

He had said, 'It would be catastrophe by which you can inherit the throne.'

The catastrophe had been named the Mahabharata.

I am grandson number one now.

The Night Patrol Redux

The dark, moonless night enveloped the city of Hastinapur. It was a Tuesday night in the Vasant month, forty years since the events of Khandava Vana.

As the first prahara of the night was fading, I was about to complete my rounds near the royal palace when the horse threw a shoe, and I stumbled in the street. *The patti with me kept their smirks to themselves.* The night may have been moonless, but the royal palace to the south of me was lit up like a house on Deepavali.

There is a famous fable of the elephant and the four blind men, Dharma, Artha, Kama and Moksha. They view the elephant as four different entities each Purushartha represents. The blindfolds have been removed. The city of serpent, Hastinapur, called Nagapura is now back to being Gajavaha, the city of elephants. Hastinapur, the City of War camps, Asandivata, is now called Shantipura.

An air of joy and contentment marked the continuous feverish festivities for the past fifteen hundred-plus nights, as if each night discovered that there was more to celebrate. In the Palace of Dharmarajya, kitchen conches continuously announced the next set of visitors to come and partake of meals. I looked towards the royal road—Pandupatha—to the west of the palace. The palaces of Bhim, Arjun, and Nakul were still awake and full of energy. Who slept when Bhim was in town?

On the road to the north towards my home, I could make out the activity in the permanent Sindhu camp, where the widows of my uncles kept a lively house and hearth for the orphans of the war.

I changed horses and turned homewards, calling it a night. My bed beckoned me. Lined up ahead, in the distance, were the houses of night owls Indrasena, Vishoka, and Samar, my boon companions, and of course the house of Durmukha, I now shared with Sahadev.

I rode past my alma mater, now the large school of the son of Krishna, Vishoka. The school that never slept, with dance performances, night song festivals, Vitandavada discussions, and Samkhya debates that go on through the night of an active university. Where the mind is free, and thought is unchained by narrow domestic walls. Vishoka kept the promise he gave to Yudhamanyu, the ersatz gandharva Vishvavasu from the Ghosha excursion.

'One day in glorious Dharmarajya, we will convert our swords and bows back into ploughs, lutes, and arani sticks and open a school together. That would be our greatest legacy. That is why we fight,' Yudhamanyu had said.

I approached my home. Old Lakha ran up to hold the reins as I dismounted.

I had just washed my hands in a bowl of water when a little hurricane slammed right into me with laughter and joyful exclamations.

I missed the stream of water intended for my legs as I picked up my son. I heard rather than saw Lakha slip in the water. His resigned squeaks to the maid told me he was fine. The maid slapped me in the back of my head as I walked away without washing my feet.

Faces and forms will change but foundations never change.

'This is the second prahar! Way past your bedtime,' I admonished little Prabhanjansuta, carrying him into our bedroom. Sahadharmini took our child and put him to bed.

I was the son of one of the hundred brothers of Duryodhana. She was the daughter of one of the 105 brothers of Kichaka. In the eyes of the world, we are one.

We met on another cattle adventure.

The grandson of 206 grandfathers is named for the one who broke their bones and killed them with his fists, mace, arrows, and a large tree.

People pass judgement daily on others who were part of momentous events. People who have no experience of the events or conditions but act as commentators. One can just document the truths and believe in Satyameva Jayate. One day, our son would understand our choices when he reads this.

'I have started my story as well,' she softly told me as the little one nodded off nestled in maternal embrace.

I turned her pages and started reading.

> The Cattle Heist of Virata
> Sairandhari stood before the King of Matsaya and stated truthfully, I am Malini, the wife of Five Gandharvas, JAYa, JAYant, ViJAYA, JAYAtsena and JAYAdbala.
>
> Kanka Vyaghrapada tried to hide his smile. The newly appointed Cowshed and Stable chiefs tittered. In the distance, from the Kitchen of the King came an uproarious laugh like a thunderclap. JAI HO!
> The persona the brothers took on the day of the Ghosha!!

Sahadharmini was shocked out of her sleep by my sudden stentorian snigger and shushed me as I stroked her somnolent son!

About the Editor and Contributors

Aditi Banerjee (curator and editor)

Aditi Banerjee is a novelist and a practicing attorney at a Fortune 500 financial services company. She is the author of *The Curse of Gandhari* (2019), *The Vow of Parvati* (2022), and *Hindu Love Stories: Dharmically Ever After*. Her latest book, *Kashi: The Valiant History of a Sacred Geography* (2024), explores the historical and spiritual significance of Kashi. A devout Hindu, she writes and speaks extensively on Hinduism and the Hindu-American experience.

Aditi holds a J.D. from Yale Law School and an Executive MBA from Columbia University. She is a member of the Indic Academy. In 2019, the Indic Academy sponsored a six-city book-launch tour across India for *The Curse of Gandhari*. She co-edited *Invading the Sacred: An Analysis of Hinduism Studies in America* alongside Rajiv Malhotra, and has contributed essays to several influential publications, including *The Columbia Documentary History of Religion in America since 1945* (Columbia University Press) and *Buddhists, Hindus, and Sikhs in America: A Short History* (Oxford University

Press). Her articles have also been featured in *Outlook* and many other notable platforms.

Pranshu B. Saxena (co-editor)

Pranshu B. Saxena is a computer scientist. He fell into the habit of recording life around him in his frayed notebooks that acted as fuel for his imagination, which sometimes leak onto the keyboard.

His love for world history and the Mahabharata found an auspicious marriage in this collection. His contributions are also included in *Unsung Valour: Forgotten Warriors of Kurukshetra*, *Flight of Deities: Saga of Destruction and Devotion*, and *Shared Roots: Tales from the Indosphere*. He was awarded a certificate of recognition for his story on Pootna in the Sharadiya Navaratri essay competition on Shaktisthalas. He lives in New Jersey with his wife, daughter, father-in-law and a lifelong collection of books.

Madhavi Girish Kunte

Madhavi Girish Kunte holds an MSc degree in medical microbiology, an MBA in marketing, and a PG diploma in intellectual property rights. In the past, she has worked as a sales executive for a stem cell banking company and a patent analyst for an IP firm. Now, Madhavi is a full-time storyteller. Reading and narrating stories across genres have been a hobby ever since she can remember. She writes stories on mythology and contemporary fiction. Her essay on 'Beej Mata' was recently published in the anthology by INDICA titled *Padma Bharati: Ordinary Indians, Extraordinary Triumphs.* She has also contributed to two other anthologies for Indic Academy, which are currently under publication. At present, she is working on her first independent contemporary fiction. Madhavi is based out of Bengaluru, where she gets to be a happy, stay-at-home mother of two adorable kids.

Shivakumar G.V.

Shivakumar G.V. is the director of Guru-Saadhaka Sachiva at INDICA. His responsibilities focus on INDICA's critical mission to cultivate leadership. He guides initiatives to serve gurus, perpetuate their legacies, enable/empower leaders committed to the Indian knowledge system (IKS) to become influential thinkers, institution builders, and public leaders, and bolster the broader IKS ecosystem. Shivakumar has embarked on an ambitious pledge to honour and sustain the legacies of 108 living and past gurus from the 20th century. His efforts will focus on organizing, making accessible, and cultivating a parampara that highlights their significant contributions to our civilization.

As an IKS research scholar, Shivakumar remains dedicated to the pursuits of knowledge around Itihasa and Puranas. His work includes developing contemporary frameworks based on IKS principles, with a special focus on the Mahabharata and Purushartha. He has been a prolific contributor to *Indic Today,* sharing his insights and knowledge with both academic and general audiences. He has delivered several stories and courses on the Mahabharata and Purushartha for aspiring leaders and students. He has curated a book, *Aryaa: An Anthology of Vedic Women,* published by INDICA. His story on Ghatotkach was published in another INDICA anthology *Unsung Valour,* curated by Saiswaroopa Iyer.

Shivakumar holds an MTech degree in computer science from IIT Bombay and a BE from the National Institute of Technology, Surat. With twenty-five years of experience in the IT industry, his expertise spans theoretical computer science, algorithms, and learning system design. He resides in Bengaluru with his family and is a devoted follower of the river goddess Saraswati.

Ramanjaneya Sharaph

A student of the Bhagavad Gita and the Ramayana, Ramanjaneya Sharaph's writing is inspired by India, Indic themes, and the feminine. A Pushcart Prize nominated author, he has written over 300 poems, four plays, several short stories, and thought pieces. Ramanjaneya writes in Kannada, English, and Hindi but is also fluent in three other languages.

Ramanjaneya is a resident of the prestigious Himalayan Emerging Writers Residency. his work has appeared in *Bridges Not Borders: Anthology of South Asian Writing, Amar Ujala, TMYS Review, Anthologies of India Poetry Circle, The Hive Publishers,* and *Indic Today,* besides platforms such as The Himalayan Writing Retreat and Indic Academy. He is currently working on a novel based on the Panchakanya.

A chartered accountant and an MBA, Ramanjaneya advises founders and CEOs of large corporations on strategy, growth, and finance. He lives in Mumbai with his wife.

Kavitha Sankaranarayanan

Kavitha Sankaranarayanan is a scientist by profession and passion. She heads a research laboratory, where she mentors PhD candidates who aspire to become scientists. She is a mother of two, is passionate about literature and writing, and is an active blogger. She has authored numerous publications in the scientific domain, and this is her first contribution to a book on Indian mythology.

Paras Artwani

Paras Artwani is a serial entrepreneur. He has a medical background but moved into the field of software to pursue his passion. Paras loves to delve into the fascinating world of philosophy and Indian culture, which has inspired the story in this anthology. He is a seeker who is always open to learning from various masters and is actively involved as a volunteer at Sri Aurobindo Ashram and Ramakrishna Math.

Neena Mukherjee

With a master's degree in English literature, Neena Mukherjee blends academic expertise with a passion for history, anthropology, mythology, and Indic fine arts. She is at home in both poetry and prose, and her work showcases her versatililty in Hindi and English languages and a deep understanding of diverse cultures. Besides writing, she is associated with Sangam Talks, where she actively volunteers to write and edit, contributing significantly to the dialogue on cultural and historical topics. Her work not only illuminates the past but also inspires a thoughtful appreciation of the arts and humanities in contemporary society.

Raghu Ram Sola

Raghu Ram Sola works as a technical specialist on advanced driver-assistance systems (ADAS) for a prominent automotive parts manufacturer.

He is a writer by passion. Encouraged by his grandfather, Raghu Ram finds joy in everything related to the Mahabharata. This is his debut work, and he hopes it will lead to many more.

Ananya Ganesh

Ananya Ganesh's interest in the Ramayana and Mahabharata piqued at the age of four and has now become a lifelong pursuit. A gifted writer, her work has been selected for exclusive writing scholarships. She is currently studying biology and psychology and hopes to pursue a career in the sciences.

Ananya is a talented graphic designer and has been involved in community-related projects, such as Carbon Footprint Reduction Project, for which she received the 2022 John 'Mac' McQuown Award for Sustainability. She is the president of IISP MUN, a conference that she co-founded in 2022, currently among the largest MUN conferences in India. Besides work, Ananya loves to travel, enjoys photography, and reads voraciously. She lives with her brothers and parents in Pune, India.

Sumathi Sridhar

Sumathi Sridhar is a financial analyst–turned mythology enthusiast. She runs a YouTube channel, Kulture Katha, where she shares lesser-known stories from the fascinating universe of Indian lore. Sumathi has an advanced diploma in comparative mythology from Mumbai University, where she is also a visiting faculty member.

Sumathi writes and speaks on mythology in English and Tamil. Her book *Deivangalin Aayudhangal* traces the iconographic evolution of Indic deities and their weapons over the Vedic, epic, and Puranic periods.

S. Anuradha

S. Anuradha published her debut novel, *The Friendless God*, in 2017. The story is set against the backdrop of the Ram Janmabhoomi–Babri Masjid conflict and tracks the lives of a religious son and an atheist mother through the worlds of Carnatic music, Kalamkari painting, and gardening.

She has edited a lecture series on 'Shiva Samhita', a medieval Yoga-Vedanta text in Sanskrit, which was published by Motilal Banarsidass under the title *Advaita Vedanta of Shiva Samhita*. She has also written about the history of the Hindu Centre, a Singapore-based voluntary organization that promotes the study of Hinduism. Anuradha is a financial journalist by profession and lives in Singapore.

Battu Sri Charan

Battu Sri Charan has an undergraduate degree in E&ECE from IIT Kharagpur and is working as an engineer for a semiconductor company. When work gets stressful, he likes to dote on his half-year-old nephew. He reads widely across genres—fantasy, sci-fi, finance, astronomy, philosophy, and other obscure things. Battu hopes to become a writer someday.

Shambhavi Tripathi

Shambhavi Tripathi is a lawyer with over three years of experience. She currently works as an in-house counsel for one of the leading biotech companies. She is also a gold medalist in forensic science. Besides work, Shambhavi enjoys reading, cooking, and spending time with her loved ones. While she has written several articles, research papers, petitions, and contracts, her contribution to this anthology is her first attempt at creative writing.

Shantheri Mallaya

Shantheri Mallaya is a tech journalist with eighteen years of experience at renowned tech media houses. Professionally, she has played diverse roles—an editor, an event content anchor, a panel moderator, a speaker, a mentor, a tech observer, and a researcher—but enjoys the most when in conversation with tech communities. Besides work, Shantheri is an avid reader, cinephile, podcast buff, blogger, writer, and storyteller. She dabbles in theater and has worked in English and Kannada productions, both onstage and backstage. She is also an honorary trustee of Chiranthana, a Bengaluru-based not-for-profit for special needs. Shantheri has co-authored a novella, *The Game of Pawns*. She has a bachelor's degree in commerce from Bangalore University and a postgraduate degree in journalism. She has also completed a certification course in guidance and counselling from the Indian Institute of Psychology and Research (IIPR).

Rajesh Ramachander

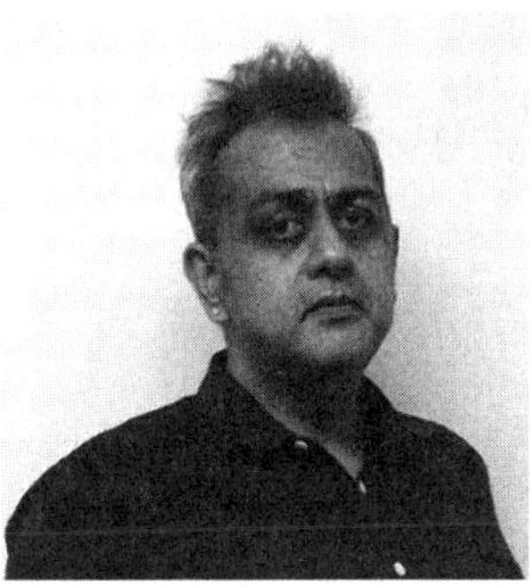

Rajesh Ramachander is an engineer with a diverse range of interests. He works at the cutting edge of artificial intelligence, where the only constant is to push the boundaries of possibility. Beyond engineering and AI, his deep passion to uncover the world's authentic history has him delve into Puranas to reveal hidden narratives and unexplored truths. His interest in the intersaction of technology, history, and spirituality drives his quest to bridge the gap between the ancient and the modern. In his free time, he explores ancient texts, connects the dots, and matches the patterns to illuminate the hidden narratives.